T0368108

Manifest Your Magnificence

The Energetics of Being

Joan E. Walmsley

BALBOA.
PRESS

A DIVISION OF HAY HOUSE

Balboa Press books may be ordered through booksellers or by contacting:

Balboa Press
A Division of Hay House
1663 Liberty Drive
Bloomington, IN 47403
www.balboapress.com
1 (877) 407-4847

Because of the dynamic nature of the Internet, any web addresses or links contained in this book may have changed since publication and may no longer be valid. The views expressed in this work are solely those of the author and do not necessarily reflect the views of the publisher, and the publisher hereby disclaims any responsibility for them.

The author of this book does not dispense medical advice or prescribe the use of any technique as a form of treatment for physical, emotional, or medical problems without the advice of a physician, either directly or indirectly. The intent of the author is only to offer information of a general nature to help you in your quest for physical, emotional, mental and spiritual wellbeing. In the event you use any of the information in this book for yourself, which is your constitutional right, the author and the publisher assume no responsibility for your actions.

Front Cover Image stock imagery © Shutterstock Roman Sigaev

Any people depicted in stock imagery provided by Thinkstock are models, and such images are being used for illustrative purposes only. Certain stock imagery © Thinkstock.

Print information available on the last page.

ISBN: 978-1-5043-4103-5 (sc)
ISBN: 978-1-5043-4104-2 (hc)
ISBN: 978-1-5043-4105-9 (e)

Library of Congress Control Number: 2015916001

Balboa Press rev. date: 10/06/2015

Contents

To my mother, Grace Mary Winifred Walmsley,
and my father, Kenneth Curzon Walmsley.

The tragedies and sacrifices of their lives propelled me
onto a path of exploration that began over thirty
years ago and is ongoing.

With love.

Preface

I was first introduced to the concepts of energy—energy fields, vibrations, frequencies—and multidimensional existence by my father, Kenneth, when I was at the ripe old age of seven. He was an electrical design engineer who worked in the field of telecommunications. On the one hand, he was a very practical man, as most engineers are; and on the other hand, he was deeply spiritual. I loved to just be with him and experience his energy and essence. It was as rare and beautiful as a delicate flower, and I was enraptured by our conversations. They enabled me to make sense of some of the "paranormal" occurrences of my young life that to me were absolutely normal. This was back in the 1950s, when conversations on the subject of energy and its relationship with consciousness were far less common than nowadays. Little did I know, our conversations would form the foundations for *Manifest Your Magnificence: The Energetics of Being*.

My beloved mother, Grace, rooted the family in Christian values; she was as beautiful as her name and was the hub of family life. Her prolonged struggle with depression and cancer and finally her long, drawn-out death catapulted my father into a long-term breakdown and an ongoing estrangement from my sister and me when I was age twenty-nine. He died still estranged from both of us nine years later. The great sorrow engendered by these two tragic converging events would be pivotal in thrusting me into a deep search for the meaning of life.

I had opted for the world of business and commerce as a young woman, and once again, this was not usual in those days. What may seem very natural now in the twenty-first century, as more and more women have found their voices and independence, was certainly an uphill struggle for the trailblazers in the '70s and '80s of the twentieth century. However, I was fortunate that my various positions would take me all over the world, introducing me to many different cultures, particularly those of the East, and bringing in their wake extraordinary and unexpected material abundance.

Alongside my professional career, my disillusionment with organized religion and deep inner turmoil following the complete collapse of my family led to an immersion in Eastern philosophy and a twenty-year study of the great Chinese, Indian, and Tibetan spiritual traditions.

By this time I was forty-nine and had traveled the world. From a purely materialistic viewpoint I was a successful businesswoman, and yet over the next three years, my life literally started to deconstruct, piece by piece. My long-term relationship ended, my thriving business was suddenly terminated by totally unforeseen events, and I was forced to sell my home and all my possessions. What I did not sell, I gave away. Through what seemed like major crises then, I had reached another crossroads in my life. I looked out at my disintegrating world and realized there was something radical going on. At the same time, I had a deep longing to make a difference in the world, but I did not know how or where.

Some years earlier, my sister, June, had gifted me a book called *Hands of Light*, written by the acclaimed teacher and author Barbara Ann Brennan. As soon as I read it, I knew one day I would study with her.

In 2005, while practicing yoga with another very gifted teacher in the United Kingdom, I had what can only be described as a peak experience of knowingness and beingness, and shortly after this I enrolled to begin a prolonged and advanced training in personal energy management. As my training progressed, it became abundantly clear to me that if I wanted to make a difference in the world, then the change must start with me. This resulted in a deep personal transformational process that was life changing.

Over the past ten years I have once again been traveling, this time in North and South America, honing my skills, learning more new skills with a variety of incredible and wonderfully gifted teachers, developing new techniques, and working with the people and the land of wherever I happened to be. In 2011 at the age of sixty, I undertook a program of intense physical training, completely transforming my physical body so that it would mirror its new energetic template.

I knew in 2005 that this book would be written. "So why has it taken so long?" you might ask. The answer is twofold:

Science is now able to evidence what was once only theory. This book could have been written earlier, yes, but then it would have been without the support of the very newest revelations from the scientific community, particularly the research around placebo effects, mind-matter interaction, scalar energy, DNA, and the emerging electrical, fractal, and holographic nature of the universe. It takes time for new ideas and paradigm shifts to gather momentum and fully embed into public awareness. Science itself is now demanding this shift. Now is the time.

On a personal level, it has taken me almost a lifetime to consciously enable the reprogramming and recalibration of my own personal energy system while obtaining the emotional, psychological, spiritual, and scientific knowledge at multidimensional levels required to transmute my own physical and nonphysical matter into a higher vibration. In order to be able to share the process with others in a meaningful way, I had to use the construct of time to slow down the experience of bringing the lower vibrations of my system into full contact with the higher frequencies of my being. For me, the transmutation of the material substance has occurred with a full conscious awareness of every single stage, accompanied by knowledge and understanding of the root cause of the initial fragmentations across the time line, thus enabling the restoration of the original DNA template. This also enables an accelerated and clear transmission of transformative energy for others. All this was accomplished while remaining grounded in a typical 3-D business environment. At the time, I did not realize that this too was a necessary and imperative part of my training.

My deep transformational work commenced concurrent with a move to Toronto, Canada, to take up a post with a business-communications training company. This was no coincidence, for as it turned out, there was much work for me on many levels in this part of the world. This was a crucial aspect of my overall training, as it allowed me to develop my own personal energy-management skills not only with private clients but also to coach in real-life business settings, as well as complete a new coaching training that enabled me to enhance my work with children and youth. This gave me a firm footing of groundedness in 3-D, while at the same time I was exploring and holding the higher dimensions.

Everything we experience in our external reality is determined by the vibrational frequencies of our own energy signature. An understanding of energy and our energetic nature is crucial to creating and maintaining all permanent change in any and all aspects of our lives and our perceived realities.

This is a huge statement and opens up many questions, but it is nevertheless a statement I have tested, lived, and embodied time and time again, only to discover that modern science is now well on its way to supporting the truth of this premise. The knowledge and information now coded into this personal energy matrix forms a resonant template that is able to activate, promote, and facilitate the transformational process very quickly for individuals in all age ranges, groups, and organizations at a time when the new incoming cosmic energies supporting global transformation are fully supporting this. All is synchronous and in perfect timing. And so in this moment of the now, I invite you to join me on the journey to your magnificence.

Acknowledgments

My life to date has been so rich and so full of wonderful and wondrous beings that I am humbled as I begin the recall of the many who have helped me on my way. Those who particularly stand out in my memory are mentioned below, and yet there are many others, too numerous to mention but nevertheless a part of my journey. I honor, acknowledge, and bless all my teachers.

My dear sister, June, illuminated the way with her practical gift of a book and the enormous gift of her presence in my life.

Beloved friends Sylvia (now transitioned) and Ray Flinn, Amanda Rowe, Julie Marriot, and Carol Tillett saw, listened, and heard me in my moments of deepest sorrow and despair.

To my dear friend Susan Eaves—my deepest gratitude for allowing me to be part of your own journey and for your ongoing encouragement to write.

To all the patriarchs I have worked with and who mirrored back to me my own unbalanced energy aspects and my complete denial of the feminine within: without you I would never have rediscovered her.

To my soul brother Frank Medliecott Shipley—our twelve years together and twelve years apart brought me face-to-face with my shadow self, light and dark. Bless you for then and now. I treasure our friendship.

To my soul brother Gerard Hutton—through his yoga I developed a love and knowledge of the physical body moving, while simultaneously integrating its higher aspects. Through the harmonic induction of his exquisite vibrational field, I experienced firsthand knowledge of the beauty of the galactic dimensions and the cosmos within.

To Barbara Ann Brennan, for demonstrating the healing power of the written word and modeling the true meaning of leadership: one who goes first into the unknown, no matter how crazy the impulse seems to the linear mind or to commentators who do not hear the music or see the vision. I honor your great courage and bravery in your surrender to higher will.

To the Barbara Brennan School of Healing faculty in the United States between the years 2005 and 2012 and Susan Hewitt in Europe for such dedicated mirroring and modeling of presence. Your gifts of love and dedication are only outweighed by your humanity and compassion.

With special gratitude and appreciation to my mentor, supervisor, and outstanding example of dedicated service to the transformation and healing of the human and animal kingdoms, Dr. Catherine Nelson, PhD.

To the BBSH graduating class of 2009 USA and Advanced Studies Brennan Integration Work graduating class of 2012 USA—what a roller-coaster ride that was, in and out of class. I am so blessed to have been with you then and to be with you now in my heart.

Shar Napp, dear soul sister and school buddy, blessings for all the work we did together over the years. We had such deep sharing and so many good times together. I miss you.

To my dear friends and work colleagues in Canada, deepest gratitude: Susan Lynne; Doris Poirier; Lidia Mattucci; Marcia Wilson; Lional Andris; Santino; Constantin; Dave Newby; Roger and Jazz Davies; and the various teams and networks at McLuhan & Davies and Think On Your Feet International, Inc.—all of whom played crucial roles along my journey into the deep dive of self-discovery.

To Sifu Matthew Raymond Cohen at Sacred Energy Arts in Santa Monica, California, whose integrated approach to martial, yogic, and healing arts provided me with fully integrated yogic teacher training. My time in California turned out to be an important phase in my personal transformative process.

To Sang Il Jo of Trainer Jo's in Toronto for training my physical body with such care and professionalism and providing me with lifelong knowledge of practices for nutrition and well-being.

To Susan Howson, founder of Magnificent Creations Limitee, Toronto, Canada, whose program Kids Coaching Connection trained me to effectively mentor kids, reintroduced me to my own child within, provided me with the first half of the title of this book, and confirmed to me that I could manifest my own magnificence.

To the Masters of Seggau, the group with whom I completed my master of science degree at Inter–Universitaires Colleg, Graz, in Austria. This led me to research the science required to write this book. The process as well as the research proved to be another treasure chest of gifts.

To my close friend and soul brother Karl Pernull, whose intellect and counsel are matched only by his great heart.

To my soul brother Christof Melchizedek, a powerful indigo worker and founder of the Limitless program—such a great inspiration. Thank you for allowing me to experience what can be achieved online and demonstrating the power of focus and dedication.

To my beloved soul sister, Tiara Kumara, founder of the Children of the Sun Foundation and creator of I Am Avatar Yoga and the Morphogenesis programs. Words cannot begin to express what joy our friendship brings and my gratitude for our Peruvian Amazon expedition together, an experience of outstanding magnitude and power. You inspire me to do great things.

To soul brother and sister Toby and Ivonne Alexander, whose diligent work developing scalar wave programming for repatterning and activating existing and dormant DNA formed the basis of my certification to facilitate and teach these specific protocols.

To scientists the world over, many of whom appear in this book, whose diligent work is providing humankind with many answers and even more questions about the nature of our existence.

To the Devas of the Angelic Realms and the animal, plant, and mineral kingdoms—you have played such an enormous part in enabling me to open my heart and mind fully to all life, with love and appreciation.

And finally, to the spiritual master and guardian source aspects of this being that hold this projection in physical form. I have been aware of this presence and guidance in my life since the age of twelve. Through this connection and presence, I experience the magnificence of source being in this moment of now and live in awe and thanksgiving.

Introduction

> Truth has to be repeated constantly, because error also is being preached all the time, and not just by the few, but by the multitude. In the press and encyclopedias, in schools and universities, everywhere error holds sway, feeling happy and comfortable in the knowledge of having majority on its side.
>
> —Goethe

If we check out the daily news, we could be forgiven for believing that we are a doomed race living on a planet that is heading for self-destruction. More and more chaos appears to prevail in many of the established systems of world governance, and every day we read of atrocities and unacceptable suffering in one part of the world or another. Yet the world is in the process of a major transformation and transition, even though this may not be apparent in mainstream media reportage. This is an era of awakening consciousness on a grand scale. Many are moved to respond to the gentle but persistent calling of their own inner being to recognize and bring forth the gifts of their own deepest wisdom.

Technological advance has enabled us to connect instantly with others all over the world. What is not yet fully realized by the majority is that we are able to do this anyway, without a cell phone or computer. This book is an introduction to the energetic nature of our being. People are sharing and caring about one another much more than may seem immediately obvious. People are connecting with their hearts, and these connections are strengthening daily. There are many examples of the magnificence of "ordinary" human beings that confirm the interconnectedness of all life. "But what has this to do with energy?" you might ask. The following pages confirm how deeply we are all connected, and through the understanding of our energetic nature and conscious experience of our connections to all that is, we will see how each of us through our simple being can and will bring more and more light into the dark places of our world—until finally we have transformation on a global scale that ushers in peace, goodwill, and prosperity for all as our collective reality.

The establishing of right relationship and the will-to-good among all living beings and all the sentient life on planet earth allows humankind to create genuine peace and abundance for all, not just the few. To accomplish this requires first that we establish right relationship with self. This must be the strong foundation from which we build a new world together. When we realize that we are not separated from our source or one other, the will to serve one another becomes our natural way of being. It can be no other way. Ultimately, the magnificence of which I speak is nothing less than getting to know the self as an aspect of source energy and being that. A side effect of not only understanding the concept but actually experiencing the reality is that we begin to live content and fulfilled lives, all our relationships thrive, we understand our purpose, we eradicate limiting belief systems, there is no more repetition of negative behavioral patterns, we live in radiant health, and we achieve our fullest potential as human beings, becoming conscious cocreators with source. Through our cocreations, all aspects of life are enhanced and improved, and this is reflected back to us in the world we inhabit.

The task at hand is no less than to bring source energy fully into our material form, while embodying the knowing that we are not separate from our creator or each other. We are all one being. In order to know this experientially, we emerge into physical life and thereby into the realm of duality on the material plane of earth so that we may experience the many aspects of the source in our own being and in the mirror of other beings. The true reality is there is only one of us in myriad different forms. In this book I challenge you to experience this for yourself as you manifest your magnificence and discover who you really are.

The underlying theme throughout the book is one of synthesis and synergy. Synthesis is defined as the combination of elements to form a connected whole; synergy is the cooperation of two or more elements to produce a combined effect greater than the sum of their separate effects. *Manifest Your Magnificence* explores the synthesis of science and spirituality; the mind with the body; the higher self with the lower self; energy with consciousness; the synergy of scientific disciplines as scientists work in intentional unison to explore creation; and the synergy of empowered individuals combining their unique, individual magnificence to collaborate to shift planetary consciousness. The convergence of science and spirituality is currently well underway and becoming stronger daily with each new revelation from the scientific community. This reorientation may not yet be consciously realized by the protagonists, but it will be self-evident after an exploration of the evidence. It is my intention that the book do what it can to bring their obvious commonality into more public awareness and be instrumental in furthering the cause of unification between the two branches of human knowledge.

Science is now providing us with a greater understanding of the energetic nature of our being and its connection to our consciously perceived reality. *Manifest Your Magnificence* recounts, in detail, the personal synthesis that occurs within a human being when a thorough exploration of the inner world is undertaken, resulting in a shift from a physical-based perception to an energy consciousness-based understanding of reality and the reorientation of experiences this engenders. When all aspects of our being are accessed, experienced, and integrated, the manifestation of magnificence is a natural and organic outcome, and the life is transformed. The book includes proven energetic, experiential practices that introduce the reader to an understanding and management of the personal energy system and assist the acceleration of this synthesis.

Finally, it is my deepest intention that through an immersion in the energy of the information presented here, there may be a realization of what can be accomplished by unified consciousness in action. By approaching the problems of our personal lives, our families, our businesses, our communities, and the global community at large with an awareness of powerful synthesized and synergistic solutions, there can be immediate improvement of world conditions and radical and rapid transformations for the greater good of all—all through our individual and combined intention and action.

What follows may challenge your current belief system way beyond your comfort zone. That is good because this is where true growth occurs. Anyone who has been successful at anything will tell you real achievement happens outside the status quo. We grow by pushing ourselves past the safety of familiar boundaries.

Why Now?

This is an unprecedented time in the history of humankind. Never before has there been the opportunity for such rapid personal, group, and planetary transformation and evolution on such a grand scale. As we move through the material, it will become very clear that the entire universe is supporting this transition. It is happening whether we are conscious of this or not, but through our conscious awareness of the promptings of our own inner guidance systems, we can accelerate the process, reduce resistance, and expedite the benefits of the positive outcome, individually and collectively. "Transformation of what?" one might ask. Answer: everything and anything. By transforming thoughts, emotions, and outdated belief systems, clearing out old programming and conditioning, consciously choosing to take full responsibility for experienced reality, living from true purpose, and being consistently and consciously connected to pure source energy, anyone can overcome all challenges and thrive and grow beyond his or her wildest dreams. All becomes possible. You can manifest your magnificence now!

Instead of investing in a blame culture and giving your personal power away to a belief system that leaves you powerless; instead of believing life is something that happens to you rather than something created by you; instead of projecting out on to others that which is not perceived or understood to be created by the self; and instead of believing you are separate from others and from your source, you can know the self as the complete, whole, creative, resourceful, all-knowing, unconditionally loving being that you naturally are. This automatically brings an individual into a state of beingness in which peace resides and knowingness that all is one. You will experience that when the inner perspective changes, everything in the outer reality changes. It is as simple as that. And as you begin to manifest your own magnificence by increasing your energetic vibration and attuning to the higher frequencies of life (which literally means becoming more light-filled), all benefit. We are not separate from each other, our planet, or our source but rather are purely different aspects of the same being and same consciousness. We are seriously interconnected with each other and all that is manifest and unmanifest in the cosmos. This is a connection that transcends time and space.

This is not New Age hocus-pocus, psychobabble, or mysterious elite magic. There is now hard scientific evidence becoming available, and growing daily, that confirms what the great teachers, mystics, and masters have been saying for thousands and thousands of years and what many are now beginning to perceive, experience, know, and live. Every single one of us is a powerful creator who creates his or her own experience with intentions, beliefs, thoughts, feelings, attitudes, and words and has the power to directly affect the material world, each other, and the planet. There is no question; the evidence reveals that science is now reconciling with ancient wisdom through direct demonstration and not theory alone to develop a new model for the future.

For Whom?

The book has been created as a labor of love, with gratitude and appreciation for my own journey and the many gifts I have received along the way. One of those gifts is the deepest urge to share the knowing of my own lived experience to assist others in activating and reclaiming their own power. This is no less than the power to remove all impediments to their connection to their higher aspects and live in full alignment with their true purpose. It is for the many who are moved by the call of their inner being to create a better life and a better world for themselves and their children. It is for those who are called to step into their own mastery, whether they are in the home or in the workplace. It is for educators, leaders, businesses, and medics. It is for the healers of the planet. It is for "ordinary" men and women, for you will come to see there is no such thing as ordinary. It is particularly for the youth of our planet, including those who have been labeled with an acronym or condition that supposedly defines them, such as Autism, ADD, ADHD, ASD, or Asperger's syndrome. This book is for all who are struggling to make sense of the world they have been born into, with or without an acronym.

Everything and everyone in our lives has its foundation in *energy*. I have discovered this is a term that is used widely and yet with much confusion. When asked, many people, including energy practitioners themselves, cannot articulate the definition of *energy* meaningfully without reverting to a dualistic approach. Not because of incompetence but because energy consciousness and the science of energy are only recently emerging as one unified whole. The bridge is growing stronger daily, and yet there are those for whom science is a scary proposition. It has its own language.

Similarly for scientists, the other half of the equation, the more esoteric approach also has its own terminology, and yet through discernment and ongoing revelation, one may see they are both sides of the same coin. Therefore this book is positioned for both the rational thinker and the seeker of ancient wisdom, conditions that are not mutually exclusive. I have found that very often it is only semantics that divides the expressions of the human experience. The science presented here is very basic and simplified as much as possible, purposed to act as an introduction to a new way of thinking about the nature of objective reality and to support the material in parts 2 and 3. The intention is to make this scientific knowledge easily accessible and comprehensible to all and particularly those who may not be familiar with science and its methods.

The principles outlined in the second part of the book are a deep dive into the elements of human consciousness and will undoubtedly challenge all who are not familiar with this type of transcendental perspective. They are meant to, but in a space of non-judgment, compassion, and love, the path is cut. In its structure of presentation, the first two parts of the book really represent, respectively, the masculine and feminine principles of human existence, the two hemispheres of the brain, the rational thinker and the intuitive knower, the concrete mind and the feeling nature. The thinking mind is the powerful creative tool of our manifestations, but our new highest creations, aligned with true purpose, cannot be birthed without the nurturance, experience, and wisdom of love. We can know a concept intellectually, but we must feel, be, and live that knowing too. The balancing between these two aspects creates harmony, equilibrium, and coherence and is achieved by developing a practice of ongoing self-inquiry and energetic clearing such as described in part 3. The practices outlined here are an introduction to managing your own energy. They are energetic tools purposed to assist the unification of both aspects of human existence, bringing them into a perfect balance and an alignment. In this state of coherence the human energy system is able to attract, accumulate and hold more light particles and transmute physical matter into finer and finer substance, vibrating at higher and higher frequencies.

Part 1: Synergy and Synthesis

Part 1 is an encounter with the incredible world of the newly unfolding science as revealed through fact, theory, and experiment. It is an exploration of the new scientific revolution that is currently underway and demonstrates how the emerging scientific model is now facilitating a new understanding of the nature of our reality. This multidisciplinary approach allows us to see the connections and similarities now occurring in what at first may seem unrelated research. An incredible picture emerges as we spend a little time familiarizing ourselves with the work of some of the greatest scientists of the past century, upon whose genius rests the foundation of our current knowledge. This is combined with new findings based on the most amazing technological advances in detection available more recently. Our encounters confirm that the very nature of matter reveals it is an illusion and there is a distinct possibility the physical world that we call consensual "reality" is our individual and collective creative process that manipulates physical matter using consciousness, sound, light, and energy projecting out into the many dimensions of the material plane, including those that are not yet visible to the human eye. We will see how it is possible that we co-create and call forth that which we experience as our reality by our very own thought process and that our visible "reality" is not actually solid and fixed, but fluid and wavelike, and can be altered by the power of intention, thought, and imagination. We will investigate the holographic principle and consider the feasibility of the concept that we are living in a holographic universe and we are living holograms.

From here we will explore the world of energy and the various energy fields that affect our existence in physical reality—the source field, the planetary field, the morphogenetic fields, and finally the human bioenergy field, including our energetic DNA. Their relevance to our physical life will be demonstrated as we see that we are energetic beings in constant two-way communication with the living energy matrix, both visible and invisible, of all sentient life and the environment in which we live, whether we are consciously aware of this or not. An understanding of energy and how it behaves is paramount to all that follows. This will be explored in enough detail to allow for an understanding of the basic physics involved.

An introduction to human, planetary, and systemic energetic anatomy reveals how deeply our destiny is connected to and woven into all sentient life, our planet, and ultimately the cosmos. An exploration of the personal energetic anatomy of the human being leads us to the discovery that our physical body is a miraculous and magnificent creation that is a living matrix of energy—a complete energy system that registers every thought, feeling, and emotion and is communicating constantly with the energy system of others, as well as the planetary, cosmic, and source fields. We will see there is the possibility our minds are not in the brain, as conventional thought posits. We will discover our brains as processors, but the heart regulates all physical body systems and is profoundly affected by our inner and outer environments. We get to discover our magnificence at the DNA and cellular level and how physical life itself is generated from the genetic coding arising from an energetic template that can be literally programmed and reprogrammed by us. This section also includes some very basic scientific definitions that I hope will be useful for those who are not familiar with the scientific language of energy.

Part 2: The Keys to the Kingdom

Part 2 addresses the subject of consciousness in depth—its electrical nature, its cosmic origin, and its expression in the human being. Here we study the nature of the energetic signature created by the vibrational frequency of our consciousness and the links to psychological and physiological function and dysfunction. We will explore the creative process as it is linked into the evolutionary life impulse, how and why we create the reality we do, and how and why we need to build coherence in our bioenergetic field. This section includes an exploration of the dimension of intention: its importance in the creative process, the cause and effect of its dysfunction, and its role in creating the resonance fundamental to balancing all our multidimensional energies into a coherent and unified whole.

The exploration of the first seven elements of human awareness begins with a review of the personality self and the energetic fields of consciousness that correspond to the form life or physical life of our being. Here there is attention to the physical body, its cellular intelligence, and the effects of movement, breath, nourishment, hydration, and rest. This is also the arena of the emotional nature of our feelings and our mind content in the form of thoughts, attitudes, belief systems, and the ego that currently runs our lives. It will be demonstrated how our feelings and thoughts can keep us locked in old paradigm thinking, in outworn cycles of behavior and fearful illusions about a reality that no longer serves us or anyone else. We will explore human sexuality and balancing the masculine and feminine energies and how this relates to the creative cycle. Emotional and mental stability are fundamental to building a coherent energy system; and feelings versus emotions, the foundations of psychological health, environmental conditioning, energetic imprints and energy signatures, the child consciousness within all, and the nature of the three minds all are discussed in depth, and participatory practices are made available and highly recommended.

From here we move to the transpersonal self and the major power center of the body, the sacred human heart. Here we experience the bridge of transcendence that is opened by the heart center, introducing the personality self or lower frequency self to the higher frequency aspects of our being. We become connected to causal or soul energy and its purpose and the higher vibrational aspects of love/wisdom, higher will, and higher mind. As the human personality is introduced to and becomes influenced by these higher energetic frequencies, we will see that eventually the entire organism comes under their supervision, true purpose is revealed, and the human life comes under the full direct guidance of its own soul in order to become fully aligned with the still higher aspect of itself, the monadic higher self (spirit).

The heart is the center of relationship and connection to all other life. It is only through our relationship with others that we can truly know the self and expand our consciousness. This section involves a review of psychoenergetic interaction and all the implications for our relationships with others; the behavioral strategies the ego uses to keep the true greater self imprisoned and separate and prevent us from creating that which we intend; the mask self that denies the truth of who we are and what we are feeling and creates a false projection; and the shadow self that lives in the recesses of our subconscious mind and of whom we have no conscious knowledge, yet can powerfully direct all our relationships and our creative outcomes. We will encounter our projections and transferences of reality and see how we actually live most of our lives not in the truth of the present moment, but in the shadows of a past that is gone or the fantasy of a future that is not yet arrived. We will consider the acts of connection, forgiveness, and personal love and the transforming energy released by their influence. The cohesive power of the higher frequency energy of that which we call love/wisdom, the foundational energy upon which the entire solar system rests, is recognized and experienced as sourced from within our own being and not an external relationship.

The final chapters in this section deal with the expression of your magnificence and how this will look for you in the outside world of your new reality. They are concerned with the ability to surrender to the higher will and hear and follow its discreet (and sometimes not so discreet) but persistent guidance. We consider the nature of pleasure and the payoff derived from staying in a destructive, negative intentionality and the possible lack of motivation to go further into the unknown depths of our being. We explore the great power and meaning of sound and speech and how these are utilized in the process of creation.

As the lower aspects of the energy field are charged, cleared, and balanced, this allows an unimpeded flow of energy from the higher aspects of our bioenergy field. In this section the significance of the head energy centers, together with the part visualization and imagination play in the creative process, is described. As the contact with the higher frequencies increases and this energy penetrates and permeates our entire being, it touches ever more deeply into the lower energies still held in the shadow of our conscious knowing. Often this can generate even stronger negative resistance than previously encountered. The ways we can deal with this resistance are documented in the section on dualism and resistance.

There is an introduction to the anatomy of our energetic DNA and how this can be reprogrammed using light, sound, energetic clearing, and activation codes of a new harmonized earth reality. Clearing at this level activates and expedites the entire transformational process for those who are willing to unconditionally surrender to the unknown and step into their full mastery. Part 2 ends with the integrated state of consciousness known as at-one-ment or unity consciousness and how this is frequently experienced.

Part 3: The Energetic Highway

Part 3 provides energetic practices, meditations, affirmations, invocations, and evocations to aid and accelerate your passage through this material. These give you an energetic foundation for your transformational journey into change. No one can do this work for you. Your dedication, focus, and commitment are paramount. However, it should be stressed that much of this work requires the reflection and support of others, and the optimal way to benefit from your experiences is to do this work either on a one-to-one basis with an experienced facilitator coach or, even more effectively, within a group setting. In my own experience, a mixture of both methods has proved the most fruitful. Group work can support and greatly expedite your progress due to the power and intention of a collective morphogenetic energy field. It is something to consider. This also provides perfect opportunities for the reflection of issues that may be held in shadow and thus more difficult to access. You are a multidimensional being, whether you experience this awareness yet or not. Presenting concepts in book form requires a linear approach; however, experiences may not follow the order of the book. It is highly likely they will not, as any change in any one aspect of our energy system affects all levels of the multidimensional energy body. What occurs and when it occurs for each one is perfect for the individual's particular path.

PART 1

Synthesis and Synergy

I have long believed in and advocated a dialogue and cross-fertilization between science and spirituality as both are essential for enriching human life and alleviating suffering on both the individual and global levels.

—His Holiness the fourteenth Dalai Lama

The day science begins to study non-physical phenomena, it will make more progress in one decade than in all the previous centuries of its existence. To understand the true nature of the universe, one must think in terms of energy, frequency and vibration.

—Nicola Tesla

CHAPTER 1

Background

Science is an ever-evolving body of knowledge. It is not a fixed set of laws that never changes, nor should it be. It evolves as our knowledge and understanding of our universe increases. Its theories grow and expand, while retaining those ideas and knowledge that remain reliable as an explanation of what is perceived. This way it incorporates and integrates the older established knowledge with newer data to form a wider picture. Scientists question and explore and change their views when fact and logic force them to do so. They base their views on what can be verified through experiment or what can be deduced from experimentally confirmed hypotheses. They ask how, not why. Science is an enterprise that systematically builds and organizes knowledge in the form of testable explanations and predictions about the universe. It has assumed there is an objective reality shared by rational observers and governed by natural laws that can be described by observation and experimentation.

How Science Works

Although there is some controversy in scientific circles around the scientific method, the elements of good scientific practice cannot be and should not be ignored. They include controlled and disciplined observation, with careful and unbiased measurement, and a requirement for public consensus agreement that these measurements are correct. Phenomena must be independently and repeatedly measurable to allow this consensus to form. Only this repeated replication creates stability for any hypothesis.[1] It is a valuable process that allows us to keep moving forward, develop and test theories, and ultimately add to our self-knowledge.

It is an interesting phenomenon that science works toward gaining a concrete and absolute factual knowledge, and yet so much of what is held as consensus is based on assumption and uncertainty. This is the great paradox. However, even though one cannot deny the incredible advances science has made, particularly over the past hundred years, there is still so very much more to explore. The latest developments in quantum physics, astrophysics, cymatics, cosmology, plasma science, neuroscience, biology, biophysics, epigenetics, and molecular biology are converging to provide a new worldview of who we are and where we came from that is very different from the one we think we know. There is a slow emergence of reconciliation between the ancient, intuitive, mystic, and metaphysical views of the spiritual world with the findings of science through scientific exploration. What is emerging is a picture of consciousness, as these two seemingly opposed worlds begin to discover their real similarities rather than polarize in their differences. As we move forward in our search for knowledge, this is a time for synthesis and synergy. As Carl Sagan wrote, "The very act of understanding is a celebration of joining, even if in a very modest sense with the magnificence of the cosmos. Science is not only compatible with spirituality; it is a profound source of spirituality."[2]

3-D Reality—Current Mainstream Views

What follows is a brief review of where we are as a global community in terms of scientific exploration, understanding, and mainstream views. The term *energetics* in the book title refers to the principles, components, and applications of energy. If you believe you are not interested in science or that it is not relevant to what follows, this is step number one in challenging belief systems that condition your thinking. A very brief review of how current mainstream views developed leads us on into the newer and incredibly exciting revelations of modern science. This will certainly facilitate your progress and support clarity of purpose as you approach the self-inquiry sections in part 2. It has been humbling to research these topics, for it is clear how the courageous men and women over the past three centuries have pioneered new frontiers, sometimes at the expense of their lives, to provide you and me with incredible knowledge about ourselves and our universe. Their work has formed the foundation for the knowledge that is becoming available now, and rather than be now dismissed as "incorrect," it can be integrated and viewed as a necessary step along the way of our ever-expanding global consciousness. And it continues.

Our scientific awareness is an evolutionary process as we develop more and more sophisticated methods of research and detection. I urge you not to skip part 1, even those among you who may have a reasonable knowledge of current scientific data. This section covers many disciplines, and it is this multidisciplinary approach that gradually reveals the incredible connections between events that might have previously seemed unrelated. It is the story of a new emerging paradigm.

Newton, Darwin, and Descartes:
The Historical Context

Scientific views inform our concept of self. We are the product of our scientific heritage. How we learn to think about ourselves is based on the scientific models scientists use to describe our physical world. Our concept of the self is changed as new scientific theories evolve and new evidence is presented, provided the new information is disseminated. Science gains knowledge through conducting research. However, the current general view of physical reality and the universe is based on models that no longer adequately explain the phenomena of our experienced reality. The majority of educated people, including education systems, medical research bodies, corporations, governments, and indeed some of those in the mainstream scientific community itself, still hold a dualistic worldview of mechanical materialism and a separate spirituality that manifests in some kind of religious expression.

Newton, together with Darwin, gave us a description of a mechanistic universe, existing independently from humans, created by accident, with no purpose and doomed to endless scarcity and competitive struggle before ending in heat death by a decline into disorder. Still, the most popular view that prevails is that "out there" is an external reality that controls our lives and is composed of separate objects behaving in a predictable way. The most separate of these are the human beings, who are disconnected from their source and each other. The old scientific paradigm view based on the Newtonian model posits that all objects exist within a three-dimensional geometry of length, width, and height and move in space according to fixed laws of motion. Matter was considered to have fixed boundaries, and to influence matter in any way required force applied from outside the object. Everything is isolated and not connected, and we cannot affect the material world by what we think or do.

It was also Newton that discovered mathematics could accurately describe the physical world, an incredibly valuable legacy to the modern scientist. Newtonian physics is referred to as classical physics and is the mathematical formulation of common sense. It makes *basic assumptions* about the fabric of our reality that correspond to how the world appears to our senses. These are assumptions only based on the perceptions of the five physical senses. The classical physics way of regarding the world appeared sufficient to explain large segments of the observable world. It worked for most things at the physical human scale. It is common sense. Classical physics holds that the universe is made from solid objects made from smaller building blocks called atoms. This physics relied on reductionism, the philosophical position that holds that a complex system is nothing but the sum of its parts, and if we break down the components and study them in isolation, this gives rise to an understanding of the whole system. The problem is this philosophy is no longer feasible. When we break down atoms to their smallest parts, we find these parts behave very differently from what was predicted by Newtonian physics.

Similarly, the premise of Darwin's theory of evolution is a widely held notion that all life has evolved from nonlife in a purely naturalistic and undirected way: that humans have evolved from simplistic ancestors over a period of time by way of random genetic mutations within the organism's genetic code, and by the process of natural selection, these mutations are preserved because they aid survival. In other words, it is the survival of the fittest. Over a period of time, the mutations accumulate, to result in the creation of an entirely different organism, us. However, even Darwin himself agreed that reductionism could not account for the development of such complex systems as the eye, ear, and heart. In 1859 he wrote: "To suppose that the eye with all its inimitable contrivances for adjusting the focus to different distances, for admitting different amounts of light, and for the correction of spherical and chromatic aberration, could have been formed by natural selection, seems, I freely confess, absurd in the highest degree."[3]

Molecular biologist Michael Denton wrote of Darwinism as a theory in crisis. "Although the tiniest bacterial cells are incredibly small, weighing less than 10^{-12} grams, each is in effect a veritable micro-miniaturized factory containing thousands of exquisitely designed pieces of intricate molecular machinery, made up altogether of one hundred thousand million atoms, far more complicated than any machinery built by man and absolutely without parallel in the non-living world."[4] And yet, this theory is a prevalent worldview that continues to be taught to our children today.

Rene Descartes was one of the most prominent philosophers, mathematicians, and scientists of the seventeenth century and had a profound influence on the history of Western philosophy. He is probably best known for the statement "I think therefore I am." His premise that the body (matter) and mind (intelligence) are two independent substances and not connected has been the basis of allopathic medicine for over three hundred years. But we will see there is hard evidence now that this is simply no longer a truth. To his great credit, Descartes initiated the model for explaining natural phenomena with science-based observation and experiment, the foundation of modern science. For this we must be grateful to him, for it is through this scientific method that we continue to be curious and evolve our knowledge of our universe and our place in it.

Commonly Held Misperceptions

❖ The physical world is objectively real and exists in a fixed and objective way, whether being observed or not.
❖ Objects can only be influenced by direct contact. Action at a distance is not possible.

❖ There is a one directional fixed cause and effect sequence that occurs in that order.

❖ There are no discontinuous jumps in nature and space and time are smooth.

❖ Mind and body are separate, and mind cannot affect the material world.

❖ Genes are responsible for our biology. The body is a machine determined by its genetic codes and DNA; the engine is the brain.

❖ Health is predetermined by our genes.

❖ Consciousness is a product of the brain.

❖ The space between objects is empty.

❖ Everything exists in isolation and is not connected.

To summarize, a general current worldview is this is a clockwork universe, where objects and humans operate separately in time and space; human beings have evolved by genetic mutation to secure the survival of the fittest, with no direction or purpose; and our bodies are completely separate from our minds and spirit. These assumptions have shaped our belief system about our world, our identity, and our being and are views still held by many in the world today.

Change and Resistance

Science has evolved considerably over the past century, and there is now mounting evidence that these assumptions are simply not true. Yes, I say *century* because a lot of the information that will be presented here is not new. Many authors have presented this information before, including the scientists themselves. However, as with all paradigm shifts, it takes time for the new version to be accepted and assimilated. Even though new information exists and is incontrovertible, often, new ideas that do not fit a current worldview are either not perceived, not acknowledged, or dismissed. There is resistance by mainstream scientists to change their way of thinking, even though much of the new science is peer reviewed. This is not helped by the fragmentation of established science bodies, with their inability to correlate the results of all the disassociated disciplines. This creates a barrier to a clear overview. The left hand does not know what the right hand is doing; this kind of decentralization does not support collaboration.

There is resistance in education systems to embrace new ideas and an inability within current structures to accommodate the multidisciplinary approach required to connect the dots. There is resistance from governments and corporations to fund and support modern scientific discovery not consistent with political and financial aims. Added to this catalogue of restraint is a mainstream media that often delivers on the basis of financial and political considerations. This has ever been the case with new ideas that point to a radical change in our thinking, but the unequivocal fact remains: the old science no longer can explain the reality of our experience as human beings. Our belief systems are flawed on a very large scale, and this keeps us from knowing who we truly are and what we can be and accomplish.

What Is the New Science?

According to d'Espagnat, "The doctrine that the world is made up of objects whose existence is independent of human consciousness turns out to be in conflict with quantum mechanics and with facts established by experiment."[5]

This is such an exciting time to be alive. If we take a look at the developments in the various scientific disciplines over the past hundred years, these discoveries themselves give evidence of the magnificent creations human beings are. The science section of the book takes a look at the incredible science supporting its message. We will discover that we only see what we expect to see in our outer reality. If we change our expectation, we change the outcome of what we observe. Everything is connected or entangled and interacts with instant communication, and even though the movement of particles is random, it becomes ordered or coherent by human intention and thought. Our genes do not determine our health and well-being. Our consciousness does not arise from the brain. Mind does significantly affect matter. We are each a cell in the planetary body, inextricably linked to all species and connected to the entire solar system, galaxy, and cosmos by fields of energy. And most importantly, we are all in this together.

This may turn all your current belief systems upside down and hence not be comfortable to read. Or you may believe this information does not affect you or your life. Initially it may not seem relevant to you to investigate such disciplines as quantum physics or cosmology, and yes, the book, could have been written without this and still carry an empowering message. However, quantum physics is the study of how the smallest components of our universe behave. You and me and everything in our known universe are made from these components. Cosmology is the science of the origin and development of the universe. You do not need to be a scientist to understand the implications of the work of these great pioneers of knowledge.

CHAPTER 2

Energy—A Universal Proposition

Before starting our journey through the most incredible science imaginable, this section begins with some fundamental definitions of terms that will be used throughout the book in order to provide clarity for the reader with no or little scientific knowledge. It all starts with energy. To those in the scientific world, this word can mean one thing; to those of an esoteric nature, it may mean something else. It has been my experience as a practitioner of energy management that there is much confusion around the meaning of this term, creating a duality that is unnecessary. Therefore, I have included my own definition based on my research and my own practical experience as a conduit for receiving and transmitting energy. This book will show it is all the same energy, whichever philosophy or discipline you follow. Energy *is* what powers our world, but in a much more significant way than it may be presently seen and understood as a global norm. Let's take a look at what energy *really* is.

Energy can be described as the strength, vitality, and power derived from resources required to create an effect or outcome by informing, deforming, reforming, or transforming matter. This term can be applied to all life and all its aspects: physical, emotional, mental, and spiritual.

Energy's various manifestations lie along a spectrum comprising various effects seen and unseen in the physical world, for energy itself is not visible. For example, when electrons are forced along a path in a conducting substance, such as a wire, the result is an energy called electricity. The electrons cannot be seen in the wire, but the resulting electricity powers our appliances. There are many different types of energy known because of their effect or the work they do. Its multiple expressions include:

- ❖ electric,
- ❖ magnetic,
- ❖ electromagnetic,
- ❖ light (color is formed when light is reflected or emitted from an object),
- ❖ sound,
- ❖ nuclear,
- ❖ thermal—heat,
- ❖ kinetic—motion,
- ❖ chemical,
- ❖ biological,
- ❖ psychological,
- ❖ potential (energy stored because of a position, e.g., a drawn bow),

plus others that may yet be unknown. It can be defined as the ability or capacity to move or change matter or substance. Energy surrounds us but has no mass, and yet we can observe the effects it has on matter. It can be conserved and transformed into a different state and is perceived as being unable to be created or destroyed. The amount of energy something has refers to its capacity to make something happen, to move an object over a distance against a force.

Some Useful Definitions

Vibration

is the back-and-forth movement of an electron in a regular rhythm from its center of equilibrium. This may also be called an oscillation. These oscillations carry information that can either be stored or applied.[6] At the particle level of an atom, electrons are moving back and forth, up and down, at high speeds, causing a vibration at a certain frequency.

Frequency

is the number of times the movement occurs. The faster the movement, the higher the frequency; the slower the movement, the lower the frequency.[7]

Resonance

A most important quality of vibrating energy is sound. Everything that vibrates creates a sound,[*] which, in turn, creates resonance. Resonance is the tendency of a system to vibrate with greater amplitude at a particular frequency rather than others. When this amplitude is its maximum, this is known as the system's resonant frequency. Resonance is the phenomenon that occurs when, for example, you strike a tuning fork; another fork near it will begin to vibrate at the same frequency and create the same sound. Similarly, through this mechanism, vibrating energy will attract to itself like energy, hence the words "resonate with."

---

[*] Not all sounds are audible to the human ear. Generally any frequency above 20khz is inaudible. Any sound above this is considered to be ultrasound.
Hz = cycles per second.

All matter vibrates at a specific rate. This is the object's natural or resonant frequency, and it will vibrate strongly when subject to vibrations equal to or very close to its own natural frequency. Through resonance, a weak vibration in one object can cause a strong vibration in another.[8]

Energy Field

When electrons move within a particle, their vibrations create an excitation in space or a field of energy. Fields are the wavelike, fluid motion of particles and how forces (see below) move through space. Whether a field becomes a true wave or not depends on how or if it moves itself though space. Fields can detach themselves into packets of energy and move independently, supporting and regenerating one another along the way. This then becomes an independent wave, for example, a radio wave.[9]

Force

A force is an interaction that either maintains or changes the motion of an object.[10]

The Four Known Forces of the Universe

Gravity is the force with which an object attracts other objects to itself. The force of gravity on earth is always equal to the weight of the object.[11]

Electromagnetism is the force that causes the interaction between electrically charged particles. The moving electron of an atom has a negative charge and the proton at the nucleus is positive. They are held together by the attractive force of magnetism. The areas in which this happens are called electromagnetic fields. Electromagnetism is the force that holds electrons and protons together in an atom.

Electric fields and magnetic fields are just different aspects of the same force and are therefore intrinsically linked, so a changing electric field creates a magnetic field and vice versa.[12]

Nuclear Strong— binds the protons and neutrons in the nucleus together in an atom.[13]

Nuclear Weak—is responsible for radioactive decay and the nuclear fusion of subatomic particles.[14]

What Is Matter?

> Concerning matter, we have been all wrong. What we have called matter is energy, whose vibration has been so lowered as to be perceptible to the senses. There is no matter.
>
> —Albert Einstein

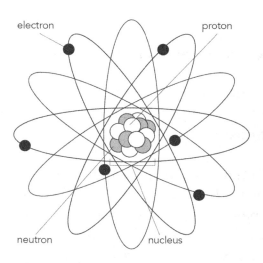

Figure 2.1. Structure of a carbon atom.

Matter is an illusory state. It appears solid because it has mass and takes up space. However, matter is simply very dense or compacted energy vibrating at a certain frequency. Atoms are mostly space and contain only 0.00001 percent substance. There are several models that describe matter: the particle/orbital view, in which the moving electrons create fields of energy and only give an illusion of solidity; the particle/wave view or dualistic quantum model, where matter can exist as a particle or a wave; and the modern unified field view that matter exists as a particle, wave, and field simultaneously in space. This is still an open line of research.

Different States of Matter

* ❖ condensate (a term given to a superatom formed at temperatures near absolute zero; the atoms stop moving due to loss of energy and form a clump in one large atom),
* ❖ solid,
* ❖ liquid,
* ❖ gaseous, and
* ❖ plasma

Waves

Waves are disturbances in a given medium that transfer energy from one location to another without transporting matter. Essentially waves are information carriers.

Light and the Electromagnetic Spectrum

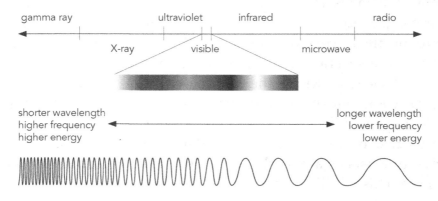

Figure 2.2. Electromagnetic spectrum.

Transverse Waves

Light waves are transverse waves, which means they oscillate (vibrate and rotate) opposite to their directional movement and can travel in a vacuum. The shorter the length of the wave, the higher is the frequency.

Longitudinal Waves

Longitudinal waves oscillate in the same direction as their directional movement (e.g., how a concertina moves) through compression and expansion and need to travel through a solid, liquid, gas, or plasma. These types of waves do not usually travel in a vacuum. Longitudinal waves traveling through the earth's interior are called telluric waves. It has been assumed, because these specific waves do not travel in a vacuum, that all longitudinal waves cannot. However, there is now important evidence showing there are certain types of longitudinal waves that can travel in a vacuum, with far-reaching consequences for science and for humankind.

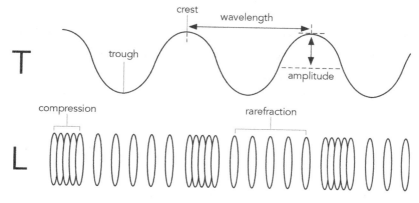

Figure 2.3.1. Waveforms.

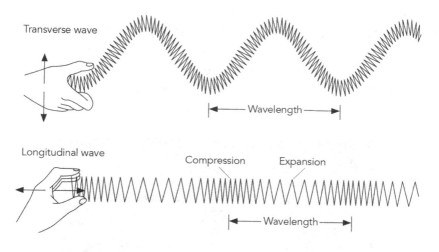

Figure 2.3.2. Wave directions.

Scalar Waves

First proposed by Tesla in the 1880s and largely ignored by the scientific community of the day, science is now evidencing the existence of scalar waves. These particular longitudinal waves have very unique properties and are greatly significant to all human life. Scalar waves are field-like as are normal longitudinal waves, but unlike the normal wave, they have been found to exceed the speed of light, tunnel through matter, pass through electromagnetic shielding, and disseminate from space. They can act as carriers, not only receiving and transmitting information but also amplifying it, causing their effects to be cumulative in nature.

"How is this meaningful to me?" you might ask.

We will begin to see the enormous implications of scalar energy and its extraordinary properties in subsequent chapters when we come to look at the physical and energetic components of the human being and the mechanisms by which they interact and connect with all other life. The incredible properties of scalar energy can account for many phenomena that have hitherto been unexplained, such as mind-matter interaction and remote viewing, to name only a couple. It also can account for many processes in the body that were previously thought to be only biochemical. For those who would like more information about the science of scalar energy, please see appendix.

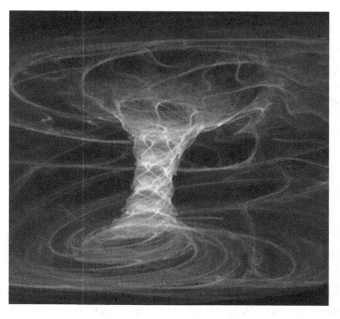

Figure 2.4. Energy vortex.

Vibration and Sound

> Each celestial body, in fact each and every
> atom, produces a particular sound on account
> of its movement, its rhythm or vibration. All
> these sounds and vibrations form a universal
> harmony in which each element, while having
> its own function and character, contributes to
> the whole.
>
> —Pythagoras (569–475 BC)

According to Pythagoras energy first manifests as vibration, and all vibration produces a sound depending on its frequency. It is the vibrating impulse or first sound that awakens matter into activity by creating photons of light and thereby all that is perceived in physical manifestation. Cymatics is the science of sound and vibration made visible. It is the term first used by the physician and natural scientist Hans Jenny in 1967 to describe the study of the effects that wave phenomena and vibration have on matter.[15]

Sound has the power to activate, manipulate, and affect matter and therefore, according to our definition, is energy. When the visual geometry of sound is studied, it is found to include many of the mathematical constants of the universe, including phi, known as the golden mean. This ratio is 1 to 1.618 and is the ideal moderate position between two extremes, visually presenting as a harmony and beauty of proportion. It is also expressed mathematically in a number sequence called the Fibonacci sequence and is found in all living things. This ratio shows up in nature, music, and art, and is even involved in the physics of black holes, thus demonstrating the connection between sound and all life.

Figure 2.5. Cymaglyph of twin sound spiral. Reprinted courtesy of Sonic Age America, LLC.
Figure 2.6. A mathematical beauty. Image courtesy of Aimee Rivers, 2010, https://www.flickr.com/photos/sermoa/4657844388/. Creative Commons attribution—no derivatives, 4.0 international public license.

In 2002 acoustics engineer John Stuart Reid in the United Kingdom, in collaboration with Erik Larsen, a design engineer in the United States, developed a new type of scientific instrument called the CymaScope™. This was built to Pythagorean proportions and is able to imprint sonic vibration onto ultrapure water. It is based on the premise that when a sound meets a surface such as water, it imprints an invisible pattern of energy. This means the vibrations of the sound are converted and become water ripples, creating geometric patterns that are actually holographic bubbles, each with a pattern on its surface. A most remarkable example of this is demonstrated by the image created by a recording of the sun's vibration. Stanford University, in collaboration with the European Space Agency (ESA) and National Aeronautics and Space Administration (NASA), while studying the physics of the sun's core, its outer corona, and solar wind regions, obtained data available from the SOHO spacecraft. CymaScope.com has imaged one of the sounds recorded from this spacecraft, literally the "Song of the Sun."

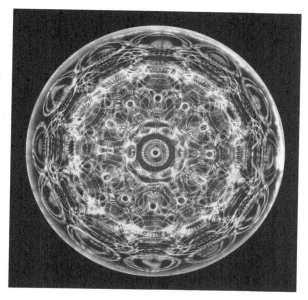

Figure 2.7. Cymaglyph: "The Song of the Sun." © Stanford University. Image courtesy Sonic Age America, LLC.

Pythagoras also developed a system of musical tuning, in which the frequency relationships are based on a specific ratio; this is the oldest way of tuning the musical scale: A = 432 Hz*, also known as Verdi's A. This interval was chosen because it was the most pleasing to the ear. Pythagoras, who was more famous for his geometry, had discovered the relationship between harmony and numbers, and it has now been realized that many of the ancient cultures unknowingly tuned their instruments using the same tuning mechanism. It can be found in such instruments as Tibetan bowls, Native American flutes, and the Indian sitar. Its mathematics has also been

---

* Currently the basis for modern tuning is 440Hz. This was made the ISO standard in 1953. Even though the difference is only 8 cycles per second, the longer wave of 432Hz is a much fuller, richer, rounded sound, and the comparable images reveal it creates a much clearer and definite pattern that resonates more deeply with the physical body and its energy field.

correlated with cosmic movement, the construction of a variety of ancient sites from the Pyramid at Giza to Stonehenge, the speed of light, the frequencies of color on the electromagnetic spectrum, and the phi ratio of all living things. Our universe is slowly revealing itself as one based on a universal language of mathematics, geometry, energy patterns, and frequencies of light and sound.[16,17,18]

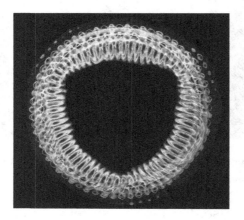

Figure 2.8. Cymaglyph of 432hertz.
Courtesy of Sonic Age America, LLC.

Holographic Sound and Light

Reid's research proposes that sound is holographic in nature. He has found that, rather than moving through the air as a longitudinal wave, as previously thought, sound moves in a sonic bubble, with the same vibration as the original source. He proposes that every atom in the sonic bubble contains all the data of the sound source. He also proposes that the sonic bubble is accompanied by low-level light emissions; and that sound and light are inextricably linked.[19]

Fractals—The Secret Codes of Creation

> To see the world in a grain of sand, and heaven
> in a wild flower,
>   Hold Infinity in the palm of your hand and
> eternity in an hour.
>
> —William Blake

All form is based on how energy moves, and all the various geometric shapes are created by spin or rotary motion of particles around energy's axis. Nature uses the five perfect divisions of the sphere or the Platonic solids as the basis for the diverse forms of matter. Shapes, forms, proportions, and rhythms are nature's toolbox for expression and evolution. Everything has a pattern, and the pattern is key to creating a specific effect. The most important patterns are repeated throughout all levels of creation. Let us take, for example, the sphere; this is based on rotational energy movement. This is the container shape for energy and is repeated throughout all life-forms, from an atom to a planet. The spiral is also found replicated many times in nature. This is another way that energy moves, spiraling upward to higher levels of vibration and frequency. These recurring patterns are known as fractals and occur repeatedly on smaller and smaller scales, each tiny part containing a replication of the whole. These fractal configurations of nature are the patterns of evolution, and they clearly demonstrate the overall intelligent-design pattern inherent in nature. Amazingly, the abstract world of mathematics can now demonstrate that shape is built into numbers.

Newton was the first to realize mathematics could describe the physical world; however, up until 1970, mathematics could only describe regular shapes. Anything irregular, such as a coastline, a mountain range, or a cloud, was outside mathematical description. It required a new geometry and a different kind of formula to translate nature's patterns into a mathematical proposition. The Mandelbrot set (set = a collection of numbers), together with the advanced computing power of twentieth-century processors, has been able to demonstrate the maps of fractal patterning that are built into number sequences—shapes that repeat and repeat infinitely on a smaller and smaller scale. The most important point to remember about this phenomenon, other than the extraordinary beauty and complexity fractals demonstrate, is that mathematics reveals them but did not create them. The patterns were already there, just waiting to be discovered. Mathematics is a concept of quantity; numbers are abstract, not physical; and the laws of mathematics are mental constructs only. But the numbers are a tool of discovery and reveal the underlying intelligent energy of the universe exhibited in the snowflake, the fern, a coastline, a mountain chain, or lightning branches.

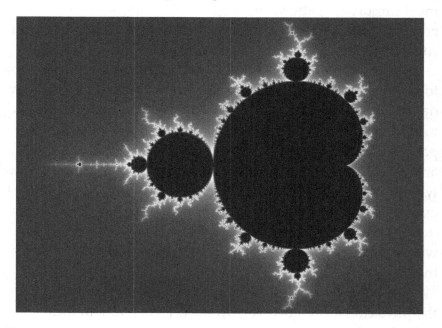

Figure 2.9. Mandelbrot-set fractal. Courtesy Wolfang Beyer, 2006, http://en.wikipedia.org/wiki/Mandelbrot_set. Creative Commons attribution—no derivatives, 4.0 international public license.

Mandelbrot recognized this when he stated he knew how to transform the formulas into pictures instantly.[20] Evidence of fractal patterns and their applications can be seen everywhere. For example, in nature the distribution of trees in a forest replicates the distribution of branches on a tree. The fractal pattern in a forest enables researchers to predict the amount of carbon dioxide the entire forest can absorb. Brian Enquist, professor of Ecology and Evolutionary Biology at the University of Arizona, states, "All of life is sustained by underlying networks and circuitry systems; full biological systems are fractal."[21]

Ary Goldberger, professor of Medicine at Harvard Medical School, discovered that the heartbeat is not constant over time and that a healthy heartbeat has a distinctive, fractal architecture. These patterns can be used as an important diagnostic tool in determining heart disease.[22] More and more physiological processes have been found to be fractal.

Ophthalmologist Martin Mainster found that the branching patterns of the retinal arterial and venous system have characteristics of a fractal, a geometrical pattern whose parts resemble the whole. More amazing research reveals the eye absorbs an incredibly large amount of information and physiological changes can occur when fractal patterns are viewed.[23]

Richard Taylor, professor of Physics, Psychology, and Art at the University of Oregon, and his research team have been able to use eye-tracking equipment to examine how people view patterns, together with EEG and MRI probes, which quantify the resulting brain activity. These experiments indicate that human beings are hardwired to respond to a specific form of fractal found in nature and that this can reduce stress levels by up to 60 percent.[24] Stress reduction is triggered by a physiological resonance when the fractal structure of the eye matches that of the fractal image being viewed. When the fractal properties of two patterns match resonance, this generates a state of relaxation in the observer. Light (color) and pattern can create change in our physiology.[25]

Peter Burns from the University of Toronto has used fractal patterns present in the structure of blood vessels to generate a mathematical model that can detect early signs of cancer in patients. Early-developing tumors can be difficult to detect by ultrasound because the vasculature that feeds them is tangled and disorganized. The fractal patterns present in healthy tissue allow a direct comparison and detection of what may become malignant tissue by monitoring the blood flow in the very early stages of tumor development.[26]

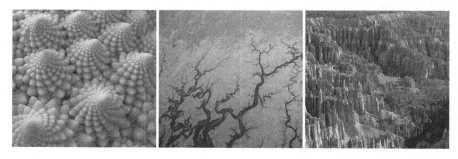

Figure 2.10. Fractals in nature. Courtesy Flickr.
Figure 2.10.1. Fractal vegetable. Paul McCoubrie, 2012. http://www.flickr.com/photos/paulmccoubrie/6792412657
Figure 2.10.2. Florida delta. Nelson Minar, 2010. http://www.flickr.com/photos/nelsonminar/5343713074/
Figure **2.10.3.** Fractal world, Bryce Canyon. Brewbooks,2009. http://www.flickr.com/photos/brewbooks/3759544955/
All images Creative Commons attribution—no derivatives, 4.0 international public license.

Science is beginning to unveil a very different picture of our universe and the active intelligence that underlies all life.

Debunking the Myths of Darwinism

According to biologist Rupert Sheldrake, Darwin's evolution theory is based on assumptions. It does not explain how one species becomes another or why a genotype stays constant when the physical appearance of species can vary so much. He believes it is an incorrect assumption to suggest that members of the same species are in competition for food sources and therefore survival, as this is not always the case; for example, wolves hunt in a pack and share the kill. The discovery of fractals is one of the strongest evidences that the patterns of evolution are not created by chance and without purpose. Darwinism is based on the foundational idea that variations in species occur by chance. However, as the fractal configuration of nature becomes more and more clearly apparent, "evolution appears to be fuelled by an innate intelligence of life moving towards greater wholeness as it recognizes and adapts to the changes in the physical world."[27] Observation of nature reveals that as change occurs, greater awareness is achieved, giving rise to more sophisticated forms with greater perception. This increased awareness becomes the key to successful survival.

Cellular biologist Bruce Lipton offers a wonderful illustration of the fractal evolutionary process based on simple cellular development. If evolution is defined as developing greater awareness, at the single cellular level he shows us this awareness would be the receptor site. This interfaces with the environment, surveying all and reporting back to the cell. The more receptor sites, the greater the awareness, and survival becomes assured. However, the cell's size limits the number of receptors it can possess. How does it increase awareness?

Simple cells group themselves together to form colonies to increase collective awareness. By joining together they demonstrate organizing forces in new directions that would be impossible for a single cell. To obtain a larger awareness requires the many cells of a colony to merge once more into a singularity by folding the membrane inward and thereby increasing overall receptor capacity. The cells then become incorporated into different cells specializing in certain types of awareness and form tiny organs inside the cell wall. This creates a new awareness in the form of a complex single cell, a eukaryotic cell. From here the single eukaryotic cells once again group together to form another complex. This process continues as ever higher levels of complexity are organized into tissue, bones, and organs, and so the survival of the group becomes more important than that of the individual and eventually together they create a single multicellular organism, a human being. The life process becomes a cycle of one to many to one to many, and so this continues. Biological evolution is established as a fractal process as the basic formula replicates itself. Lipton points out that there is no function in the human body that is not already present in a cell.[28] Just as the cells in the human body create a multicellular organization to make a whole being, the human being is now at a stage in its evolution where its survival depends on its interconnectedness with all life on the planet. Now is the time for group endeavor.

Summary

Everything is energy. Modern physics is now revealing that everything is a pure phenomenon of energy interaction, information fields, and resonance. Everything in our cosmos—universe, galaxy, solar system, planet, plants, animals, rocks, the table, the chair, you, me, and everything else—is made from substances vibrating at different frequencies, some of which are visible and some of which are not. All vibrating substance creates sound determined by its frequency, and the sonic bubble of sound is accompanied by light emission. All form is based on the movement of energy, creating patterns that are repeated throughout creation even down to cellular development. This confirms the very presence of an active intelligence inherent in all substance. The fractals we observe around us every day in the clouds, trees, vegetables, flowers, and mountain ranges remind us those patterns are in us too, and most particularly, the rhythm of our beating heart reminds us that we are one with nature, its pulse, and its cycle. Fractal evolution becomes the journey home. Humankind is evolving to unite as fully conscious elements to share awareness for the common benefit of planetary evolution. Human beings are the cells in the body of the earth, and we have reached a stage of physical development where the next stage is to inform, deform, reform, and transform the body, thus enlightening its structure and stepping into a higher frequency of vibration together. As Nassim Haramein states, "The level of consciousness of a civilisation is always equal to its capacity to reach new fractal scales of relationship in its world."[29]

CHAPTER 3

The Great Pioneers of Energy and Matter

Einstein and Planck

Physics is the branch of science concerned with the study of the properties of energy and matter, and the foundations of the current science model rest upon two major theories: Albert Einstein's special and general theories of relativity, describing the largest objects in our universe, and quantum theory, originated by German physicist Max Planck, accounting for the tiniest objects.

Einstein was considered the most influential scientist of the twentieth century. However, his early years gave no indication of his hidden genius. Born in Germany in 1879, he did not speak until he was three, and his performance at school was considered mediocre. As a teenager he found his formal education boring and useless and began studying advanced mathematics and physics in his spare time. He finally obtained his doctorate in physics while working as a clerk in the Swiss patent office and published his revolutionary *Theory of Relativity* in 1905. This described the existence of space/time, extending Newton's laws of gravitation and motion. It confirmed nothing moved faster than the speed of light, and it revealed that a tiny amount of mass can create a massive amount of energy. His famous equation was:

$$e=mc^2$$

e = energy, m = mass, and c^2 = the speed of light squared

Basically, this equation means energy and mass are interchangeable. If an object has mass, it is considered to be matter, and masses increase as the speed of light is approached.

Einstein became a hero, and his theory revolutionized physics and impacted many other disciplines, as well as philosophy and society in general. Einstein showed that the speed of light must be constant, no matter how fast an object is moving. Time gets slower the faster an object moves. Space and time became relative in his new theory. This new insight was pivotal in overthrowing 250 years of Newtonian physics. What had been thought constant and absolute was now regarded as relative.

Ten years later Einstein introduced another theory, in which space and time are like a fabric that can be curved and stretched. This new picture—in which gravity originates from the bending of sheets of space-time[30]—revolutionized cosmology and introduced a new theory of creation, the big bang theory. Although this theory is the current accepted version of gravity in modern physics, it remains only a theory.

Although he was not a great fan of quantum theory and instead preferred to think of it as only a piece of the puzzle in a grand unified theory of everything, Einstein did contribute significantly to the newly developed theory of Max Planck. He also demonstrated the dual wave/particle nature of light. In 1905 when Planck postulated that energy is quantized, that is, it exists in individual units and not just one continuous wave, Einstein proposed that not just the energy but the radiation (photon) itself was quantized in the same manner, and quantum theory was born.[31]From here on, the advance in scientific discovery that emerged as a development of this theory over the next hundred years, as scientists discovered the atoms that formed Newton's building blocks of the universe consisted of even smaller subatomic particles, has been nothing less than breathtaking in its implications. This model, which now is known as the standard model, gives us a very different view of the behavior of matter and energy.

Quantum is derived from the Latin word meaning amount, and in modern understanding it describes the smallest possible discrete unit of any physical property, such as energy or matter.

The Quantum Brigade

"The theories and discoveries of thousands of physicists since the 1930s have resulted in a remarkable insight into the fundamental structure of matter: everything in the universe is found to be made from a few basic building blocks called fundamental particles, governed by four fundamental forces."[32]

Quantum theory explains the nature and behavior of matter and energy at the subatomic and atomic levels. Max Planck won the Nobel Prize in 1918 for his theory, but there have been many scientists who have made incredible contributions to the development of what now forms the basis of modern physics. Many others have also been awarded Nobel Prizes. Their work has deep implications for the understanding of energetics.

Wave or Particle?

At the subatomic level, matter and light consist of particles that have dual properties. They can be either particles or waves. In 1905 Einstein published his paper to explain the photoelectric effect, proposing that light waves travel as discrete bundles of energy called quanta. The energy contained within a photon is related to the frequency of the light and can have particle-like interactions with other particles. This theory came to be known as the photon theory of light.

The question of whether this phenomenon also applied to matter was investigated by Louis de Broglie in 1924. He hypothesized that the behavior of energy and matter was the same at the atomic and subatomic levels and extended Einstein's work to include the theory that waves are produced by electrons orbiting the nucleus of an atom and these waves have a certain energy, frequency, and wavelength. Experiments confirmed the hypothesis in 1927, resulting in a 1929 Nobel Prize for de Broglie.[33]

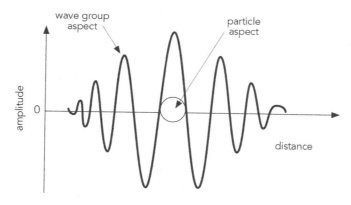

Figure 3.1. The wave particle nature of light and matter.

The double-slit experiment is a most famous experiment, first conducted in the nineteenth century, in which Thomas Young demonstrated the wave/particle nature of light.[34]

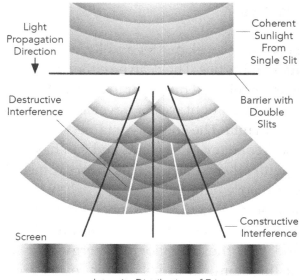

Figure 3.2. **This figure** illustrates Thomas Young's double-slit experiment showing the wave/particle properties of light and matter. Light (photons) or matter (electrons) is fired from a single source (laser or electron gun) toward a plate with two slits. Behind the first plate is a second observer plate. As the material passes through the slits, it begins to diffract (spread out in wavelike fashion). The waves create an interference pattern that shows up on the observer screen, hitting the observer screen at discrete points as particles, creating the diffracted pattern on the observer panel. This result would not be expected if the material had passed through the original two slits as particles. Thus the experiment evidences the wave and particle properties of light and matter.

The famous double-slit experiment demonstrating the wave/particle duality has been replicated many times by many different scientists. The most recent experiments, in 2012 by Radin and associates, have been refined and extended to give us modern-day evidence published in a mainstream science journal not only of the wave/particle effect but also that human consciousness influences the world we perceive.[35] The double-slit experiment is a demonstration that light and matter can display characteristics of both classically defined waves and particles. Radin's extended versions in six different experiments also demonstrate the probabilistic nature of quantum phenomena and the collapse of the wave nature of particles when being observed, indicating the inseparability of the experiment and the experimenter.

All Possible States at Once; Believing Is Seeing

Quanta (the smallest packets of energy) exist in a field of probability. The act of observing or measuring quanta can determine whether they show up as particles or as waves; until then they are in all states simultaneously. In 1926 Viennese physicist Erwin Schrodinger published an equation describing how the quantum state of a physical system changes with time and the wave function of particles. The total of all possible states in which an object can exist—for example, in wave or particle form for photons (particles of light) that travel in both directions at once–makes up the object's *wave function*.[36]

In 1927 Werner Heisenberg proposed that the precise simultaneous measurement of two complementary values— such as the position and momentum of a subatomic particle—is impossible. This theory became known as *the uncertainty principle*.[37] The same year Niels Bohr proposed an interpretation of this theory called the Copenhagen interpretation, which asserts that a particle is whatever it is measured to be (for example, a wave or a particle) but that it cannot be assumed to have specific properties, or even to exist, until it is measured.[38] Simply, Bohr was saying that objective reality does not exist.

This gave rise to the principle called *coherent superposition*, which claims that while the state of any object is unknown, it is actually in all possible states simultaneously, as long as it is not observed. Energy takes on matter form when it is observed and remains only a potential otherwise. It may be forced into a different observable state each time. When an object is observed, the superposition collapses, and the object is forced into one of the states of its wave function. Therefore, observers have the ability to manifest form by collapsing the wave potential into particles by the simple act of observing or measuring the particle they expect to see. This was the first time science acknowledged that human beings can have an effect on matter.

The wave/particle theory provides us with the possibility that objects are probability waves or probabilities of connections, events, or paths that only may become event, as well as that the universe is a dynamic web of energies and energy patterns that includes the observer to become visible.

The Virtual Sea

Theoretical physicist and Nobel Laureate Paul Dirac in the 1930s proposed the antiparticle theory, which states that for every positive electron there is a negative positron.[39] He correctly predicted a negative energy state unobservable to the human eye. What was originally thought of as the vacuum of space is actually filled with a negative energy state; these particles could not be measured, because they are virtual, not physical, and therefore unobservable. If the negative energy state is stimulated by a photon (light) with enough energy, the particle may be promoted into a positive state and become physically visible. The holes left behind are the antiparticle or positron, and all particles possess this mirror state. The theory was confirmed by Carl David Anderson in 1932, who discovered the antielectron or positron in cosmic rays using a cloud chamber at the University of California.[40] To date, antiparticles have been found for all named particles in physics, confirming that the vacuum of space is a sea of virtual particles that may be brought into physical visibility by light.

Entanglement or "Spooky Actions at a Distance"

Entanglement is a term used in quantum theory that describes the way particles form a relationship that allows them to predictably interact with each other. In this process of correlation, particles that have interacted with each other retain their connection and can be entangled with each other in pairs. If the spin state of one particle is known, this allows us to know that the spin state of its partner will be in the opposite direction. Even more amazing, the measured particle has no single spin state before being measured due to the aforementioned phenomenon of superposition. This is determined at the time of measurement and communicated to the other particle, which may be separated by incredible distances. This seems to allow for communication that is not limited to the speed of light. No matter how great the distance between the particles, they will remain entangled as long as they are isolated. This has given rise to the term *nonlocality*, which describes the apparent ability of objects to instantaneously know about each other's state, even when separated by large distances, potentially even billions of light-years. This was first described in the "EPR Papers" of Albert Einstein, Boris Podolsky, and Nathan Rosen in 1935, and it is sometimes referred to as the EPR paradox.[41] Nonlocality suggests that the universe is profoundly different from our habitual understanding of it and that its "separate" parts are potentially connected in an intimate and immediate way.

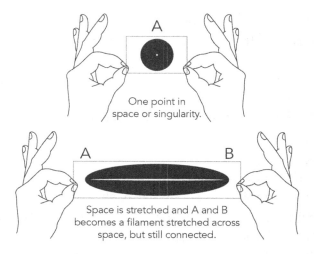

Figure 3.3. Quantum entanglement, also known as nonlocality. Particles remain connected across space and time.

In 1964, Irish physicist John Bell produced a theory to demonstrate that the results predicted and described by Einstein, Podolsky, and Rosen could not be explained by any theory that maintained the state of locality.[42] The subsequent practical experiments by John Clauser and Stuart Freedman in 1972 seem to definitively show that the effects of nonlocality are real and that "spooky actions at a distance," as Einstein described them, are indeed possible.[43] Alain Aspect, a French physicist, proved Bell's theorem experimentally in 1982.[44] The concept of entanglement, nonlocality, and instantaneous communication gives rise to the possibility of information exchange without the transfer of energy and possibly could account for such phenomena as telepathy, remote viewing, distance transfer of light and sound vibrations.

As Rolf Landaver stated, "Given that small amounts of information can precipitate huge reactions in biological systems, non-local biological effects, even if infinitesimally small, could conceivably affect other biological systems at a distance."[45]

Since Aspect's initial experiment, many scientists all over the world have continued to explore the implications and possible applications of quantum entanglement and have shown it is possible to transmit information instantaneously by quantum teleportation.

Bennett and associates stated, "The property of quantum entanglement establishes a connection between two particles in such a way that the quantum essence of the particle can be passed from one to the other, i.e., it can be teleported to another location along with all the information it embodies."[46]

Peter Higgs's Boson

The very latest discovery in particle physics has been made by scientists working with the large hadron collider in Geneva, Switzerland, a huge project helmed by the European Organization for Nuclear Research, or CERN as it is known. Using this megasize particle accelerator in July 2012, scientists found a particle believed to be the Higgs boson, named after the British theoretical physicist Peter Higgs. Nearly fifty years ago, he predicted the Higgs field, a scalar field present in all space, which gives rise to this particle. It is believed through interaction with this field and its boson that subatomic particles achieve their mass. Its discovery confirms the existence of the first scalar field and first elementary scalar particle found in nature. According to Lisa Randall, eminent theoretical physicist and cosmologist at Harvard, the particles interacting with this field could be thought of as "experiencing a new type of force, one that is distinct from the four known forces. While completing the particle theory of the Standard Model, its discovery opens up even more questions and more research for science."[47] At the time of writing, the discovery of this particle has not led to any further answers to the unanswered questions of physics. Questions concerning gravity, dark matter, dark energy, and the imbalance of matter to antimatter in the universe are currently the most active areas of research in physics as science continues its search for a "theory of everything."

A New Perspective

The old classical view of how our universe is constructed just cannot account for many of the experiences and phenomena now being reported worldwide in ever-increasing numbers. The evidence provided by the science of quantum theory has required scientists to develop new theories about the real nature of our reality; the standard model, accepted by the scientific community at large, now supersedes Newton's view but still leaves much unanswered. Currently, mainstream science accepts that Einstein's theory of relativity explains those objects that are visible to the eye and quantum theory explains what happens at the atomic and subatomic levels. Thanks to the development of new technology and more powerful probes and measuring devices now available, more and more discoveries are surfacing that remain unexplained by either theory. Scientists search for possible theories that can unify these two perspectives and continue their quest for the theory of everything. What we do know for sure is that science has now refuted some of our long-held assumptions surrounding the nature of matter and what we may believe is objective reality.

Summary

At the subatomic level, our material world is not solid. We live in a living field of probability, where particles can also be waves and flash in and out of visible existence constantly. Energy in the form of sound and light promotes them into existence, and what comes into existence can be affected by the very act of observing and intending. Everything is held together and interacts by four known forces of energy, and yet once particles that have been together are separated, they stay connected and have instant communication over vast distances. Our dive into the subatomic world reveals everything is energy and everything is connected.

CHAPTER 4

All the World's a Stage— The Principle of Holography

> In a certain sense, everything is everywhere at all times. For every location involves an aspect of itself in every other location. Thus every spatio-temporal standpoint mirrors the world.
>
> —Ralph Waldo Emerson

> All the world's a stage, and all the men and women merely players: they have their exits and their entrances; and one man in his time plays many parts, his acts being seven ages.
>
> —William Shakespeare

Several eminent scientists from different disciplines support a view that is based on the current known evidence of scientific inquiry and accounts for many of the phenomena that continue to proliferate in human experience. This is called the holographic theory. The concept of a hologram is that every piece is the exact representation of the whole and can therefore reconstruct the whole. This, of course, is based on the principle of fractals, examples of which we have already seen abound in nature; this principle has even wider implications when applied to our universe.

How Holograms Work

The hologram was first developed in 1947 by electrical engineer and physicist Denis Gabor. A hologram is produced when a single beam of coherent light, such as laser light, is focused at a beam splitter, which splits the beam into two separate parts. Mirrors direct the paths of the two beams so they reach their intended targets. Each beam passes through a discharging lens, diffusing the light from the narrow original beam. The first beam (the object beam) is reflected by its mirror and bounces off the object to be photographed (the ball) onto the photographic plate. Similarly, the second beam (the reference beam) reflects off its mirror and collides with the reflected light of the first beam on the photographic plate. This creates an interference pattern that is then captured on film. When another beam is shone through the film, a three-dimensional image of the original object will appear. A fascinating aspect of the holographic principle is that the whole object is recreated in each part of its three-dimensional image. If a holographic projection is divided into any number of pieces, each single piece incorporates a tiny and complete representation of the whole. The mathematics that describes the hologram enables any physical pattern to be transformed into waveforms and converted back to its original shape. The mathematics used is called Fourier transforms and is an analytical tool used by mathematicians and physicists to describe complex systems. They reveal the underlying geometry or patterns in a system, and Mandelbrot's discovery of fractal geometry in the 1970s confirms this. We will see that this principle is repeated many times in our exploration of the various physical manifestations of our universe.[48]

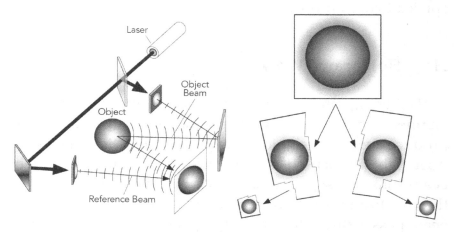

Figure 4.1.1. Hologram setup. **Figure 4.1.2.** Each part of a hologram contains the whole.

The Cosmic Hologram

Michael Talbot, in his groundbreaking book *The Holographic Universe,*[49] does an amazing job of describing the possible nature of the universe as a hologram and discusses in detail the theories of eminent theoretical physicist David Bohm, who was one of the first scientists to develop a holographic theory of the universe, which he called the implicate/explicate order theory based on quantum theory. Bohm, in his own book *Wholeness and the Implicate Order,*[50] stated that all arises from an enfolded implicate order. He asserts that the reality of our physical life is an illusion, similar to a holographic image. He believes all observable reality is underpinned by a deeper order that gives rise to all objects and appearances, similar to the way a piece of holographic film gives rise to a hologram. He calls the physical level of existence the explicate or unfolded order. It is his theory that electrons and all other particles are not permanent but sustained by a constant influx from the implicate or enfolded order, and when a particle appears to be destroyed, it simply enfolds back into the deeper level of order from which it came.

This is supported by Dirac's work, when he discovered the negative state of the particle. This constant flow and exchange between these two orders could explain how particles can change from one state to another (wave) and how quanta can be particles and wave events determined by the observer that become visible. Bohm describes the universe as a holomovement,[51] because he sees this as a perpetual movement between the two orders of reality. This also explains why reality is nonlocal at the sub-quantum level. When something is organized in holographic form, information is distributed non-locally. This he called a quantum potential that pervades all space and possesses wholeness or unity; he stated that the behavior of its parts was actually organized by the whole and suggested that this wholeness was the primary reality. At the sub- quantum level, the level in which quantum potential operates, location ceases to exist; all points in space become equal to all other points (a scalar field), and therefore nothing is separate from anything—there is unity. All particles are part of an unbroken web and embedded in space.

Further to Alain Aspect's discovery in 1982 on entanglement, Bohm interpreted his findings in another way. He posits that the reason subatomic particles are able to remain in contact with one another despite the distance separating them is not because they are communicating with one another beyond the speed of light but because their separateness is an illusion. He argues that at some deeper level of reality, such particles are not individual entities, but are actually extensions of the same fundamental essence.

Talbot describes Bohm's illustration beautifully. He asks us to imagine an aquarium containing a fish. Imagine also that you are unable to see the aquarium directly and your knowledge about it and what it contains comes from two television cameras, one directed at the front of the aquarium and the other directed at its side. As you stare at the two television monitors, you might assume that the fish on each of the screens are two separate entities. Because the cameras are set at different angles, each of the images will be slightly different. But as you continue to watch the two fish, you will eventually become aware that there is a certain relationship between them. When one turns, the other also makes a slightly different but corresponding turn; when one faces the front, the other always faces toward the side. If you remain unaware of the true nature of the situation, then you might even assume that the fish must be instantaneously communicating with one another, but this is clearly not the case.

Similar to the fish in the aquarium, Bohm argues that we are only seeing a portion of the reality of the subatomic particles. He goes even further to suggest that everything in the cosmos is one continuum, where all arises from the continuous, holographic fabric of the one implicate order. Everything, including you and me, is part of the undivided whole and yet still possesses its own unique aspects. "Separate" objects arise only as a way of making them stand out in our perception by the way we think.[52]

The Holy Grail—A Theory of Everything

Just like the quest of the Arthurian knights in search of the Holy Grail, a theory of everything, uniting the macro with the microworlds, became a main focus of scientific inquiry. Stephen Hawking, the world-renowned British theoretical physicist, is best known for his incredible contributions to cosmology, general relativity, and quantum gravity, particularly in relation to the quantum physics of black holes. This is exactly the point where Einstein's theories and quantum theory became irreconcilable.

Hawking predicted the universe had a beginning in space and time by spontaneously bursting into being as a big bang from a singularity* and would end with a black hole as the radiation dissipated. His original theory stated that once information disappears into a black hole, it is lost forever. Further developments in theoretical physics proposed the concepts of superstrings and M theory as a possible way to reconcile the macrocosmic with the microcosmic worlds. The idea that particles are point-like dots of matter is now superseded by a concept that all particles actually consist of ultra-minute waveforms called strings, whose oscillatory patterns and resonance form the universe and which vibrate in ten dimensions. The ten dimensions are compacted into the four dimensions of space-time and embedded in branes. Branes (short for membranes) are multidimensional objects that theoretically form the framework within which the strings oscillate and to which they are energetically connected. It may be that branes form the boundary of space-time and are the means by which the entire physical world is projected.[53] Hawking himself has now accepted the concept of the multiverse to help explain certain paradoxes that arose in his black hole theory.

Leonard Susskind, professor of Theoretical Physics at Stanford, known for his work on string theory and his support for the holographic principle, vehemently disagreed with Hawking about what happens to the information that disappears into a black hole; he theorized the universe is a hologram, and the information that disappears into a black

---

* *Singularity*: In the center of a black hole is a gravitational singularity, a one-dimensional point that contains infinite mass in an infinitely small space, where gravity becomes infinite and space-time curves infinitely and where the laws of physics as we know them cease to operate.[58]

hole is also stored and preserved and on the boundary of the system, the event horizon. (This becomes the photographic plate of Gabor's hologram setup.)

In 2013 Susskind, together with the brilliant Argentinian physicist Juan Maldacena and based on the experimental simulations of a group of Japanese researchers,[54,55,56,57] was able to provide some of the clearest evidence available yet that our universe is one huge projection.

The Holofractographic Model

A most recent contribution to the development of these theories has come from the work of Nassim Haramein, Director of Research at the Hawaii Institute of Unified Physics, who published a radical and groundbreaking paper in 2013.[58] In essence this paper seems to show how everything in the universe is connected through a new and alternative understanding of unified gravity and the origin of mass in the universe.

Haramein's holofractographic model proposes our reality of space and time is a limitless holographic projection originating from the quantum potential field. He posits it is not the collapse of the stars that creates black holes but the nature of space-time itself to move toward zero volume at all points. Einstein showed us that space-time bends. By tweaking Einstein's theory, Haramein proposes the container of space -time has two distinct movements. Not only does it curve in toward the black hole at its center, but at the same time it curls, creating a spiraling vortex that sends energy expanding outward. As per Susskind and Maldacena's theories, he suggests that black holes are radiating objects as well as imploding holes. He suggests that the movement of the space-time continuum itself creates a double torus, which is expanding and contracting on itself endlessly. Imagine space-time curving inward toward the point of singularity, but at the same time it is curling like the vortex in a whirlpool. He believes these natural movements are the source of spin at all levels, whether an atom, a solar system, or a galaxy. Objects are forced to spin because space-time itself curls, and as it moves toward singularity, it approaches the speed of light, generating a centrifugal force that in turn creates an expansion. The expanding space is eventually overcome once again by the curvature, and the cycle begins again. He is suggesting this continuing cycle of expansion and contraction creates the forces known as electromagnetism and gravity.

His theory goes on to describe the universe as an infinitely repeating fractal that generates a harmonic scale of toroidal systems (dimensions) that organize matter, and he further states that every atom is a complete representation of the cosmos on a smaller scale. He is suggesting space defines matter and creates mass through the spin movement inherent in all space. Haramein describes the fractal geometric structure of the space-time continuum and how, from the energy of the quantum potential field, movement collapses infinite potential into a differentiated form of a photon, an atom, a man, a star, a galaxy, and even a universe based on holographic, fractal, geometric patterns. His paper implies that cosmic objects from the atom to a universe can be viewed as toroidal black hole systems, each embedded within another expressed in defined dimensions of the space-time continuum. In Haramein's fractal holographic universe, all things are seen as black hole-type structures, where everything is centered by a singularity. The black hole is simultaneously inside the radiating part and the visible part that can be seen. Thus he posits our manifest universe is actually inside a black hole. Creation is happening continuously at the boundaries of all black holes (and at the micro level of you and me; all have the absolute and infinite potential within their own physical form). He describes our universe as the inside of a gigantic black hole, with everything we see on the inside as being the outside of other smaller black holes, which appear as radiating objects, such as stars, planets, and galaxies. It is a beautiful theory and, like many great theories, includes an intuitive process.

His science, as well as his lack of credentials, has been criticized, and his theory requires further expansion and development from a scientific perspective. This does not mean he is not correct. Much of what he predicts is slowly being evidenced, and it must be said his intuitive approach does offer a new perspective for the scientific community to investigate. There is ample evidence from nature itself of the fractal geometry that underlies all creation. Science continues its search for the theory and evidence of everything. What we do know for sure is that science has now refuted some of our long-held assumptions surrounding the nature of matter and what we may believe is objective reality.

Consciousness and the Holographic Brain

Over fifty years ago, neuroscientist Karl Pribram also became convinced of the holographic principle and proposed there was evidence that suggested the brain functions in a holographic way. Pribram was puzzled as to how and where memory was stored in the brain. At that time conventional thought was that each memory had a specific location somewhere in the cells of the brain and that everything that was ever experienced was recorded. These memory traces were called engrams. However, no-one knew what they were made of or where they were located, and they were never found. Pribram discovered the work of neuropsychologist Karl Lashley, who as early as the 1920s had trained rats to run a maze. He then proceeded to remove various portions of the rats' brains and retested them. It was found that no matter what portion or how large a portion of the brain was removed, the rats could still navigate the maze. This indicated to Pribram that memory might be distributed throughout the entire brain. Further experiments revealed that our vision could also be holographic. Pribram's research on cats' optic nerves demonstrated that 98 percent of the nerve could be removed before disenabling complex visual tasks. His experiments over the next seven years discredited the prevailing view that a photographic-like image becomes projected onto the cortical surface of the eye. Pribram believes that memories are not encoded *in* the neurons but in the wave patterns of nerve impulses created by the electrical activity in the neurons that crisscross the entire brain, creating endless interference patterns that store information. It is the same way the patterns of laser light interference crisscross the entire area of a piece of the film containing the holographic image. In other words, the brain itself is a holographic plate.[59] A series of experiments with salamander brains undertaken by Paul Pietsch, initially to prove Pribram wrong, actually provided more positive evidence and therefore even more credence to his theory.[60]

Holograms possess a huge capacity for information storage. By changing the angle at which the two lasers strike the piece of photographic film, it is possible to record many different images on the same surface. It has been demonstrated that one cubic centimeter of film can hold as many as 10 billion pieces of information. Thus Pribram's holographic brain theory also explains the puzzle of information storage in the brain: how the human brain can store so many memories in so little space. It has been estimated that the human brain has the capacity to memorize something like 10 billion pieces of information during the average human lifetime, roughly the same amount of information contained in five sets of the *Encyclopaedia Britannica*. The ability to quickly retrieve whatever information we have stored becomes understandable if the brain is functioning according to holographic principles.[61]

According to Pribram, the brain is able to translate the frequencies of light and sound, as well as other frequencies it receives via our senses, into the concrete world of our perceived reality by encoding and decoding these frequencies—just like our photographic example, which, via the lens, is able to translate the wave patterns into a coherent image of a star. Pribram believes our brains comprise a lens and uses holographic principles to mathematically convert the frequencies it receives through the senses into the inner world of our perceptions. "Over the last thirty years there has been more and more evidence that the cerebral cortex has cells which encode in the frequency domain."[62]

If we put Pribram's theory together with Bohm's theory, then what we consider to be objective reality is really only a secondary reality, an incredible illusion. Prime state reality is that which consists of a multitude of different frequencies from which the holographic brain selects some and transforms them into sensory perceptions that in turn form our view of our objective reality. But if this is so, who or what decides what should be selected? If we go back to our original example, the photographic hologram, what is equivalent to the laser beam that precipitates this cascade of interactions? From where does the photon of light appear that changes the positron to the electron and brings it into observable reality from Bohm's implicate order? Is this consciousness, thought, mind?

Quantum Computation in the Brain

In support of Pribram's view, as recently as 2013 other brain researchers have confirmed quantum vibrations are present in the microtubules of the neurons in the brain. An apparent unlikely coupling of genius developed in the form of Stuart Hameroff, a prominent anesthetist and professor of Psychology and Consciousness Studies at the University of Arizona, and British mathematical physicist Sir Roger Penrose. Both were working independently in very different disciplines and came together to develop a theory of consciousness over twenty years ago. Their orchestrated objective reduction theory suggests quantum computation is taking place in the brain cells, operating via the cells' microtubules, and is affected by sequences of electromagnetic pulses. Electrons in the microtubules become "entangled" and are unstable in space-time. They are probabilities only until the wave event collapses into actuality. According to Hameroff and Penrose, "in our view, a 'proto-conscious' source of mind is omni-present in the universe as OR (objective reduction) events which shape reality." They suggested quantum vibrational computations in microtubules were "orchestrated" (Hameroff's "Orch") by electromagnetic pulses or waves carrying information and memory stored in microtubules, and the wave of probability is then collapsed by information from the mind field by what Penrose calls "objective reduction." The microtubules in one neuron are connected to other microtubules in other neurons by the quantum tunneling of the electrons, resulting in waves of neural activity that are perceived as conscious experience.[63]

Twenty years ago, when first published, they faced strenuous opposition. However, the theory was corroborated in 2013 by a research group led by Anirban Bandyopadhyay, PhD, at the National Institute of Material Sciences in Tsukuba, Japan, and MIT, whose team discovered warm temperature quantum vibrations in microtubules in brain neurons.[64] Additionally, based on his laboratory work, Roderick G. Eckenhoff, MD, at the University of Pennsylvania suggested that anesthesia also acts via the microtubules in the brain neurons.[65] These very recent findings refute the widely held classical view that the mind is in the neurons of the brain or that the brain produces consciousness. They uphold the view that the brain is merely the processor of consciousness. Deepak Chopra says "these events indicate that an invisible agency (consciousness) is producing orderly, intelligent, information-infused activity at the very interface where space-time emerges."[66]

Further phenomena associated with the brain can be explained by the holographic model, such as the ability to remember and forget, the ability to recognize familiar things, photographic memory, associative memory, the transference of learned skills, the vastness of our memory, the scaling of body movements, and movements as waveforms. Neurophysiologists are now beginning to accept that some aspects of memory are stored holographically.

Psychoenergetics—A New Emerging Scientific Discipline

Another eminent physicist, William A. Tiller, started his scientific life as what he describes as an orthodox physicist at the Department of Material Science at the University of Pennsylvania. Subsequently, from 1964 to 1998, he was professor of Material Science and Engineering at Stanford and fellow to the American Academy for the Advancement of Science, with three books and 275 papers published. However, alongside his already prolific work, as early as 1970 Tiller began to challenge orthodox science's unstated assumption instigated by Descartes' original view that "no human quality of mind, emotion, intention or consciousness could influence a well-designed target experiment in physical reality." According to Tiller, since the time of Descartes, this had been an unwritten law upheld by the orthodox scientific community, and subsequently this community neglected the consideration of human consciousness. Conversely, Tiller believes in order to expand the framework of scientific knowledge, this community must include intention and consciousness as important scientific variables in the research of the future. To this end he has developed a new branch of science called psychoenergetics. His research is now providing incredible experimental data. He has experimentally described two unique levels of existence.

Tiller postulates that the vacuum (quantum potential field) with its negative energy state and unobservable particles is the territory where subtle energies may exist. Tiller says, "An interaction exists between this chaotic virtual particle sea and physical matter. It is this fundamental interaction that determines the ground state energies of all the atoms and molecules and all the condensed matter present in the universe."[67] He subscribes to the holographic principle and has developed a model that for the first time includes consciousness and which he asserts does not violate any of the fundamental laws of physics. He sees the human as a much higher being than merely a physical one who, through the mechanism of conscious awareness, has created a "multi-dimensional mind domain perception," which in turn creates a vehicle for our experience within the cosmos, our local universe, our solar system, our planet, and our physical bodies. Tiller affirms a holographic view of the universe in his proposition that the mind is a "simulator" of our experience that we view from a higher perspective outside the "simulator."[68]

He describes the simulator as comprising two interpenetrating spaces, each with a number of dimensions that possess their own structure, substance, and emanations. He suggests that these two spaces have a mirror relationship with each other: one is electromagnetic and is in the dimension of time and space (physical and visible), where mass travels at or less than the speed of light. He calls this D space. The second space is the domain of magnetic matter and is a domain of frequencies, subtle and invisible to the normal senses, and is negative matter that travels at faster than the speed of light. He calls this R space. These two mirror dimensions interact with each other through the mediation of a particle Tiller calls the deltron. According to his theory, this particle acts as a coupler between the magnetic information wave of the vacuum with the electron/atom/molecule level, and this coupled state allows influence of properties, materials, and space at the physical level.[69]

He describes a holographic model where the original light beam is provided by the higher aspect of self. It becomes influenced by the frequency patterns built at mind level and then projects them onto the two screens, which in this case are the network grids of the two joined spaces (positive and negative space.) The waves traveling through these networks demonstrate qualities of the energy consciousness. Substance at these two levels interacts with the potentials stored on these grids, and an "event wave" arises from the various potentials stored here. A response is created by a thought, feeling, or action, and the essence of this is fed back to the mind grid; the alterations that subsequently occur on the mind grid cause a change to the holograph that is projected. This then changes the collective potentials stored there by interaction with substance, and this in turn alters the following sequence of events in time.[70] Simply put, how we think, feel, and act imprints the space around us and is reflected back to us as our reality. Tiller's theory offers a scientifically described mechanism for the possible nature of our observed reality and the inclusion of consciousness.

Summary

❖ Our higher aspect is the laser beam.
❖ Our mind/consciousness, influenced by thoughts, intentions, visualizations, and feelings, is the object.
❖ The physical brain and its neuron network provide the photographic plate, which stores the information and

processes by encoding and decoding the information of the interference patterns created by our mind/consciousness frequencies.

❖ Space-time and the underlying quantum potential field are the mirrors (Tiller's D space and R space, Bohm's implicate/explicate order).

❖ The hologram is the appearance of our thoughts, intentions, feelings, imaginings, and visualizations as a physical reality.

This model is of high significance. Tiller himself states it is a work in progress and is still incomplete. However, it gives us a scientific framework for a model of manifestation taking place when a concept or belief is transmitted from the higher invisible frequencies of mind into the more dense levels of three-dimensional space-time.

In support of this new scientific discipline, William Tiller has published four seminal books, 150 scientific papers, ten white papers, and two DVDs. His statement in a recent recorded interview concerning his work that "he wished to leave a body of work that will make sense to those who follow"[71] reveals a man who is not only brilliant and humble but is living his magnificence. Even though of necessity he had to initially approach this work on an avocational basis and much of his data are still neglected by orthodox science, history will undoubtedly record him as one of the founding fathers of the new science of the future. This theory provides us with a scientific explanation for the different phenomena that are known to exist because we can observe their effects, for example, telepathy, higher sense perception, distance healing, remote viewing, mind-matter interaction, and so on. There are thousands of experiments over the last fifty years or so that provide evidence that these phenomena exist and happen with an increasing frequency. It appears science itself is supporting, even though orthodox science is perhaps reluctant to accept, what mystics have known for centuries. Physical reality is a complex illusion. What we perceive as our objective reality "out there" is actually a vast space resonating with waveforms, a frequency domain that transforms into our "seen" world only after it is sensed or perceived. Our quantum experimenters have shown us that event waves collapse into particles only when being observed, and the newest branches of twenty-first-century science are in the throes of a scientific revolution that for the first time includes the human being and consciousness in the equation.

CHAPTER 5

Fields of Energy

The field is the sole governing agency of the particle.

—Albert Einstein

When electrical charges flow, they create magnetic fields in the surrounding space. This is a law of physics. As we move further on in our exploration of energy, now it's time to investigate the various existent energy fields. This can be a confusing area because there are many different types of fields and many different names for the same fields. Some can be measured, and some cannot yet be. There are those that are physically measurable, such as electromagnetic and magnetic fields generated by all physical matter that has stationary electrical particles (electric field) and moving electrical particles (magnetic field). Also we will see later in this chapter the new sophisticated technologies that are now available to measure those frequencies that are not yet visible to the human eye.

Space, Time, the Vacuum, and the Plenum

David Bohm stated "Space is full not empty. A plenum which is the ground for the existence of everything, including ourselves. The universe is not separate from this cosmic sea of energy [72]."

Let us picture space as the container for all the known fields of energy—all particles and all matter. Space, sometimes called the vacuum, is the ground state of being. It is not empty, but contains a plenum of energy and quantum potential that can be activated into existence by electrical charges that move to create fields of information that inform substance. This energy and potential exists in space throughout the entire universe. Time does not exist in this domain. There are various terms given to the quantum potential field. In literature, there are Bohm's implicate order,[73] Tiller's R space,[74] McTaggart's the field,[75] Wilcock's source field,[76] and Brennan's universal energy field (UEF),[77] to name but a few. In the language of physics, the terms *quantum field* refer to the theory itself and uses the terms *zero point field* as the descriptor of the actual field, referring to zero point energy as the lowest possible energy that a quantum mechanical physical system may have. In metaphysics, the vacuum that is actually a plenum state has been described as the void, Brahman, or infinity.

Because various names exist for the same thing, this can cause confusion. In this account let's assign the terms *quantum potential field* to denote the underlying space of the absolute where all is connected, where there is no time, and from which all objective reality arises. And similarly let's assign the terms *cosmic holographic field* to the container in space and time that holds all the various energies, together with manifested objects such as dimensions, universes, galaxies, solar systems, planets, you, and me. I have personally observed and experienced this field as being filled with points of white light with small tails sometimes, swimming in and out of existence, sparks and larger flashes of light, gossamer hexagonal-shaped webs of light energy, clouds of color, geometric shapes, and liquid plasmoid-type shapes, with boundaries that bend and melt.

The Casimir Effect

The Casimir effect is a scientific experiment largely used as scientific evidence of the existence of this energy field. This was an experiment devised in 1948 by the Dutch physicist Henrik Casimir.[78]

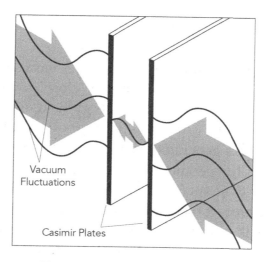

Vacuum Fluctuations

Casimir Plates

Figure 5.1. The Casimir Effect

Two mirrors were placed into a vacuum parallel to each other with a space in between. It was found that the two mirrors were being pushed together by an unknown force. The experiment revealed that even in a vacuum supposedly consisting of "empty space," there were energy fluctuations. Because space is filled with fluctuating electromagnetic waves, the space between the mirrors could not sustain all the frequencies of the electromagnetic field, particularly those wavelengths comparable to the length of the plate separation.

So the amount of zero point energy on the inside of the plates was less than outside. This gave rise to zero point energy on the outside of the plate that tried to push the plates together. It increased in strength the nearer the plates became and then disappeared once they were together. This became known as the Casimir force and is how we now know there is energy in what was once believed to be a vacuum. Nearly fifty years later this was actually measured in 1996 by atomic physicist Stephen Lamoreaux at Yale.[79]

The Cosmic Environment and the Planetary Energy Field

After the mind- and space-bending science of the cosmic landscape, our journey now brings us closer to home and on to an investigation of the earth's energy field, often called the magnetosphere. The earth has a magnetic field created by electrical currents generated by movement in its molten core; it is also called the geomagnetic field. It extends out from the earth's interior to about 370,000 miles above the earth. Its main function is to protect the planet from cosmic radiation or solar winds, as this is sometimes called. It forms a magnetic bubble around the earth that diverts most of these particles into a circular path around the earth.

The Schumann Resonance

The earth also emits natural extremely low frequency standing waves that oscillate between the earth's surface and the upper atmosphere or ionosphere. These electrically charged layers of the earth's upper atmosphere create a spherical waveguide around the earth, allowing frequencies such as radio waves to pass through. Tesla had certainly intuited this with his early work on wireless energy transmission, but it was not until 1952 that Otto Schumann predicted mathematically, and then 1954 that he finally detected, this global electromagnetic resonance now called the Schumann resonance.[80] The surface of the earth, the ionosphere, and the atmosphere together form one gigantic electrical circuit, a circuit naturally excited by lightning strikes.

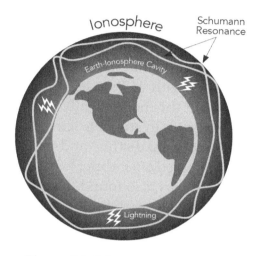

Figure 5.2. Schumann resonance.

The lowest frequency range of the Schumann resonance is at a frequency of approximately 7.83, 14, 20, 26, 33, 39, and 45 Hz, with a daily variation of about ±0.5 hertz. The daily increase and decrease are caused by variations in radiation from the sun. Similarly, solar activity, such as sunspot cycles, coronal mass ejections, and geomagnetic storms, all have an effect. All matter is vibrating energy, and all living things have a natural resonant frequency; therefore it will probably be no surprise to find all biological systems resonate in this frequency range. The 7.83 Hz is the same frequency associated with the human brain wave alpha state conducive to meditation, creativity, and relaxation. Dolphins produce sound waves at this frequency. H. König, Schumann's successor at Munich University, discovered that the dominant brain wave rhythm of all mammals is the alpha or resting state of 6–8 Hz. When two vibrating systems resonate with each other, like the human brain and the earth's global electric circuit, they can be said to be in tune or in resonance with each other, and there is a rise in amplitude of the wave likely to result in a feeling of well-being.

To test the effect of interruption of the Schumann resonance, Rutger Wever, from the Max Planck Institute for Behavioral Physiology in Erling-Andechs, built an underground bunker, screening out magnetic fields. Between 1964 and 1989 he conducted 418 studies with 447 students. Student volunteers lived for four weeks in this hermetically sealed environment. Wever noted a divergence in students' circadian rhythms and that they suffered emotional distress and migraine headaches. The symptoms disappeared after a brief exposure to 7.8 Hz while still in the bunker.[81] It was also found that similar complaints were reported by the first astronauts and cosmonauts deprived of Schumann waves in space.

Even more astonishing, while researching how water retains the memory of substances dissolved in it, Luc Montagnier, Nobel Prize winner for the discovery of the HIV virus, found that DNA sequences communicate with each other in water by emitting low frequency electromagnetic waves and this takes place in an ambient electromagnetic frequency range of 7 Hz. In January 2010 in this groundbreaking experiment, Montagnier placed two test tubes adjacent to each other connected by a copper coil and subjected them to a frequency of 7 Hz. The apparatus was shielded from other electromagnetic influences. One test tube contained DNA, and the other contained just pure water. After sixteen to eighteen hours, both samples were subjected to the polymerase chain reaction (PCR), which is a method routinely used to amplify traces of DNA by using enzymes to make copies of the original. It was found that the same fragments of DNA were retrieved from both test tubes, even though one contained only water. The result was only obtained after the DNA sample had been subjected to several dilutions and both samples exposed to the low frequency electromagnetism of 7Hz Montagnier's team is suggesting that DNA emits low frequency electromagnetic waves that imprint the structure of the molecules into the water. Montagnier claims this structure is then preserved and amplified through quantum coherence effects and the enzymes use this energetic template to produce DNA that matches the sent information pattern.[82] This experiment has been replicated twelve out of twelve times and also repeated with another DNA type.[83] The wider implications of these incredible experiments will be discussed in greater detail when we move to the energetics of the human body. However, this does demonstrate the importance of the life-enhancing frequency of the Schumann resonance of the earth's field and the deep connections we have to this. Even our DNA resonates at the same frequency as the earth's field, and DNA signaling is stimulated by this resonance. This clearly demonstrates our energetic connection to our planet and the implications this can have for the well-being of all life.

Earth's Energy Pathways

A ley line is a straight line connecting three or more prehistoric or ancient sites, sometimes regarded as the line of a former track and associated by some with lines of energy and other paranormal phenomena. The term was originally adopted in 1921 by Alfred Watkins, an amateur archaeologist, in his writings about the ancient pathways of the British landscape. Many of the sacred sites of the world are associated with areas of the planet that are purported to be based in areas of high energetic activity, built upon the node formed where these lines cross or used to cross. Some have likened these "power nodes" to the acupuncture points of the human body and the ley lines themselves as the physical out-picture of the more subtle energy grid of the earth, similar to the energy meridians ascribed to acupuncture along which pass energy and information in the human body. Sites such as Stonehenge in the United Kingdom, Mt. Shasta in the United States, Machu Picchu in Peru, and the Pyramids in Egypt are just some of these high vibrational centers forming these power nodes associated with the energy system of the earth.

The Hartmann and Curry grids are subtle energy grids named after the two German doctors who discovered them. The Curry grid has a reach of about 4.5 m and is aligned in the direction southwest to northeast. The Hartmann grid has a reach of about 3 m and is aligned north/south and east/west and could possibly be connected with the natural telluric or earth currents. These are natural electric currents flowing on and beneath the surface of the earth, including the oceans, generally following in a direction parallel to the earth's surface.[84] These natural currents are believed to originate from moving charged particles from the solar winds that follow the earth's magnetic field's rotation, generating the telluric currents that flow across the earth's surface. As the earth has been rotating around the sun for many millions of years, these electromagnetic waves have settled across the earth's surface and crust, interacting with electrons and ions and stabilizing into grids of low frequency, longitudinal electric waves.[85]

These natural standing waves of energy are stable and consistent, and according to scientist and dowser Jiro Olcott, when a conductor such as a large crystalline stone is placed into the energy grid, a corresponding resonance of energy can be detected in the stone. This resonance can be amplified if the stone is placed on a node where two or more underground streams cross.[86] On the basis of this information, we can further understand the development of the earth's sacred energy sites and how combined earth and solar energies create an energy source that can be stored, used, and amplified. It must also be noted that the artificial electromagnetic radiation created by human-made systems such as electric power cables, TV, radio, and mobile phones also form part of the telluric currents and can have a potentially harmful effect on human life, as their frequencies often can be disruptive and unbalanced.

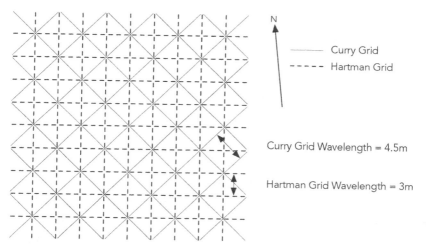

Figure 5.3. The Curry and Hartmann energy grids.

In the geophysical world, a ley line is a straight fault line in the tectonic plates of the earth's crust. When these plates move, magnetic energy can be released through these cracks in the crust. These movements are driven by the earth's inner heat emanating from its molten core, and as we now know, when energy moves, a field is created. It has recently been discovered that the earth's crust is moving twice as fast as it did 1.2 billion years ago.[87] Scientists were puzzled by this phenomenon because, due to the normal aging process of the earth, the speed should be decreasing not increasing. Astonishingly, it is now believed that this movement is caused by the presence of large amounts of water in the earth's lower mantle.

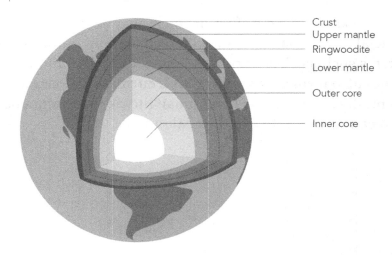

Crust
Upper mantle
Ringwoodite
Lower mantle

Outer core

Inner core

Figure 5.4. The crystal layer of water ringwoodite recently found between the upper and lower mantle of the earth's crust.

The discovery of ringwoodite in March 2012, a new crystal that contains 1.5 percent water and is formed only at very high pressure, was made at the transition zone between the earth's core and upper mantle. This has confirmed to geoscientists that there are huge deposits of water deep within the earth held in crystal form.[88]

This is an important discovery, referring back to Montagnier's DNA experiment. The medium for his experiment was water, and an electromagnetic wave emitted from the DNA resulted in the transfer of information and the imprinting of an energetic template in the water of the second test tube. The presence of water within these crystalline structures provides and evidences yet another medium for information transfer for the planet. The earth's core itself holds yet another big surprise.

The Crystalline Forest at the Earth's Core

Developments in seismology have proved to be so very beneficial to scientists researching the composition and structure of the inner earth. Their "journey to the center of the earth" has been rich in its rewards, and it has revealed an incredible landscape of surging white hot metal and a beautiful forest of crystal. The inner core of the earth is almost the size of the moon and is believed to be composed of an iron-nickel alloy. In order to understand the form this may take under the conditions found at the earth's center, Professor Kei Herose set about recreating those conditions in his lab at the SPring-8 synchrotron near Osaka, Japan. After ten years of trying, he finally succeeded. He created an extremely powerful vise using the tips of two diamonds and then pressurized a sample of iron-nickel to 3 million times atmospheric pressure to a temperature of around 4500 C. He discovered under these extraordinary extreme conditions, the crystalline structure of the iron-nickel alloy changed. In fact, the crystals rapidly grew in size. He believes crystals at the earth's center could measure up to 10 km, aligning like a forest to point to each pole.[89] This core creates the magnetic field so vital to life on the planet. It helps the honeybees to find their hive; turtles, butterflies, and birds use it in migration. And of course, it is essential for our own well-being. It seems fitting this "planet within a planet" turns out to be one of such great beauty. Perhaps we can begin to see how a communications network is emerging as we piece together the findings of different scientific disciplines and view the whole, not just the parts. An information matrix, linking the electromagnetic fields, energy pathways, power nodes, and inner crystalline structures that create, store, and pass information around the planetary body, is being revealed.

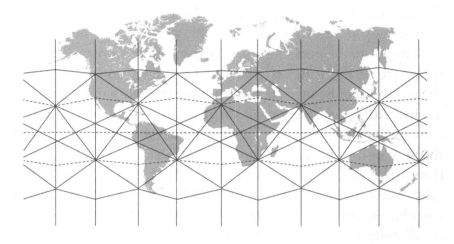

Figure 5.5. Earth grids.

The Local Planetary Neighborhood

At this point it is useful to look at what is going on in our local planetary neighborhood. This may give us an answer to the question of why now is an incredibly optimum time in our history to be undertaking transformational work. In a sense, whether we consciously choose to do this work or not, change is unavoidable; it is part of our evolutionary process, and we will see much is happening energetically in our part of the cosmos.

Astronomy, Astrology, and the Precession of the Equinox

Astronomy is one of the oldest natural sciences and is concerned with the study of celestial objects, their physics, chemistry, and evolution. In the twentieth century it became known as astrophysics. Cosmology is a related, but distinct, discipline that studies the universe as a whole. In the early twentieth century, the International Astronomical Union (IAU), whose role it is to name and define all things astronomical, created the official constellation boundaries, which are still used to this day.

Astrology, on the other hand, consists of various methods or systems used to gain insight on the relationship or connection between astronomical events and phenomena arising in the human world. It uses as its basis the study of the planets and stars within our own solar system, using the progression of the twelve constellations or signs of the zodiac that most of us are familiar with. From the astronomical perspective, any predictive dates may not agree with the computations of astrologers. Much has been said about the coming of a "new age," which has been linked to the earth's passage into the constellation of Aquarius. This is not an astronomical term but an astrological one. However, fortunately, new technology is allowing us to examine our universe in greater detail than ever before, and we can now turn to this for evidence of shifts in the energetic environment of our planet and solar system and what they may mean for humankind as our study of energy progresses. With this background, let us take a quick look at the real motion of the earth in its solar system.

The earth's rotation on its axis is not fixed. Over a period of 25,620 years, it executes a very slow precession. This means there is a very real movement as it undergoes a change in the orientation of its rotational axis.

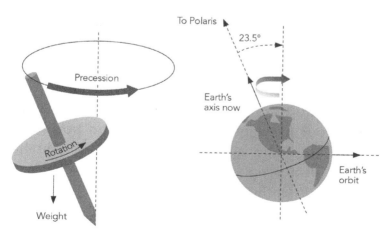

Figure 5.6. Earth changing its rotational axis.

In astronomy the equinox is the event when the sun can be observed directly above the equator. So the precession of the equinox is the sun's apparent position moving slowly west as observed on the same day each year (the vernal/spring equinox). This of course is dependent on the position of earth. With the passing of the years, this point shifts approximately one degree every seventy-two years. In order to complete this cycle, the earth takes 25,620 years to move through each of the twelve astrological zodiac constellations, spending approximately 2,135 years in each. When the March equinox point moves out of the constellation of Pisces and into the next constellation (Aquarius), this is officially said to be the start of the new cycle.[90]

According to the Belgian astronomer Jean Meeus, who uses the IAU boundaries for the definitions of the constellations, the March equinox point will pass from Pisces to Aquarius in AD 2597. However, from an astrological perspective, history demonstrates the influence of the energies associated with the shift of an age usually begins to be experienced from between five hundred and eight hundred years prior. Thus, from a scientific point of view, although we are currently still in the age of Pisces, earth is being strongly influenced by Aquarian values, progressively leaving the one and progressively entering the other. As far back as the 1700s, revolution in Europe gave us the values of freedom, equality, and fraternity, which could be viewed as heralding the new values associated with the astrological influences assigned to the "new Aquarian Age." Whether you subscribe to this view or not, as a civilized society, these are values we are still charged to create for all, establishing our freedom in constructive and positive ways that respect the rights and opinions of others: equality of opportunity, brotherhood, unity, peace, and the will to do good, ending all conflict and feuds.[91]

It may be a wiser choice not to get locked into specific dates in linear time of predicted events, but to open to what is being recorded in the now. According to a holographic, quantum perspective of being, this means that any predicted outcome of any event can be changed, as everything is only a possibility until we, either as an individual or together as a collective consciousness, manifest the event by collapsing the wave of probability into reality. In effect, time and dates become malleable. The positive qualities associated with the arrival of a new golden age can be experienced right now in this moment. It is simply a matter of our choice.

Energy in Interstellar Space

Although even now no one can say for sure for sure whether the earth is in or out of the constellation of Aquarius yet, a look at the scientific data to see what is actually happening energetically in and around the planet unearths some very surprising and convincing results. In recent years, sensors recorded a torrent of solar wind particles streaming into the magnetosphere. An international team of researchers also has discovered a puzzling surplus of high-energy electrons bombarding earth from space. The source of these cosmic rays is unknown, but it was thought to be close to the solar system. The results were reported in the 24 December 2009, issue of the journal Nature.[92] To study these most powerful and interesting cosmic rays, NASA funded scientists from Louisiana State University, who sent a series of balloons to fly through the stratosphere over Antarctica. The cosmic ray detector found a significant surplus of high-energy electrons. "This is a big discovery," said researcher John Wefel of Louisiana State University. "It's the first time we've seen a discrete source of accelerated cosmic rays standing out from the general galactic background."

Also in December 2009, NASA reported the discovery of an interstellar magnetic field just outside our solar system by their two unmanned spacecraft, Voyagers 1 and 2. This magnetic field is apparently holding together an interstellar cloud through which our solar system will pass for the next ten thousand years or so; it has been called "Local Fluff" by scientists at

NASA. IBEX (Interstellar Boundary Explorer) data show that our solar system is currently located within the boundary of this local cloud, which was not supposed to exist and confirms the Voyager 1 and 2 discovery. The cloud itself is immersed in a much larger expanse of hot gas called the "Local Bubble." The energy being detected is from a different, larger energy field that is cutting through the sun's magnetic field; this incoming energy is creating a band or ribbon effect, called the IBEX ribbon.

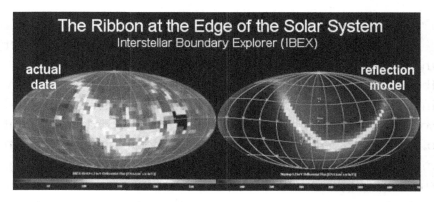

Figure 5.7. The Ibex ribbon courtesy of NASA. http://science.nasa.gov/ science-news/science-at-nasa/2009/15oct_ibex/

New High Frequency Cosmic Rays in Earth's Atmosphere

In June 2014 it was reported by the European Space Agency that the earth's magnetic field was weakening much faster than predicted and this could be evidence that the magnetic pole was preparing to "flip." Data collected by the SWARM satellites indicated a dramatic decline over the western hemisphere and an increase in strength over the Indian Ocean. This is a normal, natural event that occurs every 250,000 years or so, and the results of a flip in the magnetic poles is not life-threatening. However, when it does happen, it means that afterward for a time the earth's magnetic field is very weak; this would allow more cosmic rays to penetrate the surface.

NASA has also predicted that the sun's magnetic field or heliosphere will become compressed as it passes through this interstellar cloud and more cosmic rays reach the inner solar system. This seems to be evidenced in the recent activity of the Van Allen belts. These are two radiation belts created by the highly charged particles of the solar wind that becomes trapped by the earth's magnetic field. Shortly after the launch of the NASA twin Van Allen belt probes in August 2012, a third radiation belt was seen to be forming due to intense activity in these belts.

Figure 5.8. Image courtesy of NASA showing third radiation ring. Recent observations by NASA's Van Allen probes' mission showed an event in which three radiation zones were observed at extremely high energies, including an unusual medium narrow ring that existed for approximately four weeks. http://www.nasa.gov/mission_pages/rbsp/images/index.html?id=346161

This was a narrow belt formed between the two usual belts; it existed for approximately four weeks before dispersing. This new belt of radiation was the result of a solar storm of plasma particles that would usually be repelled and dispersed by the earth's magnetic field. In a study of this phenomenon by a team at UCLA in 2013, it was reported that this third belt consisted of a different type of electron, which had very different properties and behaviors from those found in the other radiation belts. These extremely highly charged particles, called "ultrarelativistic electrons," were found to be moving close to the speed of light, were not influenced by a low frequency electromagnetic pulsation (modeling earth's magnetic field) that would typically disperse them, and could penetrate the shielding of spacecraft. Their properties were the same as the scalar energy waves discussed earlier. Yuri Shprits, a research geophysicist at UCLA, and his team discovered that on September 1, 2012, plasma waves produced by ions that did not typically affect energetic electrons "whipped out ultra-relativistic electrons in the outer belt almost down to the inner edge of the outer belt." Only a narrow ring of ultrarelativistic electrons survived the storm, and these remnants formed the third ring. "I believe that, with this study, we have uncovered the tip of the iceberg," said Shprits. "We still need to fully understand how these electrons are accelerated, where they originate and how the dynamics of the belts is different for different storms. This study shows that completely different populations of particles exist in space that change on different timescales, are driven by different physics and show very different spatial structures."[93]

Solar Mysteries

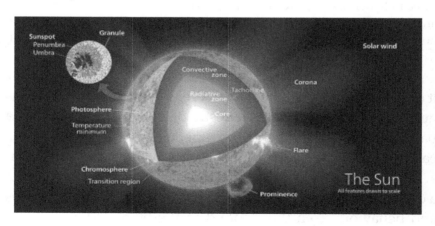

Figure 5.9. Anatomy of the sun courtesy of Kelvinsong, ©(CC BY-SA 3.0) (http://creativecommons.org/licenses/by-sa/3.0)], via Wikimedia Commons. En.wikipedia.org

Our life on earth is inextricably linked with the sun and the light it provides. This incredible star is constantly sending a stream of energy our way in the form of the solar wind, which pulsates and flows through space creating electric and magnetic fields of energy. If we refer back to the radiation rings of the Van Allen belt and recall that these consist of particles from the solar stream and other cosmic particles, the discovery made in 2012–13 by Schprits while investigating the temporary appearance of a third Van Allen belt indicates that newer higher frequency electrons are coming into our atmosphere. We know from our earlier exploration of quanta that energy carries information and that all in our universe is connected. This pulsating stream of energy from the sun is sending out information in all directions through space.

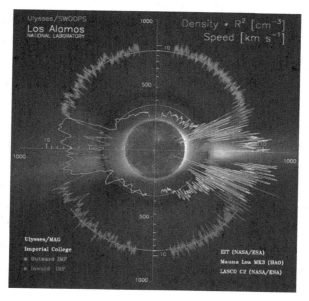

Figure 5.10. Image of solar wind observations over Ulyssees' first full polar orbit. McComas et al., *Journal of Geophysical Research*, Vol.105.10419–10433, 2000.

Without this amazing source of energy, we could not physically survive. Through photosynthesis, sunlight converts carbon dioxide and water into oxygen and carbohydrates in living organisms that humans and the rest of the food chain then consume. This is a miracle in itself that we take so much for granted. Photons interact with our skin to create vitamin D. Ultraviolet light can destroy harmful bacteria and viruses. Infrared light is used to treat a variety of physical disturbances. Through the human energy system, we will see that light charges the seven regulatory centers of the body, stimulating glands that secrete hormones affecting physical bodily functions, consciousness, and personality. More astonishing still, UV light is absorbed, stored, and transmitted by our DNA.[94,95]This is of high significance, as later we will see the evidence that reveals our DNA is actually capable of being reprogrammed by information carried by an electromagnetic wave carrier. Earth and everything on it are deeply and intimately connected with the sun, as are all the planets in our system.

The sun's magnetic field is called the heliosphere and extends out to form a teardrop shape encircling our solar system. This field of energy is produced by the flow of electrically charged ions and electrons in the plasma within the sun. This "great conveyor belt," as it is called, is a massive current of ionized gases that takes forty years to complete its cycle. Its flow also creates the magnetic fields thought to be responsible for sunspot activity. Sunspots are places where intense magnetic lines of force break through the sun's surface, and the number of sunspots that occur in an eleven-year cycle forms the solar cycle. According to Timothy Ferris of the National Geographic Journal, "Magnetism is the key to understanding the sun as magnetic fields are at the root of all the features we see on and above the sun. The loops and streamers that we can see in the corona above the surface of the sun are shaped, supported, and threaded through with and by magnetic fields."[96]

However, there are great unsolved mysteries concerning this great ball of fire. NASA solar physicist David Hathaway has been monitoring the conveyor belt speed for some time.

In 2010 he reported that the belt had been "running at record high speeds" for the previous five years, and yet the numbers of sunspots were dramatically lower then and have continued to be all through the present cycle, which began in 2008.[97]

Another great mystery is the nature of the coronal heating process. The corona is the outer atmosphere of the sun and maintains the extremely high temperatures in the upper atmosphere that accelerate the solar winds. The surface of the sun is around 6000 degrees C, but the corona is hotter than 1,000,000 degrees C. Usually it would be expected that temperatures would drop the farther away from the source of the heat, but in this case not so.

According to NASA the precise causes of solar flares and coronal mass ejections is yet another great solar unknown. Solar flares are massive explosions on the sun's surface that release energy in the form of gamma rays, X-rays, protons, and electrons and occur usually within the neutral space between oppositely directed magnetic fields. Coronal mass ejections, or CMEs as they are commonly known, are very large bubbles of gas that are threaded with magnetic field lines ejected from the sun over a period of hours. They can disrupt the flow of the solar wind and also produce disturbances that can affect the earth's atmosphere. Solar physicists have developed various theories but as yet not developed a model that fully explains or can predict these events.

There is mounting evidence that the prevailing view of the formation of galaxies and the birth of stars and planets is highly flawed. The mystery of why the sun is so much hotter at its corona than at its core may indicate the sun is not powered by nuclear fusion at its core, as the current model suggests, but by electrical energy that is naturally present in deep space. There is mounting evidence to suggest that the universe is an "electric universe" and that solar flares, the corona, and sunspots are all powered by electric currents.[98,99,100,101,102,103]

Magnetic Portals Connecting the Sun with the Earth

In 2008 space physicist David Sibeck, at Goddard Space Flight Center, announced that the evidence for magnetic portals connecting the sun with the earth is incontrovertible. Every eight minutes a portal opens, and tons of high-energy electric particles flow through this opening before it closes. These energy flows are called flux transfer events or FTEs. On the dayside of earth (the side closest to the sun), earth's magnetic field presses against the sun's magnetic field. Approximately every eight minutes, the two fields briefly merge or "reconnect," forming a portal through which particles can flow. The portal takes the form of a magnetic cylinder about as wide as earth. The European Space Agency's fleet of four Cluster spacecraft and NASA's five THEMIS probes have flown through and surrounded these cylinders, measuring their dimensions and sensing the particles that shoot through. "They're real," says Sibeck. Every eight minutes earth and all its inhabitants are receiving information from the ruler of our solar system.[104]

The Heavenly Bodies

There have also been marked changes to other planets in our solar system recorded over the past decade.

The Martian atmosphere is getting thicker. It is twice as dense as NASA predicted. Jupiter's energetic charge has risen so high that there is actually a visible tube of ionizing radiation that's formed between the surface of Jupiter and its moon Lo. Uranus and Neptune also are becoming brighter. The magnetic fields of Jupiter, Uranus, and Neptune are changing. Jupiter's magnetic field has more than doubled, and Neptune's magnetic field is increasing. The Russians say that all three of these planets are becoming brighter and their atmospheric qualities are changing. The Russians also report that Uranus and

Neptune appear to have had recent pole shifts. The brightness and magnetic fields of the planets are also changing. Venus is showing marked increases in its overall brightness.[105]

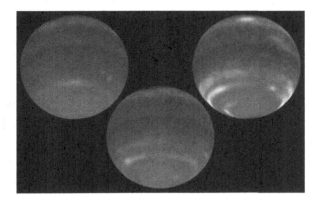

Figure 5.11. Images of Neptune taken between 1996 and 2002 show increase in brightness. Images courtesy of NASA. http://hubblesite.org/newscenter/archive/releases/2003/17

The Galactic Core

In 2005 Scott D. Hyman reported in *Nature* the discovery of "a powerful bursting radio source towards the galactic centre, consistent with coherent emission processes." At the center of our galaxy is a huge black hole called Saggitarius A. According to astrophysicists, black holes are formed by the death of a star. A black hole is a region in space where there is infinite mass and zero volume. This creates a massive pull of gravity where nothing, not even light, can get away. According to the theory put forward by researcher Paul LaViolette, this core has its own energy source, which is not created in the usual two known ways: joining elements or breaking down elements. He calls this genic energy that is spontaneously generated from a catalyst of some kind coming from outside our galaxy. There is evidence that the core produces matter at the highest rate anywhere in the galaxy and this is expelled out in the form of explosions. The last one occurred at the last ice age. He has cross-referenced data with other scientific disciplines and tree ring records using radiocarbon dating and ice core records using evidence of nitrate peaks and has been able to chart evidence for thirteen small bursts from the galactic center in the last 53,000 years. [106,107] LaViolette, president and chief researcher of the Starburst Foundation, was the first to demonstrate that cosmic rays radiated from the active core of an exploding galaxy are able to penetrate far outside the galaxy's nucleus and bombard solar systems like our own residing on the periphery. He coined the phrase "galactic super-wave" to refer to such a cosmic barrage. Galactic superwaves are a recent discovery. Until recently, astronomers believed galactic cores erupted very infrequently, every 10 to 100 million years. They also believed that interstellar magnetic fields in the galactic nucleus would trap the emitted particles in spiral orbits, causing them to reach the earth very slowly. For these reasons, most astronomers did not believe that core explosions in the Milky Way had any relevance to earth. However, in 1983 LaViolette presented evidence to the scientific community indicating that galactic core explosions actually occur about every 13,000 to 26,000 years for major outbursts and more frequently for lesser events. The emitted cosmic rays escape from the core virtually unimpeded. As they travel radially outward through the galaxy, they form a spherical shell that advances at very close to the speed of light.[108,109]

In 2010 the gamma ray space telescope, FERMI, recorded and released footage that revealed two gamma ray bubbles extending out from the galactic center north and south, each twenty-five light-years across, had been discovered. Their shape and emission suggest the structure was formed as a result of a large and rapid energy release, but the origin of this remains a mystery. This is a phenomenon that has not been seen before. Doug Finkbeiner, an astronomer from the

Harvard-Smithsonian Center for Astrophysics, said, "We don't fully understand their nature or origin." It seems this was a sudden and impulsive event. Gamma ray energy is the highest known form of light. David Spergel of Princeton University says, "Whatever the energy source behind these huge bubbles may be, it is connected to many deep questions in astrophysics." This supports LaViolette's discoveries.

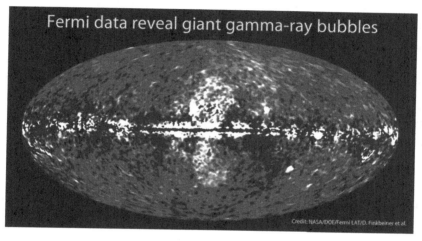

Figure 5.12.1. Gamma ray bubbles. Image Credit: NASA/DOE/Fermi LAT/D. Finkbeiner et al. http://www.nasa.gov/mission_pages/GLAST/news/new-structure.html

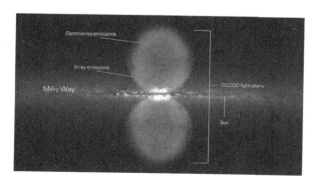

Figure 5.12.2. Gamma ray emissions. Image credit: NASA's Goddard Space Flight Center. http://www.nasa.gov/mission_pages/GLAST/news/new-structure.html

The Electric Cosmos

There appears to be a lot going on in our planetary neighborhood, much of which is unexpected and unexplained by the existing theoretical models. The latest advances in technology enabling imaging and recording from high-powered telescopes and probes into deep space are providing astronomers and cosmologists with a new picture of the universe and challenging long-held assumptions about the nature of galaxies, stars, the solar system, and planet earth. The new emerging science of plasma cosmology is suggesting that electrical energy plays a much more significant role than previously believed and the current standard model construct based on the assumption that gravity alone organizes the cosmos and keeps things running is not entirely correct. This does not mean gravity is replaced or forgotten. It simply means the moving flow of charged particles that fills space and its implications must be added into the considerations of scientific research and theory.

"From the smallest particle to the largest galactic formation, a web of electrical circuitry connects and unifies all of nature, organizing galaxies, energizing stars, giving birth to planets and in our own world controlling weather and animating biological organisms.

There are no isolated islands in an electric universe."[110]

Most of the observable universe consists of plasma. This is an astonishing fact and probably little known and even less understood. This is a substance that is so hot its atoms and molecules have ionized by breaking up into their constituent parts. This sea of charged particles can behave similar to a gas, except it is strongly influenced by electric and magnetic fields and is a highly effective conductor of electrical energy. The sun is composed of plasma. Stars and galaxies are plasma. The interstellar substance radiating between stars and galaxies is plasma. "99.9 percent of the Universe is made up of plasma," says Dr. Dennis Gallagher, a plasma physicist at NASA's Marshall Space Flight Center. "Very little material in space is made of rock like the earth."[111] This is a profound statement and cannot be disregarded just because it does not fit in with other theories. Space is full of actively charged electrical particles. Any movement of these particles forms an electric current, and this gives rise to magnetic fields and electrical events, some of which are described earlier.

In 1889–90 the Norwegian Kristian Birkeland paved the way for today's more advanced research in his pioneering expeditions to the arctic pole to take the first measurements of the earth's magnetic field; he suggested that charged particles from the sun guided by the earth's magnetic field created the celebrated aurora borealis. His claims were disputed for decades, but the theory was confirmed in the 1960s and seventies by measurements taken by satellite. In 1973 the existence of these electric currents was confirmed, and these field-aligned currents are now called the Birkeland current.[112] These are scalar waves. Birkeland was an experimentalist, and the term *Birkeland current* refers to the natural configuration of current flow in plasma.

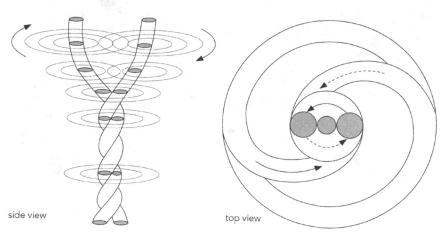

Figure 5.13.1. Birkeland current, side view. **Figure 5.13.2.** Birkeland current, top view.

This first description of current flow in plasma was considered essential to the understanding of space. Thus, Birkeland's work was highly influential to Hannes Alfven, a Swedish scientist and Nobel Laureate in Physics in 1970, who is considered to be the founding father of space plasma physics.

Originally trained as an electrical power engineer, Alfven later moved into researching plasma physics, making contributions to the understanding of the behavior of aurorae, the Van Allen radiation belts, magnetic and electrical fields in cosmic plasmas, and the effect of magnetic storms on the magnetosphere of the earth and the dynamics of plasmas in the galaxy. Alfven's description of the sun's electric circuit predicted in 1986 has now been verified by the Ulysses spacecraft.[113]

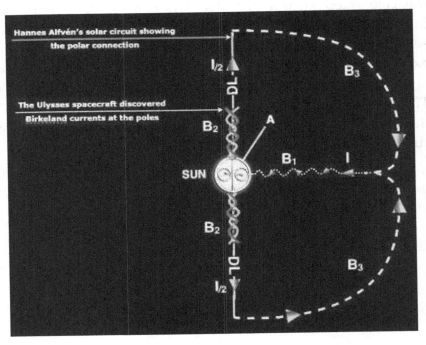

Figure 5.14. Alfvén's heliospheric circuit. The sun acts as a unipolar inductor (A), producing a current that goes outward along both the axes (B_2) and inward in the equatorial plane along the magnetic field lines (B_1). The current must close at large distances either as a homogeneous current layer, or—more likely—as a pinched current. Analogous to the

auroral circuit, there may be double layers (DLs), which should be located symmetrically on the sun's axes. Such double layers had not yet been discovered. Credit: Original diagram by H. Alfvén, NASA Conference Publication 2469, 1986, p. 27.

As previously described, unexpected radio, infrared, ultraviolet, and X-ray wavelengths in space and high electrical space events are now visible due to the development of high-resolution equipment. Their existence means electric currents and fields are pervasive. This intense electromagnetic activity across the cosmos requires a vast complex of electrical fields and electrical circuitry, as Alfven had predicted. A body of factual and theoretical knowledge is being steadily built to support the electric universe view.[114] Plasma cosmology is suggesting that electrical energy is responsible for the creation of spiraling galaxies and the incredible galactic clusters in deep space. Factual knowledge is from direct space observation and laboratory experiments and is not only from theoretical inventions based on purely mathematical assumptions such as the big bang, dark matter, dark energy, neutron stars, and black holes. This does not mean the numbers are not important. Hannes Alfven was the most prominent plasma scientist of the twentieth century, and his work provided the foundation for plasma cosmology. This work was supported by rigorous mathematics, but even he warned against disconnection from laboratory observation.

In his 1976 book, Alfven wrote, "We have to learn again that science without contact with experiments is an enterprise which is likely to go completely astray into imaginary conjecture."[115]

There appears to be a crisis developing in the world of astrophysics as current theories are slowly being dismantled by the new, unexpected, factual evidence provided by twenty-first-century space telescopes. Our solar system, including our sun, is not solid and rocklike but a plasma containing masses of electrically charged particles. These particles, through precipitation, diversification, and solidification and a corresponding steadily lowered vibrational rate, eventually reach the band of frequencies that represent the electromagnetic spectrum and can be observed, measured, and physically evidenced in the aurora borealis. This is enabled by the transfer of information through scalar energy by the pair of electric currents (Birkeland currents) entwining around one another to form double helixes. Any matter existing between these two electrical spirals undergoes a massive compression. According to plasma cosmologists, this is happening throughout the universe. However, this is not just a theory. This process has been replicated and confirmed in laboratory experiments, which show the central vortex created by the electrical arcing is pinched into zones of spherical compression and the matter within is subject to lesser and greater degrees of melting. This spiral-building pattern is recalled in the familiar spirals of DNA that hold the blueprint for human life and repeated in the formation of galaxies. This means all current theories held of how the universe was created are called into serious question.

More information about the science supporting the theory and factual observation of the electric universe can be found at www.holoscience.com. This site contains a wealth of cutting-edge science and discovery free from any restraining influences. Here can be found the work of scholars from many different disciplines who are converging to overcome the status quo and provide a paradigm shift in astrophysics, astronomy, and cosmology. This is important work, for it is through our exposure to this information that we move closer and closer to an understanding of our own nature and being.

As Thornhill wrote in 2007, "Electrical theorists remind us that when an entire paradigm is thrown into doubt, it's time to revisit all assumptions. This is necessary even if the accepted paradigm has hardened around its mathematical foundations. It's time to look again at the evidence. Pay attention to new data. And most importantly, follow the surprises, the things that don't fit. In such circumstances, evidence will often shout its message to us, as key patterns emerge, previously unseen."[116]

Summary

It appears that planet earth and our solar system are being subjected to new higher frequencies of coherent light particles coming in from the sun and the galactic core. Simultaneously, our entire solar system is passing through a highly charged interstellar cloud of energy and the earth itself is party to this as she accommodates her energy field to allow this influx. If we think of this as an information transmission, then our planet and its inhabitants are in the process of receiving copious amounts of information from cosmic, galactic, and solar sources and our beloved planet earth is an intelligent, living, conscious entity receiving new information. This brief glance at the cosmic environment indicates that all matter is in a process of being activated, excited, charged, energized, and transformed in some way. Space is not empty, and what appears to be solid and rocklike is plasma filled with electrical currents and with vast, intricate webs of electromagnetic fields of energy. Everything is connected, and everything that happens in our solar system affects our planet and our being.

CHAPTER 6

The Energetics of Being

Morphic and Morphogenetic Fields

Our brief sojourn so far into the world of modern science has shown us that much of what we have been conditioned to believe simply is no longer valid. We have come to realize we are beings of energy interfacing constantly with a universe of energy. This of course is mirrored in our biological system. Studies in biology, molecular biology, biophysics, epigenetics, and neurophysics are revealing that our human biology is governed by energetic information transmitted by fields of energetic wave patterns acting upon the genetic code in our DNA. These wave patterns are actually the blueprint for our physical life. But how does this energy organize itself into different types of matter?

A morphic field holds the information of a species, and morphic fields are many and varied. The morphic field that shapes the growing organism is called a morphogenetic field.[117] These fields enable the transfer of information from one generation to another and between the units of like species. Theoretical biologist Rupert Sheldrake developed his theory of the existence of these fields as early as 1981. "I came to the conclusion that for understanding the development of plants, their morphogenesis, genes and gene products are not enough. Morphogenesis also depends on organizing fields."[118] These are fields of information that control the biology above the biochemical level and apply equally to the animal and human kingdoms. According to Sheldrake, genes organize the information of our cells but do not explain the organization itself. The Human Genome Project has discovered that man has only 25,000 genes, the same amount as a chimpanzee. This came as a shock to the researchers; they were expecting somewhere in the region of one hundred and fifty thousand. So the big question became, why are we different? The study of the new science of epigenetics tells us that our genes do not cause our biology.

According to cellular biologist Bruce Lipton,[119] our genes contain the blueprint for the one hundred thousand or so proteins that are the building blocks of the body, but each gene has a possibility of around 30,000 variations, all of which are influenced by the cell's environment both in and outside the body. Lipton's research on the function of the cell membrane was a major breakthrough in our understanding of our biology. By applying the principles of quantum physics to the communication processing system of cells, he discovered that the cell membrane is the "brain" of the cell. It functions as an interface between the inner and outer worlds of the cell. It is a liquid crystal semiconductor with gates and channels, using its natural charge to allow signals to enter the cell or vice versa.[120] His research between 1987 and 1992 at Stanford University's School of Medicine revealed that the environment, including energetic messaging from positive and negative thought patterns, operating through this membrane by turning genes on and off, was the controlling factor in the behavior and the physiology of the cell, not the genes themselves. His papers were published, and it was these papers, now validated by many other researchers, that birthed the new science of epigenetics.

The discovery that our DNA and cells are governed by their environment is truly monumental. Why? Because this means it is programmable by us. As we will discover later when we review the properties and research of our miraculous DNA on just how this is possible, this places the responsibility for our own health and well-being fairly and squarely under the control of our own being. No matter which blueprint or hereditary gene we are born with, we are masters of our own destiny and have a choice. The morphogenetic fields work by transferring their encoded patterns to the random patterns of activity through resonance of frequency. Sheldrake uses the example of a cell and its microtubules and asks, "What determines that they form in one part of the cell rather than another when the entire cell is filled with their components?"[121] There needs to be an organizing principle of matter.

The morphic and morphogenetic field is not static. It is constantly changed every moment by each and every unit. It evolves over thousands and thousands of years and holds the information of an entire species in its energy packets or quanta and transmits this information through what Sheldrake calls morphic resonance. If we accept we are living holograms, then we each hold the all within our individual blueprint. Through resonance our energy field can connect with this memory store. Sheldrake posits there are fields of energy that organize the activity of the nervous system and through resonance convey a collective instinctive memory. Each unit of a species contributes to and draws from the collective memory of the species. This allows patterns of behavior to spread very rapidly. Examples of this are the maneuver wave of flocks of birds and the movements of schools of fish in the animal kingdom.

In terms of human social behavior, the phenomenon of the rapid spread of an idea was described brilliantly by Malcolm Gladwell in his book *The Tipping Point*.[122] Once a critical mass of energy has been reached, through the physical laws of harmonic induction and sympathetic resonance, the dispersion of information becomes inevitable. Remember the tuning fork. This phenomenon is of great significance when we come to examine our own energy-management system and how this can affect the whole. We will see in the following chapters that the human body is actually an energy field of standing stationary scalar, electromagnetic waves that are organized and structured and contain information patterns. Each physical body part has an organizing field or template through which it takes form. All fields are holographic, which means even if they are cut, as we have seen with Lashley's rat brains, the entire field remains, and as Montagnier's DNA experiment reveals, even if the DNA is removed from the test tube, the imprint remains in the solution.

The Human Bioenergy Field

Science has now confirmed the existence of the human energy field. Biologist and biophysicist James Oschman wrote in 2000, "It has now been confirmed that the energies so thoroughly studied by physicists surround and penetrate and are produced by all living things. In a few decades scientists have gone from a conviction that there is no such thing as an energy field around the human body, to an absolute certainty that it exists. Living organisms have bio-magnetic fields around them that change moment to moment in relation to events taking place within the body. They give a clearer representation of what is going on in the body than electrical tools such as electrocardiogram and the electroencephalogram."[123] As scientific knowledge and understanding of the world of energy continues to expand, this provides a rich opportunity for humankind to explore its own place within this outstanding cosmic connection framework.

The human bio field consists of many different types of energy fields that surround and interpenetrate the physical body. All the matter of our miraculous form is constantly creating electric, magnetic, and electromagnetic waves of varying frequencies of light and type that permeate, penetrate, and emit from the entire physical body. Our DNA, cells, tissues, bones, organs, thoughts, feelings, intentions, beliefs, causal body (soul), and monad (spirit) all create fields of different energy frequencies that contribute and combine to create the complex living matrix of energy that is the human being. This personal energy field permeates and extends out from the physical body and constantly interacts with other personal fields of the human, animal, plant, and mineral kingdoms, as well as the morphogenetic, planetary, solar, galactic, cosmic, and quantum potential fields. It does this in several ways, and through the advances in science many of these fields are now measurable. This has come about as traditional scientists, following the standard scientific method, have started to see the importance of the role energy plays in the biological process. Science has now given us evidence of some of the fields of energy directly observed and experienced by energy therapists and others. It has been known for some time now that the activities of cells, tissues, and organs generate electrical fields that can be detected on the skin surface, and we know that when energy moves, it creates a corresponding magnetic field in the surrounding space. But these fields are very fine and subtle, and originally there were no instruments available sensitive enough to measure them. Because of this, biologists assumed they had no significance. However, there are now instruments available that can detect some of these energy fields around and penetrating the body.

Anatomy of the Bioenergy Field

The physical body and its personal energy field interface with its environment through a network that is created by a number of energy vortices, which are located at the major nerve plexi in the physical body and correspond to the glands of the endocrine system. They run from the base of the spine to the top of the head and are centered into an energy stream running vertically and parallel with the spinal column from the perineum to the brain. These are rotational vortices absorbing energy in the form of different light frequencies to nourish the specific organs and glands associated with each of the regulatory centers. Each has its own energy field and is connected to meridians or subtle energy pathways of the physical body. These energy pathways are associated with the acupuncture system of traditional Chinese medicine and are believed to be embedded within the fascia of the physical body, which allow the energy to be distributed into the bloodstream and extracellular matrix, bringing energy and information to our bodies at the cellular and DNA levels. "Many of the observations of the energy therapists down through the ages, observations that science has previously found unacceptable, are being validated and explained by researchers around the world," according to Oschman.[124]

Our own personal bioenergy field consists of many different layers, each corresponding with the rotating vortices of energy located at the major nerve plexi. Not only do the vortices feed the physical body, but they also are the gateway to the various dimensions or frequency bands of our consciousness and the energy field associated with each level. Each level represents a field of energy particles vibrating at a different frequency, which comprise the totality of the overall field. It is constantly changing from moment to moment and consists of structured levels of standing scalar energy as well as unstructured levels of flowing transverse waves of electromagnetic energy, which can be perceived as a plethora of flowing iridescent colors interpenetrating and surrounding each other. Each succeeding vortex and field from perineum to above the head and beyond is composed of finer and finer substance and higher and higher vibratory energy. Information from these fields of energy can be sensed, seen, felt, or heard, sometimes tasted, sometimes smelled, depending on an individual's focus, evolutionary development, and conscious awareness. Many energy practitioners around the world, including myself, can give testament to this fact. I have personally found sense access can vary from person to person, depending on how their energy field interacts with my own.

The personal bioenergy field forms the blueprint or template for everything that occurs in the physical body. Each level includes a psychological, as well as a physical, function. As we have seen, mind and body are not separated. Each level of the body field also represents a different level of consciousness or awareness. The vortices of energy spin clockwise, bringing in waves of their own frequency into the energy system of the body. They each have a different frequency, color, and sound. The healthy wave patterns of an optimally healthy system can become distorted or blocked in any one or all of the different body energy fields, depending on the nature of the problem. Emotions, thoughts, feelings, belief systems, intentions, and all the physical aspects of the body such as DNA, genes, cells, tissues, organs, and bones—all carry different frequencies and contribute to the overall flow of information in the body system. A distortion in one or all of the body fields can cause energy blockages in the overall system that prevent the free flow of energy and can shut down a vortex completely so that energy cannot reach a particular area of the body. If energetic information cannot reach a part of the physical body, distortion and ultimately disease occurs in this location. Physical disease is created first in the energy field before manifesting in the body. There is no energy without a consciousness aspect, and a fully optimized energy system means an awakening to and remembering of the real self. This is health, and health is wholeness at all levels.

The Evidence

As early as the 1920s, a theory had been put forward by a distinguished researcher at Yale School of Medicine, Harold Saxton Burr, who theorized that diseases could be detected in the energy field of the body before physical symptoms appeared. He was convinced that energy fields provide the blueprint for living systems, and if the field could be altered, then disease could be prevented. Of course this was an idea way ahead of its time, but now with more sophisticated measuring devices, this is being confirmed in medical laboratories around the world.[125]

Around the same time, in Russia, biologist Alexander Gurwitsch, who was convinced of the existence of a biological field, was performing his famous onion experiment and discovered the biophoton.[126] This was to be validated years later when biophysicist Fritz Albert Popp, who at the time was involved in cancer research, found some peculiar anomalies in a strong carcinogenic substance. This discovery prompted him to develop a very sensitive light amplifier device called a photomultiplier to investigate these anomalies. Ironically he was funded in his project on the premise it would confirm there was no light in the cells. His photomultiplier was able to accurately measure these weak emissions of light from living cells and confirm, beyond any doubt, that low-level light emissions are a common property of all living cells.[127]

The Onion Experiment

The roots of two onions are positioned perpendicularly so that the tip of one root points to one side of the other root. Gurwitsch found that there was a significant increase in cell divisions on this side, compared to the opposite side. The effect disappeared when a thin piece of window glass was placed between the two roots, and reappeared when the ordinary glass (which is opaque for ultraviolet light) was replaced with quartz glass, which is transparent for ultraviolet light.[128]

Modern research now confirms Burr's and Gurwitsch's field hypotheses. Every event in the body produces not only electrical charges but also alterations to the magnetic fields in the spaces around the body. A study in Rome in 1982 explored biomagnetic fields produced near the head during epileptic seizures. In this case, the epilepsy was caused by tumors that did not show up on EEGs or CAT scans but were detected by biomagnetic recordings.[129] It has been found that mapping the magnetic fields provides more accurate data about physiology and pathology than electrical recordings such as those produced by the electrocardiogram (EEG) and the electroencephalogram (ECG).[130,131] One such device is the SQUID (superconducting quantum interference device), a magnetometer that is capable of detecting the subtle biomagnetic fields associated with the physiological activities of the body.

SQUID was invented in 1965 by Robert Jaklevic, John J. Lambe, Arnold Silver, and James Edward Zimmerman while at the science laboratory of the Ford Motor Company. These devices are based on the discovery of the quantum phenomenon of electron tunneling. This is the movement of electrons through solid matter. They are called Josephson effects after Brian Josephson, who in 1973 received a Nobel Prize for his work, which enabled the development of magnetometers of unprecedented sensitivity[132,133,134] In 1970 David Cohen of MIT first confirmed the electromagnetic measurements of the heart field and, two years later after improving the sensitivity of the instruments, measured magnetic fields around the head produced by brain activities. Experiments with various forms of energy practitioners have provided much evidence for the existence of the bioenergy fields. Dr. John Zimmerman began a study of a healing modality called Therapeutic Touch in the 1980s using a SQUID magnetometer at the University of Colorado School of Medicine, Denver, and discovered a huge pulsating biomagnetic field that emanated from a therapist's hands, which ranged from 0.3 Hz to 30 Hz, with most in the 7-8 Hz range. He found that the pulsations from the therapist's hands sweep through the frequencies that scientific studies have indicated are necessary to stimulate healing.[135]

More modern research came in 1992 from Japan, confirming these findings when Seto and associates studied practitioners of various martial arts and healing methods. Studies on Qi Gong practitioners have been extended to include light, sound, and heat. They also found that the frequencies emitted from the hands of healers vary from moment to moment and are the same frequencies that trigger a healing response in a variety of soft and hard tissues in the body.[136]

In the search to provide evidence of the existence of the human energy field, science has also managed to provide compelling evidence that substantiates the healing claims of many energy practitioners over the decades. If we consider these therapies as informational exchanges between the bioenergy fields of the patient and the practitioner, we begin to get a clearer understanding of how healing becomes possible. Academic medicine is now slowly beginning to accept these therapies as logical and beneficial because of these new scientific findings. It is important to note that results can vary from therapist to therapist, and there is now strong evidence available that shows the part intention plays in these types of interactions. This will be explored more fully further on. James Oschman says, "I have shown how some of the experiences of energy therapists have a basis in biology and physics. After centuries of neglect, energetic therapies can take their appropriate place in clinical medicine. The great discoveries of biologists and of sensitive body-workers are being integrated to give us a deeper understanding of life, disease, and healing."[137]

A more recent invention is GDV bioelectrography. This is a gas discharge visualization technique developed by Russian physicist Konstantin Korotkov and is essentially the modern equivalent of Kirlian photography. Korotkov's amazing digital camera and software are able to capture and measure the photonic light emissions from the body in real time. The body literally glimmers, but this light is not widely visible to the human eye. As changes occur in the body, the light emissions alter and can now be recorded and analyzed by this device. GDV technique is the computer registration and analysis of electrophotonic emissions of biological objects (specifically the human fingers) resulting from placing the object in the high-intensity electromagnetic field on the device lens. A weak electrical current is applied to the fingertips of the subject for less than a millisecond while the fingers are scanned. In response to this stimulus, an "electron cloud" is formed, which is composed of light energy photons. The electronic "glow" of this discharge, which is invisible to the human eye, is then captured by the camera system and then translated via computer software and transmitted back in graphical representations to show energy, stress, and vitality evaluations.[138]

See figures 6.1, 6.2, and 6.3 showing some results of various readings from the GDV device. The device has been approved and received registration as a routine medical diagnostic device by the Russian Ministry of Health upon recommendation of the Russian Academy of Sciences and is now being used worldwide.

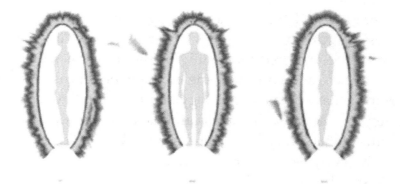

Figure 6.1. Whole body energy field front view composite of normal healthy human, computed from digital Kirlian fields of ten fingers according to algorithms based on empirical correlations with biomedical data and traditional Chinese medical theory of the acupuncture meridians calculated. GDV imaging courtesy Konstantin G. Korotkov, www.korotkov.eu.

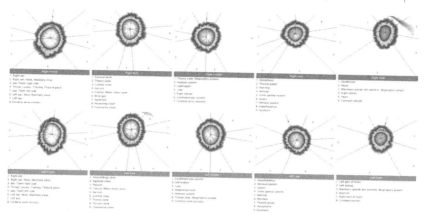

Figure 6.2. Bio-well software data showing ten finger measurements and related organs. GDV imaging courtesy of Konstantin G. Korotkov, www. korotkov.eu.

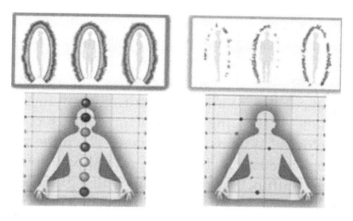

Figure 6.3. Bioenergy field and energy centers of healthy (left) and unhealthy/emotionally unbalanced individual (right). GDV imaging using Bio-well software courtesy of Konstantin G. Korotkov. www.korotkov.eu

Figure 6.3 shows the results from a case study done by Dr. Pradeep B. Deshpande, a professor emeritus at the Department of Chemical Engineering at the University of Louisville, using the GDV device and computer software. "Each Chakra (energy center) is considered to resonate at a different frequency level. With new Bio-Well® software, it is now possible to quantitatively estimate the energy of chakras (energy centers) and graphically display their level of activation."[139]

There are still not devices available to reach the intensely high frequencies of the upper range of the human bioenergy field, and yet we have seen from our exploration of cosmology, there are detectors able to locate extremely high frequency particles emanating from the sun and the galactic center in space. Perhaps it is a case of not looking for something because there is no expectation it is there. As research evolves, it is likely these higher frequency bands of the more subtle energies will eventually be detected and recorded.

Bioscalar Energy in the Human Energy Field

While she was a professor at UCLA in the seventies, Dr. Valerie Hunt developed a device capable of recording the electrical energy at the skin's surface. During this research she found energy radiating from the body's atoms emit frequencies one thousand times faster than any other electrical activity of the body. She went on in the eighties and nineties, using fractal mathematics, to analyze data from her studies of the human biofield, showing the very first chaos patterns in human biological systems. Hunt states, "When the pattern of the electromagnetism is disturbed in the body, you will get disease and malfunction."[140] Working with a group of healers who were able to observe, through heightened perception, the colors of the various energy fields of the volunteers, she was able to record the electronic signals from the skin and map the waveforms and frequencies and correlate specific waveforms and frequencies with the colors, size, and energy movements observed. Through her research she came to the conclusion that an imbalance of energies or incoherence in the energy field created disease in the physical body. This supports the view that healing is a process of rebalancing the energies within the bioenergy field. "All healing that takes place in alternative medicine is electromagnetic—everything that takes place, even the thought process, or the person's intent or spiritual state, changes the electromagnetic field and changes it almost instantaneously. If it stays changed and improved, the body heals itself, and the chemistry reorganizes."[141] Hunt believed the electromagnetic patterning of the bioenergy field could be disturbed by a number of triggers:

- ❖ genetic = the nature of the physical body matter
- ❖ experiential = lifestyle patterns
- ❖ emotional = created by the thought process

Any of these external stimuli create disturbance in the electromagnetism of the tissues, and this eventually alters the chemistry. She predicted, quite correctly, that our DNA could be reprogrammed by the emotional organization of the energy field. She also predicted, correctly, that the electromagnetic frequencies that pass through the body as waves of energy were standing energy or scalar. She termed this bioscalar. She believed this energy to be the essential electromagnetic phenomenon responsible for all healing procedures and discovered that each of us can be a generator for this. Her research has shown that we can become conductors for this energy by using our bodies as semiconductors, bringing the electromagnetic transverse waves of a particular color frequency from the cosmic field into the center of the body, creating the standing wave. Scalar energy is created when two common electromagnetic waves of the same frequency traveling from different vectors collide, canceling each other out, creating the standing scalar energy. This energy then radiates out as a field to the parts of the body that require that particular frequency. "We have found that all medical conditions are improved or eliminated by bioscalar activation, the direction is always positive as the body establishes new energy field patterns."[142]

Konstantin Meyl, a physicist in the field of electrical engineering, successfully reproduced Tesla's scalar energy experiments to provide modern science with evidence of Tesla's discovery. Applying the knowledge from this discipline to the field of molecular biology, Meyl also proposed the entire body works with scalar waves and that DNA transports information and energy with a magnetic scalar wave; neurons and the gaps (nodes of Ranvier) between the protective coating of the nerve cells (myelin sheath) indicate a longitudinal standing wave; and bioresonance medicine and homeopathy use scalar waves as the carrier. His papers and books confirm Hunt's scalar energy predictions, and we will see in our review of DNA, this view is upheld by the findings of Russian physicist Peter Gariaev in his exploration of DNA energetics.[143]

The Electromagnetic Heart

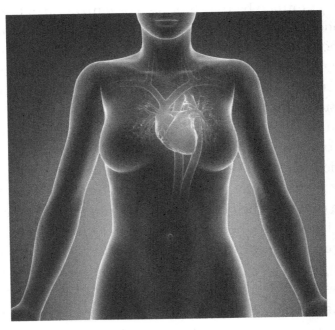

Figure 6.4. The electromagnetic human heart.

The unfolding journey into human energetic anatomy continues with a review of the human heart, the place where all wisdom resides. Here is why.

Based on over two decades of research at the HeartMath HeartMath Institute (HMI),[144] science can now evidence that the heart is a sensory organ and is a highly sophisticated communication and information processing center, emitting sound, heat, pressure waves, light, and magnetic, electrical, and electromagnetic waves, and all cells of the body are receiving information from the heart at different times through the circulatory and nervous systems. The heart is the key to everything in our biological system and is *now recognized by these scientists as a highly complex system with its own functional "brain."* Researchers at the HMI have been studying heart-brain communication and the electrophysiology of intuition and found the heart generates the most powerful and most extensive electromagnetic field in the body and the magnetic component of this magnificent energy field is far greater than the magnetic field generated by the brain. Their work also illustrates that the heart is the body's single most important regulatory organ and its smooth, ordered, coherent rhythm entrains and synchronizes with the brain. The signals the heart is continuously sending to the brain actually influence the functioning of the higher brain centers, which are involved in perception, cognition, and emotional processing, and HMI has produced evidence that these signals can be modulated by feelings.

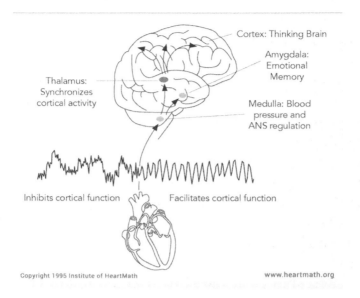

Cortex: Thinking Brain

Amygdala:
Emotional
Memory

Thalamus:
Synchronizes
cortical activity

Medulla: Blood
pressure and
ANS regulation

Inhibits cortical function   Facilitates cortical function

Copyright 1995 Institute of HeartMath   www.heartmath.org

Figure 6.5. The heart-brain function. Diagram courtesy of the HeartMath Institute, https://www.heartmath.org.

As well as the extensive neural network that links the heart to the brain and body, the heart is also communicating information to the brain and body via its electromagnetic field. All energy waves are information carriers, and the electrical component of the heart's energy field is sixty times greater in amplitude than that of the brain. HMI researchers have demonstrated not only the synchronization of the brain to the heart's rhythmic pattern but also psychophysiological coherence obtained by deep breathing and sustained feelings of love and appreciation can and do affect blood pressure, respiration, and other body functions. Positive feelings create a completely different heart pattern than negative feelings. Negative feelings create an incoherent or discordant rhythm.[145]

The research shows that information concerning a person's emotional state is communicated throughout the body via the heart's electromagnetic field. As we experience different emotions, the rhythmic beating pattern changes, becoming erratic, disordered, and incoherent when negative emotions such as anger and rage or frustration are expressed. Positive emotions of love, gratitude, and appreciation produce a smooth, ordered, and coherent pattern in the rhythm. These changes in the heart's rhythm in turn create corresponding changes in the electromagnetic field, measurable by a technique called spectral analysis at the HeartMath® Institute Research Center.[146]

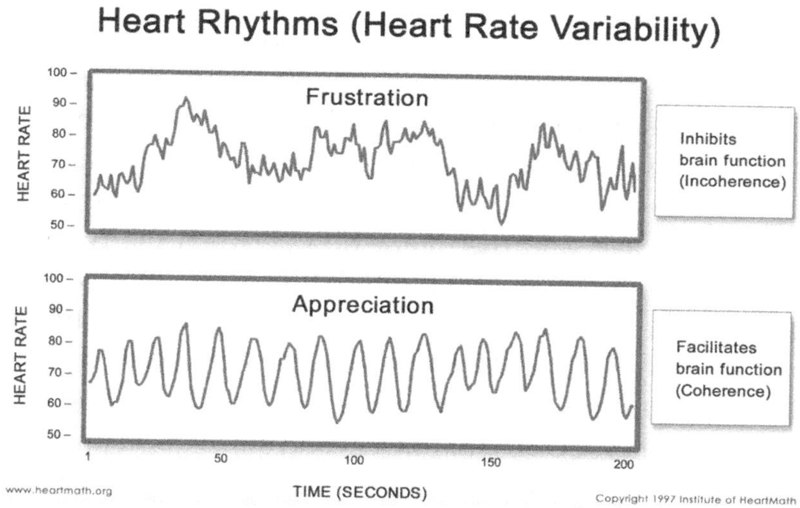

Figure 6.6. Diagram courtesy of the HeartMath Institute. https://www.heartmath.org from research showing effects of positive and negative feelings on heart coherence.

Not surprisingly, other experiments undertaken by these distinguished scientists demonstrate that heart coherence is the optimal physiological state and this underpins all learning and performance and facilitates natural healing in the body and all regenerative processes.[147] HMI defines coherence as "a calm, balanced, energized, responsive state that is conducive to everyday functioning and interaction including the performance of tasks that require mental acuity, focus, problem solving and decision making as well as physical activity and co-ordination. Heart coherence is a distinct mode of synchronized psychophysical functioning associated with sustained positive emotion. It is a state of energetic alignment and cooperation between heart, mind, body and spirit. In coherence, energy is accumulated, not wasted, leaving you more energy to manifest intention and harmonious outcomes."[148]

The heart has its own intrinsic nervous system that senses, feels, remembers, and processes information completely independent of the brain. There is evidence that the heart is "intuitive." Astonishing experiments implemented and described by Rollin McCraty at HMI have shown that the heart actually receives information before the brain and it responds faster than the brain to outside stimulation. By measuring brain wave, heart wave, and the interaction between the two, they have been able to show that the heart responds in a way that can predict if a future event will be emotionally significant or relevant to a person. Volunteers were shown two different types of photos, one set disturbing, such as a car accident or snakes; the other set were of flowers and sunsets, all randomly assigned by computer after the data were recorded. The body responded before the picture was displayed. This was a controlled experiment, with only the computer doing the selections and displays. No other person was involved. The heart responded first, sending a signal to the brain, which varied depending on the future picture. At this point the brain responded, and finally there was a physiological response.[149] This completely changes our understanding of how the body interfaces with its environment and has access to information not bound by time and space and the role of the heart. How does this happen?

According to McCraty, the neurons in the heart have short- and long-term memory capable of processing information. The neural tissue in the heart acts as an imprinter of information to and from the holographic bioenergy field. He proposes that the heart's field acts as a carrier wave for information that provides a global synchronizing signal for the entire body. He suggests the waves of energy pulsing from the heart radiate out and interact with the fields of the organs and other structures within the body. These waves encode or record the features and dynamic activity from the organ fields in patterns of energy waveforms distributed throughout the body. Through this process, encoded information actually informs (literally gives shape to) the activity of all bodily functions. We can refer back to our holographic model again, where we see patterns of organization encoded into energy waves of a system and distributed throughout the system as a whole.

Our exploration of the heart field must include the HMI research that has provided incredible evidence of an exchange of electromagnetic energy produced by the heart when people touch or are in close proximity. The researchers have been able to record results by using signal averaging techniques that show the electrocardiogram (ECG heart) of one person is registered in the electroencephalogram (EEG brain) of the other and elsewhere on the other person's body when they touch or are in close proximity.[150] It is believed that the coherent, electromagnetic field generated by the heart of an individual in a caring state may be detected and amplified by biological tissue through the mechanism of resonance and can produce measurable effects in living systems.

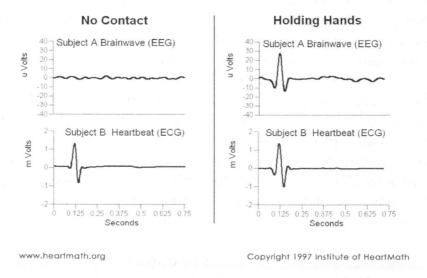

The Electricity of Touch
Heartbeat Signal Averaged Waveforms

Figure 6.7. Diagram courtesy of the HeartMath Institute, htttps://www.heartmath.org from research showing heart and brain correlation between subjects in physical contact.

It was also demonstrated in this research that the coherence of the receiving person's heart rhythm affected the result and ability to pick up the other's heart signal. The effect was not apparent in subjects with low coherence patterns.[151] Once again we see the incredible connection between living systems demonstrated and begin to realize the enormous implications of these results for all our relations with others.

Note: This study, known as the electricity of touch, describes the first successful attempts to measure energy exchange between human beings and offers a testable theory to explain the observed effects of many healing modalities that are based on the assumption that an exchange of energy takes place.

Group Heart Coherence

There are many other awe-inspiring experiments performed by the indefatigable scientists at the HeartMath Institute. They have conducted extensive research on the power of heart intelligence, intuition, and the energetic connection between all things. They have explored the intricacies of heart-brain messaging, how emotions affect human biology, and significantly, have created the Global Coherence Initiative. Through this HMI is exploring, among other things, the influences of geomagnetic fields and solar activity on our health and daily activities. It will include a very important scientific measurement component. HMI is employing an advanced sensing technology that will allow observation of changes in the earth's magnetic field in order to test the hypothesis that the earth's field is affected by mass human emotion, whether positive or negative. This monitoring system will have fourteen sensors placed in strategic locations around the world and will enable a new level of inquiry into the relationship among collective human behaviors, the earth's magnetic field, and planetary changes. Their hypotheses are: strong collective human emotions are registered and reflected by changes in the planetary field; groups of people in heart coherence can affect the planetary field; and changes in the planetary field predict earthquakes, volcanoes, and similar scale events.[152] It will be interesting to see the outcome of these group coherence initiatives and their results.

The diligent and ongoing research at HMI has clearly demonstrated the amazing effects produced by the electromagnetic energy generated by the heart. No doubt this resource within the human system will provide a fertile ground for further exploration and application. It appears to act as a synchronizing force within the body, is a crucial carrier of emotional information, and is an apparent mediator of subtle electromagnetic communication between people. The final word goes to Research Director at HMI Rollin McCraty: "The cardiac bio-electromagnetic field may have much to teach us about the inner dynamics of health and disease as well as our interactions with others."[153]

Summary

Our exploration of the complex energetics of the human energetic anatomy is slowly evidencing a very different mechanism to describe the nature of our existence than purely a physical biochemical phenomenon. Science is demonstrating a picture of energy fields of waveforms and particles, constantly storing, transmitting, and receiving information. From the morphic field of a species and its morphogenetic field developed over thousands and thousands of years to the existence of our individual complex bioenergy field now able to be measured and the properties of the powerful, electromagnetic energy field of the heart, scientific evidence is pointing us firmly in a direction that demonstrates the human physical being is a complex energetic field of energy interacting constantly with other fields of energy to transmit, receive, accumulate, and use information from all other available fields. Our DNA and cellular morphogenesis are governed by an environment of organizing waveforms transferring information through resonance. This is consistent with holographic organization. If we consider the possibility we are a holographic form in nature and holographic organization is based on a field concept of order, then information about the organization of an object and events in space and time as a whole is encoded as an interference pattern in energy waveforms distributed throughout the cosmic holographic field. This makes it possible to retrieve information about the object as a whole, or an event in space and time, from any location within the field. In effect we all hold the potential to connect to all the information in the cosmos. Our physical body is ordered based on the template of our own bioenergy field resonating with the species' morphogenetic field. The heart-brain is communicating with the holographic human bioenergy field, continuously sending information to the brain processor that results in physiological responses. Consider well the magnificence of your being.

CHAPTER 7

DNA—The Building Blocks of Life

In 1975 Hyman Hartman wrote, "What is well established in the molecular biology community, but unknown to most people, is the fact that the primary structure of DNA does actually change."[154]

In 1998 Glenn Rein and Rollin McCraty wrote, "We are therefore not necessarily stuck with the genetic blueprint passed down to us from our parents."[155]

As science is beginning now to acknowledge the importance of energetics to human health and wellbeing, much of the research into energy medicine is providing incredible evidence that our physical bodies do not work in the way the classical medical paradigm would have us believe. A review of the astonishing research into the very building blocks of life, our DNA, provides us with even more evidence to suggest that individuals have much more control over their physical condition than geneticists and the medical profession readily acknowledge. DNA research over the last fifty years has been absolutely staggering in its scope. It is unfortunate that the results of this brilliant research have been more geared to providing mankind with GM foodstuffs, cloned animals, and patented genes. However, possibly the greatest news to emerge from this phenomenal research is that each one of us has the potential to activate our dormant DNA and reprogram our already activated codons. The discovery of the incredible properties of our DNA supports the need for an extreme shift in perspective.

Properties of DNA

The DNA in our genes stores the codes for the chemical, molecular instructions that determine all cellular functions. It is the blueprint for the manufacture of all the proteins in our cells that do the work, such as cellular reproduction, breakdown of food to release energy, and transporting chemicals. It is the blueprint for physical life. Thanks to the diligent research of Alexander Gurwitsch in the 1920s and the validation and research into the nature of the biophoton in the 1980s and nineties by German biophysicist Fritz-Albert Popp, we know that our DNA emits, absorbs, stores, and transforms coherent light.[156] A miracle in itself, our DNA also turns out to be an organic superconductor capable of holding a charge and behaving as a condensate (a fluid and coherent matter where atoms are indistinguishable) that is capable of managing captive, slow-moving, solitary light waves called solitons, which continually circulate within the DNA helix, creating scalar energy.[157,158] This property facilitates the absorption and radiation of acoustic and electromagnetic information in the forms of sound and light. Solitons exhibit wave and particle duality and therefore can store information too and enable the DNA to respond to electromagnetic fields. DNA has also been found to be a living, liquid crystal, a state of matter between crystalline and liquid exhibiting the properties of both.[159] Experiments have shown that when coherent light is transmitted through crystalline-medium structures, it creates diffraction patterns or tiny holograms that exhibit spiral, fractal characteristics. Just to remind ourselves, these are repeating, fragmented geometric shapes that can be subdivided into smaller parts, each of which is a perfect copy of the whole, and are found everywhere in nature. Is this beginning to sound like familiar territory?

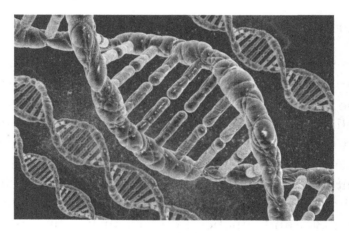

Figure 7.1. The double helix of DNA.

In the 1990s Peter Gariaev, a member of the Russian Academy of Sciences, formed a multidisciplinary group of researchers to fully investigate the amazing properties of DNA. His team included biophysicists, molecular biologists, embryologists, and linguistic experts. He and his group have demonstrated astonishing evidence for the holographic transmission and programming of morphogenetic information by our DNA.

Phantom DNA

The Russian group provided evidence of an organizing energy information field for our DNA in what has come to be known as the phantom DNA experiment. By introducing a laser (coherent) light into an empty sealed vacuum and measuring the photons (particles of light), they found the resulting pattern to be scattered. DNA was then placed in the container and the photonic pattern that developed was remeasured. The photons followed the structure of the DNA and produced this pattern. So far, these two results were exactly what the scientists would expect. The surprise came when the DNA was removed from the container and the photons in the empty container were remeasured. It was found that a wave pattern remained in evidence. The experiments took place in a vacuum. Gariaev posited "The DNA phantom effect may be interpreted as a manifestation of a new physical vacuum substructure that has been previously overlooked. This points to the presence of the morphogenetic field. It appears that this substructure can be excited from the physical vacuum in a range of energies close to zero energy provided certain specific conditions are fulfilled which are specified above."[160] Incredibly, our DNA can produce tunnel connections between different areas in space-time through which information can be transmitted.[161]

What is being demonstrated in the phantom effect is DNA interacting with an information field and demonstrating the imprint of the interaction and information transfer. Gariaev calls this field the energy information level; perhaps another description is Sheldrake's morphogenetic field. Nobel Laureate Luc Montagnier's latest experiments build upon the Russians' work, confirming that DNA can send electromagnetic imprints of itself into distant cells and fluid, which can then be used by enzymes to create copies of the original.[162]

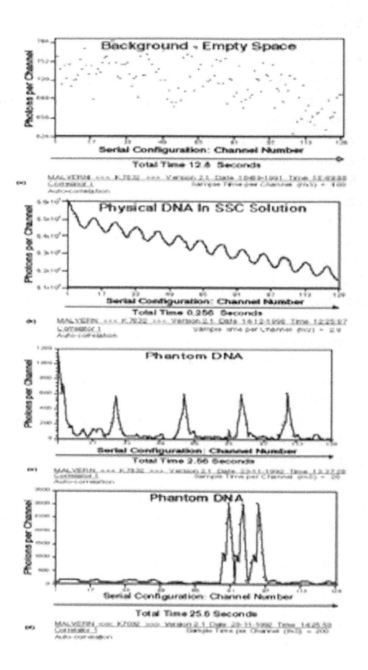

Figure 7.2. Phantom DNA.

DNA and Water

Montagnier's experiment also shows that "water memory'"
is highly significant to the process of what may be occurring
in cells, and in the last two decades, many different scientists
have been working on determining this mechanism. His work
may validate the work of the discredited French immunologist
Jacques Beneviste, who in 1988 published a controversial paper
drawing the conclusion that the configuration of molecules in
water was biologically active and coined the phrase "water
memory."

Our bodies consist of an average of 60 to 70 percent
water, rendering this an important medium for information
transfer. It is now believed there are two types of water: bulk
water or the regular H20 from the tap, and structured water,
H302.[163] This structured water is the water found inside all
cells of the body. This water has a six-sided structure, and
the small water clusters fit into and through the hexagonal
channels in the cell membrane and inside the cell. This specific
geometrical structure enables ultra-mobility and the efficient
delivery of oxygen, nutrients, protein chains, and enzymes,
as well as the speedy removal of any toxic buildup in the
cell. Investigators discovered that six-sided, crystal-shaped,
hexagonal structured water molecules form the supportive
matrix of healthy DNA. In the cell nucleus DNA is bound to
proteins to form chromosomes and is coated with a layer of
water molecules. The depletion of this matrix is a fundamental
process that negatively affects virtually every physiological
function. Research has shown the lack of this type of water
in the body is responsible for cellular aging and other cellular
problems. Studies show that 2 percent loss of cellular water
decreases energy levels by as much as 20 percent, and over
99 percent of all chemical reactions in the cell are facilitated
by water. The significance of structured water is developed
further in the section on water and cellular communications.

It is available naturally only in the body and in nature as ice, at the North Pole and various healing springs around the world, including Lourdes in France.

Holographic DNA

The properties inherent in DNA and the evidence of Gariaev's experiments reveal it possesses all the components to create a biohologram. The particle/wave nature of the DNA can be read by the biophotons stored in the chromosomes to set up a holographically produced wave field, which in turn creates a waveguide or template for the formation of the biological structure of the cells. The image is constructed according to the information in the genes that are informed by the morphogenetic field. The blueprint coded into the DNA is translated into a complex electromagnetic field that guides the molecular growth of the organism. The nervous system acts as a coordination mechanism that integrates DNA projection of the rest of the cells in the system, aligning these cellular holograms. The *biohologram*, projected by the brain, creates standing and moving electromagnetic wave patterns at different frequencies of the spectrum in order to effect different biochemical transformations.[164,165]

Another experiment, called the cell mirror effect, demonstrates the transfer of information at a distance. V. Kaznacheyev and his group in Russia performed a series of experiments to investigate this phenomenon.[166] Two identical cell cultures were placed into hermetically sealed glass containers separated from each other by a quartz barrier. A pathology was introduced into one of the cultures using a laser light, and within two to three days, the second cell culture displayed the same pathology. When the quartz barrier was replaced with glass, the experiment did not work. The DNA inside the healthy cells had somehow been rearranged to transfer the DNA of the virus to the other cell. Once again we see evidence of information stored in a field of energy transported by coherent light, with distance as no barrier.

Yet a further experiment demonstrates the ability to reprogram DNA. In 2000 Budagovsky in Russia recorded a fragment of a tissue of a raspberry plant on a hologram using a red laser and then transmitted the hologram to a raspberry plant tumor (callus). After several months the callus developed into a raspberry plant.[167] Gariaev and his group continued with more advanced experiments to demonstrate how what he now calls Wave Genetics™ can be used for healing purposes. His experiments reprogramming DNA codon sequences using modulated laser light have profound implications for human well-being.

The Language of DNA

Gariaev also discovered the language of DNA. The current accepted language of DNA's code is written in only four "letters," called A (adenine), C (cytosine), T (thymine), and G (guanine), which represent the four base nucleotides that make proteins. The meaning of this code depends on the sequence of the letters A, T, C, and G in the same way that the meaning of a word is determined by the sequence of alphabet letters. The cells read the sequence to make the chemicals that the body needs to survive. Gariaev's group discovered an even higher-level language was present in DNA. The sequence of nucleotides within the DNA molecule mirrors the sequence of syllables in human language and follows similar grammatical foundations. His group confirmed that DNA can be modified by rearranging the codons in the DNA string into different sequences. They discovered the grammatical syntax of the DNA language and were able to modulate coherent laser light, as well as radio waves, and add meaning to the carrier wave and thus were able to reprogram in vivo DNA in living organisms using the correct resonant frequencies. Using a laser biocomputer to transfer healthy codes of organs from healthy rats into diseased rats, he was able to regenerate the pancreas and spleen in the diseased animals with an overall success rate of 90 percent. These experiments took place in 2000 in Moscow, 2001 in Toronto, and 2005 in Moscow, all using the same protocols and based on the principles and technology of Wave Genetics.[TM168] It appears that human language has been actively developed from our DNA and it responds to speech, provided this can be modulated on the correct carrier frequency. Ultimately, this means our DNA can be reprogrammed by sound, voice, words, and sentences, provided they are at the correct resonant frequency. Chromosomes damaged by X-rays have been repaired with this method. Information patterns of different species have been transmitted, completely reprogramming genomes.

Gariaev confirms his research is inspired by the work of many other researchers in this field, but he has been largely influenced by two in particular: Rupert Sheldrake in the United Kingdom, and Russian Alexander Gurwitsch, who, around 1920, realized there was a necessity to introduce the concept of biological field of a chromosome, as complementary to genes, in order to account for special organization of an organism. It was Gurwitsch who actually originated the morphogenetic field theory and discovered the biophoton in 1923.

What About the Junk?

Currently 95 percent of our DNA is commonly referred to as "junk DNA"; no one in the scientific world knew its function. Gariaev's wave genetic theory posits that this mysterious portion of our DNA is actually a "super-code or wave level operating at a higher level than the RNA and proteins. That the genome is a quasi-intelligent system and the function of the wave level of genetic coding is to program the space/time organization of an organism."[169] In Gariaev's Wave Genetics™ theory, the codes are realized as dynamic gene holograms in the liquid crystal of the chromosome. According to his theory, there are two types of information being processed at this level. First is the short-term information, which regulates the everyday metabolic processes of life. He posits that the information on the gene hologram is the result of interference patterns of spatial light and sound images of the current condition of the cells recorded on the intercellular water structure. These images are then "read" by the light and sound radiations of the chromosomes, transmitting information to the neighboring cells about the condition of the cell sending the information. This operation is performed by each and every cell in the organism and forms a combined, unified informational space, which functions like a DNA wave biocomputer, constantly processing information in real time.

The other type of bioholographic information is that of the morphogenetic field. We have seen from Sheldrake's work that this is fixed for an organism and is built up slowly over time. Gariaev believes that the DNA biocomputer uses its intelligence and, operating with its own linguistic structures similar to human language, makes intelligent decisions regarding regulation of the structure and function of the organism and its parts. This is extremely important information, for this also means the DNA biocomputer is programmed according to the current condition of the cells as well as to what is held in the morphogenetic field. What we think, feel, say, do, and intend affects our cells and therefore our DNA. In effect, if there are adverse conditions present in our overall system in the form of negative thoughts and feelings, this will form energetic blockages in our DNA. Similarly as its electromagnetic field is in communication with the morphogenetic field and planetary field, any traumas or disturbances held here also affect our

DNA. We are not separated from our species' energy field nor our planet's energy field; any blockages in either can halt our progress toward health and well-being and result in disease. The great news is that by the same token we can reprogram our DNA. Gariaev has given us firm evidence that the codons can be rearranged to reverse the disease process by using modulated electromagnetic waves (coherent light or sound waves). This has enormous implications for our species. This means a coherent bioenergy system can regenerate our cells, prevent disease, and reverse the aging process.

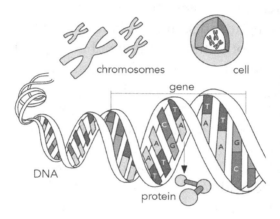

Figure 7.3. DNA components.

DNA and Sound

In 1988 Susan Alexjander, composer, together with biologist David Deamer, measured the vibrational frequencies of the four DNA bases and subsequently translated them into "sound." They found that perfect harmonic ratios exist within the frequency data of DNA. Based on the reactions of people who listened to the music created from their own DNA, she suggests that our bodies may have a way of recognizing their own electromagnetic patterns through the resonance of tone. She writes, "These particular DNA ratios, originating in light, are profoundly arresting to the ear. It is tempting to speculate that the body is recognizing itself, and is communicating this to the psyche."[170]

The Lost Solffegio Frequencies

The Solffegio frequencies were used in the tunes of ancient Gregorian chants; they were believed to impart great spiritual blessing when sung in harmony at religious services, but according to church authorities, they were "lost" many centuries ago. The original scale was developed by a Benedictine monk, Guido dArezzo (AD 991–1050), who developed them to facilitate the learning of chants and songs. The syllables are traced back to a hymn composed for John the Baptist, which itself was believed to open up a channel to the higher planes. They were rediscovered by Joseph Puleo in 1974. They are based on the old Pythagorean tuning system, with the numbers 3, 6, and 9 being the root vibrations. Tesla wrote, "If you only knew the magnificence of the 3, 6 and 9, then you would have a key to the universe." Based on ancient writings of the Apochrypha,* each tone has been designated a specific function, creating a particular effect.

Note	Hertz	Contributes to Effect of
UT	396	Reducing Guilt and Fear
RE	417	Cleansing trauma and past destructive influences
MI	528	Transformation and miracles. Returns Human DNA to original perfection
FA	639	Easing Relationship Issues
SOL	741	Encourages healthy lifestyle and diet.
LA	852	Raising awareness and aids in communication with the higher dimensions

---

* Apochrypha = additional biblical writings not considered authoritative by religious bodies.

Figure 7.4. The six primary Solffeggio tones.

In 1998 Glen Rein of the Quantum Biology Research Lab in New York performed experiments with in vitro DNA, exposing them to different recordings of musical styles, including Gregorian chants, using a technique that converted the music to audio scalar waves. He used two-phase opposite sound sources from the same music to self-cancel the waves and create scalar audio waves. With a CD player, an amplifier, and a spiral-like self-canceling coil, four different styles of music were played to test tubes containing in vitro DNA. After one hour the absorption of UV light of the DNA test tube samples was measured. It was found the Gregorian chants had caused a 5 to 9.1 percent increase in the absorption of UV light due to the unwinding of the DNA helix. Sanskrit chanting caused a similar 5.8 to 8.2 percent effect. Classical music caused a 1 percent increase, and rock music yielded 1.8 percent decreased absorption. Glen Rein finally concluded that the audible sound waves of the Solfeggio scale can cause resonance in DNA and can have healing effects.[171]

The hexagonal shape of the healthy water molecule is six-sided. In numerology the number 6 is considered to be the most harmonious of the single-digit numbers, associated with unconditional love, balance, and harmony. According to Pythagorean mathematics, the mid-Solffeggio tone MI 528 Hz has its root in the number 6.

$$(5 + 2 + 8 = 15; 1 + 5 = 6)$$

Note	Hertz	Contributes to Effect of
UT	396	Reducing Guilt and Fear
RE	417	Cleansing trauma and past destructive influences
MI	528	Transformation and miracles. Returns Human DNA to original perfection
FA	639	Easing Relationship Issues
SOL	741	Encourages healthy lifestyle and diet.
LA	852	Raising awareness and aids in communication with the higher dimensions

The transformational properties of the MI frequency 528 Hz have been widely publicized. Mathematician Victor Showell describes 528 Hz as being fundamental to the ancient pi, phi, and golden mean ratios evident in nature's designs. He posits that 528 Hz is an essential component in the geometries of circles and spirals (both types of energy movement) and consistent with DNA spiraling and hydrosonic structuring.

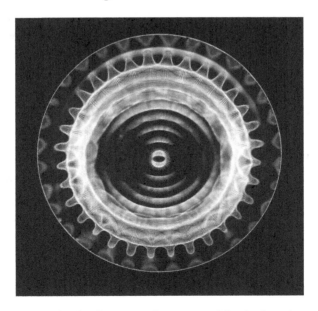

Figure 7.5. Cymaglyph of 528 Hz. Courtesy of Sonic Age America, LLC.

DNA Responds to Focused Intention and Positive Emotions

Another astonishing experiment conducted by Rein and McCraty at Heartmath® Institute demonstrated that positive emotions and focused intention expand and unwind the DNA helix and the coherence of the subject's physiology improves due to improved coherence of light emissions from the DNA.[172] By contrast, feelings of fear, anger, and rage contracted the DNA helix and reduced the subject's physiological coherence. These are incredible findings when we see real evidence that our emotions actually change the DNA that regulates all processes in the body and in our energy field.[173]

Summary

The research continues; however, the implications are nothing short of miraculous. Our own DNA can be reprogrammed by coherent light and sound. Human speech, provided the words are modulated to the correct carrier frequencies, can affect our DNA. We have seen how it responds to positive emotions. Healthy, structured water in the cell nucleus forms its supportive physical matrix. DNA has its own energy field, as does every living cell; if we recall that there are different bands of frequencies that comprise our overall bioenergy field, this means that our DNA also is multidimensional and receiving, transmitting, transforming, and storing at all these different levels. Are you beginning to see how truly incredible and magnificent is the creation you are?

CHAPTER 8

The Living Crystalline Matrix

James Oschman wrote in 2003, "The most exciting property of the living matrix is the ability of the entire network to generate and conduct vibrations ... modern biophysical research is revealing a wide range of properties that enable the body to use sound, light, electricity, magnetic fields, heat, elasticity and other forms of vibrations as signals for integrating and coordinating physiological activities, including those involved in tissue repair."[174]

A glance at the latest brain research and the whole question of consciousness appears to reconfirm the holographic nature of our brain, and Pribram's theory, developed so long ago, can provide us with answers to the many unsolved questions of how human beings really function. Gariaev and his team of researchers have demonstrated the incredible properties of our DNA and its holographic nature. It is exciting and provocative material. These very recent findings refute the widely held classical view that the mind is in the neurons of the brain or that the brain produces consciousness. They uphold the view that the brain is merely the processor of consciousness. From a biological point of view, we can now see clearly there are flaws in the current neurochemical view of information transfer within the body. The belief that the brain is the driver and the nervous system, via neurotransmitters, is the transporter of the signals from the brain, triggering a cascade of neurochemical reactions, just cannot account for the complexities of the demands of the organism or for the speed with which information is communicated. Nerve impulses and chemical reactions are too slow to explain the process. Neurons start firing synchronous pulses throughout the brain simultaneously. The coherence of the firing is faster than the physical ability of the cells to physically communicate with each other. This reveals that the brain is communicating at a higher level than the physical nerves.[175]

Our physical bodies are made up of trillions of cells, and our DNA is like a biocomputer, sending information from the electromagnetic fields of the body to all these different cells on carrier waves of light and sound. Information sent via the electromagnetic fields and biophotons of the body is instantaneous, system-wide, and nonlocal. Based on the work of Pribram, Hameroff, and Penrose, the holographic brain principle is a distinct possibility. The brain does not have a precise address. It is not a localized system. It behaves more like an antenna and quantum processor. The cells, the brain, the heart, and our DNA all have perfect conditions that allow information transfer from electromagnetic waves inside and outside the body. So through what medium does this principle actually work in our physical bodies?

Oschman proposes what he calls a "living matrix,"[176] formed by the perineural system or connective tissue that surrounds each of the nerves and reaches into nearly every part of the body. The connective tissue forms the bulk of the human body tissue, and its configuration determines the overall form, architecture, and mechanical and functional properties of all its parts. It encases and separates the circulatory, nervous, musculoskeletal, and digestive systems and the various organs, forming a continuous and interconnected system throughout the body. All movements are created by tensions carried through this connective tissue fabric. It is a liquid crystalline structure, with many of the molecules positioned in regular crystal-like lattices that include the lipids in the cell membranes, the collagen in the connective tissue, the actin and myosin molecules of the muscles, and components of the cytoskeleton of the cells. As any movement occurs, these structures produce large, coherent vibrations that move throughout the matrix and are radiated out into the environment. These are called Frohlich oscillations and produce light emissions, predicted by Gurwitsch, detected by Popp, and now verified by many others as part of the human bioenergy field. All of its components are semiconductors, meaning they can conduct and process vibrational information and can convert energy from one form to another. Oschman echoes Garaiev's metaphor of the biocomputer and likens the connective tissue to a microprocessor. It possesses piezoelectric properties (pressure electricity), which means every movement of the body and every pressure and every tension anywhere in the body generate a variety of electric signals or micro-currents, sending electromagnetic waves throughout the entire system. Most importantly the living matrix has connectivity with all cell interiors.

Cells also have their own connective tissue connecting the musculoskeletal system or cytoskeleton of the cell. The evidence from Hameroff and Penrose confirms that the cellular matrix functions in cell communication and information processing and that holographic images are stored in the microtubular lattice of the cells. The cytoskeleton of each cell can be viewed as a programmed electronic computer that can store, recall, and process information. Does this sound familiar? Soliton (single) waves traveling through neural and nonneural cells leave memories in the form of patterns of cytoskeletal structure and/or vibrations. This information can then be read and used to make informed decisions about cellular activity.

The collective functioning of all the cytoskeletons could give rise in the brain to what is referred to as thoughts, ideas, and images. Thus "the living matrix" forms one continuum of communication for the entire molecular system of the body, conducting vibrating energy containing information to all parts of the body and alerting each part of the organism what is taking place in each other part. Disorder and incoherence are created in this continuum when the energy (information) flow is restricted, and disease results. Memories are stored within this system. Similarly any infections, physical injuries, or emotional traumas can alter the fabric of the cells and its extracellular matrix so any energy vibrations passing through these tissues become changed by the information stored there. It is through this mechanism that our consciousness becomes influenced by what is stored in the tissue.[177]

Water and Cellular Communication

The most abundant compound on earth and within the physical body and at the center of all life is water. No one can physically exist for more than five days without it. We have already seen its significance in supporting the healthy functioning of our DNA, and similarly water is a dynamic component in the functioning of the "living crystalline matrix." It surrounds every molecule in the body, and due to its polarity (i.e., positive and negative electrical charge), it creates cohesion and basically holds everything together. Water and ions associated with molecules form continuous interacting chains that influence structure and function and allow transfer of energy and information throughout the matrix. As Mae Wan Ho states in her book *Living Rainbow, H2O,* "Water is the means, medium and message of life, the 'rainbow within.' This is because its liquid crystalline state enables molecules to line up and move coherently together, which creates the colors of the rainbow when viewed with a polarizing microscope."[178] According to Ho, body consciousness, which she defines as possessing sentience, intercommunication, and memory, is distributed throughout the liquid crystalline matrix that connects all the cells of our bodies, and brain consciousness associated with the nervous system is embedded in body consciousness and coupled to it.[179] She states that water plays a crucial role in all our conscious experience, and this is supported by evidence that anesthetics work by releasing and replacing the healthy water from the protein and membrane interface of cells. When this happens we lose consciousness.[180]

Gerald Pollack, one of the premier research scientists in the world of water physics, in his book *Cells, Gels and the Engines of Life*,[181] reveals that the cell's cytoplasm is more like a gel than an aqueous solution. He hypothesized that the water molecules become structured in an organized liquid crystalline state when they interact with the charged surface of proteins and water stays in the cell because it is absorbed into the protein surfaces. His book shows water is essential to everything a cell does. His subsequent laboratory research, detailed in a second book *The Fourth Phase of Water*,[182] confirmed the existence of this highly structured "fourth phase" of water, H_3O_2. He describes this as EZ or exclusion-zone water because it so effectively excludes impurities, is more viscous and dense than ordinary bulk water, has a negative charge, is more alkaline, and holds energy much like a battery. His work confirmed the hypothesis of Gilbert Ling, who had argued for over forty years that the water in the cell was aligned in multiple layers on the water-loving surfaces of membranes and proteins.[183]

Amazingly, Pollack and his team found the key ingredient to creating this structured water is light (electromagnetic energy), whether visible light, ultraviolet, or infrared. Infrared energy is the most effective, and heating is equivalent to applying this type of energy. "There are various kinds of light therapy using different wavelengths. We found that all wavelengths—some in particular—of light, even weak light, build EZ. If EZ is critical for the health of your cells, which I think is clear, these therapies have a distinct physical chemical basis."[184] This possibly accounts for why infrared saunas, light therapy, spending time in the sun, and laser therapies work so well. They are building healthy EZ water in the cells and possibly recharging damaged cells' EZ water by promoting increased capillary flow. It seems due to the mechanism of the EZ water function that radiant light and heat derived from sources outside, as well as inside, the body enhance the flow of blood through the capillaries and that the entire cardiovascular system could be assisted by radiant energy. Pollack also confirms why living tissue heals more quickly when subjected to high amounts of oxygen under pressure greater than the normal atmospheric pressure. His experiments confirm that when H_2O is put under pressure, more H_3O_2 (EZ water) is produced. When oxygen content is increased, more EZ water is built, particularly in injured areas of the body. Pollack also found that EZ water absorbs UV light. This is measured at around 270 nanometers. Interestingly water samples from the Ganges and the springs at Lourdes in France have shown spikes at the 270-nanometer level, suggesting that they contain a high level of EZ water. These waters are known to have unexplained effects on living systems. This is congruent with the findings of other investigators and researchers.

The research continues. The effects of sound and vortex energy on water are being investigated. However, so far it seems there is little doubt that when certain kinds of energy are introduced into ordinary bulk water, the health-enhancing, ordered crystalline EZ water is naturally built.

Summary

It becomes apparent that the water-abundant nature of our physical structure is key to our interface with the various organizing fields of energy responsible for the healthy functioning of the physical form. Through the living crystalline matrix of the connective tissue and its connectivity to cell interiors, information is disseminated in the form of vibrational energy flow. Consciousness is inextricably linked to energy and distributed throughout the body, mediated by the water present in the body and its crystalline layers of cells forming a living communications matrix. The largest component of our physical substance, a gel-like fluid water solution, is no less than a living electrical battery built and supported by light.

CHAPTER 9

Consciousness and Mind

Consciousness is a stage of awareness. It is not bound to specific points in space or time, but infinite and unbound. It is not localized to our bodies or brains but arises from the action of light (electromagnetic waves) upon material substance. Matter arises out of consciousness and becomes informed by it. Human beings are basically a system of energetic patterns held together by information. The human physical being is actually a coherent field of light energy drawn together by information from the electrical signals present in the unique bioenergy field of its individual aspect in accordance with how the individual is interpreting and defining reality through the senses. What we see, hear, touch, taste, smell, feel, intuit, and know informs our consciousness.

The mind therefore is the sum total of all these electromagnetic signatures of all our atoms and molecules and the energy fields they produce. Through these structured fields, if there is energy flow then the system has all the information the 70,000 trillion cells need to function and is coherent. If the flow of energy is stopped for any reason, the system becomes disturbed, which results in emotional, mental, spiritual, or physical incoherence. Dissonance at any of these levels, if not addressed, eventually manifests in the physical body as a physical disease. This distortion can be halted if new information is introduced into the system. By accessing the correct information we bring back coherence to the system. This is true for all systems, macroscopic and microscopic. There is ample evidence now available that our minds affect matter.

Mind-Matter Interaction

The first double-slit experiment was performed by Thomas Young in 1803. Subsequently, it has been repeated many times by various researchers and has confirmed consciousness and our physical reality are intertwined. A more modern and complex version of this experiment has recently been conducted by Dean Radin at the Institute of Noetic Science in 2012. Radin confirmed, "Observations not only disturb what has to be measured, they produce it. We compel the electron to assume a definite position. We ourselves produce the results of the measurement."[185]

The HeartMath® Institute has shown quantitative evidence that our feelings affect our hearts and DNA, but what about our thoughts and intentions? Is there scientific evidence to support the effects of thought and intention on physical matter?

Placebo and Nocebo Effects—What You Believe Affects Your Physical Body

The placebo effect is a phenomenon that healers have known about for centuries, and it seems that neuroscience is now very seriously researching it. Genuine placebo effects are psychobiological phenomena producing measurable changes in the body and account for almost a third of all healings. Scientists and doctors alike are finding that the effect is much more powerful than previously imagined. Patients suffering pain, depression, and even Parkinson's disease have been treated with sugar pills, saline injections, and even sham surgery. Irritable bowel sufferers have been given fake acupuncture. Women with polycystic ovarian syndrome, a common cause of infertility, have been given bogus remedies. The results have shown they feel better, cope better, move better, and conceive better. A most convincing study took place in Virginia in 2002.

> The patients were divided into three groups. The surgeons shaved the damaged cartilage in the knee of one group. For the second group they flushed out the knee joint, removing all of the material believed to be causing inflammation. Both of these processes are the standard surgeries people go through who have severe arthritic knees. The third group received a "fake" surgery, the patients were only sedated and tricked that they actually had the knee surgery. For the patients not really receiving the surgery, the doctors made the incisions and splashed salt water on the knee as they would in normal surgery. They then sewed up the incisions like a real operation and the process was complete. All three groups went through the same rehab process, and the results were astonishing. The placebo group improved just as much as the other two groups who had had surgery. The belief they had surgery reduced their pain and allowed them to resume activity. Even after being told the truth of the situation, the improvements lasted through the six-year follow up to the trial.[186]

Another article, published in 2002 in the *American Psychological Association* by University of Connecticut psychology professor Irving Kirsch titled "The Emperor's New Drugs," reports the discovery that 80 percent of the effect of antidepressants, as measured in clinical trials, could be attributed to the placebo effect. The professor had to file a Freedom of Information Act (FOIA) request to get information on the clinical trials of the top antidepressants.[187]

Perhaps just as important to note, however, is the existence of the shadow side to the placebo effect, known as the nocebo effect. This is when a patient has a belief of a negative outcome or is given negative attention or information from a doctor or therapist. This is just as powerful, and we will explore the power of negative thoughts more deeply in the next part of the book. For example, if a patient treated with a placebo is told he might experience nausea, he's likely to feel nauseous. If it is suggested he may get a headache, he may. Patients given nothing but saline who thought it was chemotherapy have actually vomited and lost hair. If a patient is told he or she is going to die, he or she probably will.[188]

Focused Intention: What We Intend Manifests

Some of the most important experiments with focused intention involve water. The results of these experiments are highly significant given water's major contribution to the composition of the human form and the living communication matrix of the body. Once more we turn to the diligent and conscientious work of William A. Tiller who, for the past forty years, alongside his traditional science work at Stanford University, has been investigating the effects of human intention on both the properties of materials—inorganic and organic, nonliving and living—and on what we call physical reality. He discovered it is possible to make a significant change to the property of a material substance by consciously holding a clear intention to do so. His research shows the ability to change the acid/alkaline ratio (pH) in a vessel of water without adding chemicals simply by creating an intention to do so. Even more incredible, he has been able to "store" a specific intention within the electrical circuit of a simple electronic device. This was done in order that the experiments could be precisely replicated.

A group of four experienced meditators (two men and two women), who were all stable, inner self-managed, capable of deep heart coherence, and able to enter and sustain a deep meditative state, imprinted the electronic device with the intention to activate the indwelling consciousness of the system so that the device increases or decreases the pH of the experimental water by one pH unit compared to the control (i.e., to increase or decrease the H content by a factor of 10). The device can be placed next to a vessel of water at any location, and in this way others have been able to replicate these experiments at multiple locations around the world. This also demonstrates that our thoughts and intentions, when coherent, produce electromagnetic waves carrying information that can be stored within an electric circuit. The results show the pH of the experimental water was increased and decreased by one pH unit depending on the intention. Tiller states these results are consistently reproducible.[189]

Meta-Analyses of Mind in Action

Dean Radin, researcher and author, is chief scientist at the Institute of Noetic Sciences (IONS) in California and is adjunct faculty in the Department of Psychology at Sonoma University, California. He has degrees in Electrical Engineering, is a Doctor of Psychology, and has authored several books and published multiple research papers in peer-reviewed journals on the subject of parapsychology. In his book *The Conscious Universe*,[190] Radin does a brilliant job of providing us with several important meta-analyses of experiments that provide evidence for how intention affects animate and inanimate matter. His meticulous scientific method has done much to provide the scientific community and the public at large with information that is regularly ignored, hidden, and denied by established institutions and various scientific disciplines that are lagging behind in their worldview. The significance of meta-analyses is they take into account many experiments that have been repeated and repeated over a long period of time by many different researchers. They also include the bad studies as well as the good. In the scientific community, in accordance with the procedures of scientific method, the repeatability of experimental results is fundamental to the process and is the way theory becomes practice. It allows public confidence to form and creates a consensus so the evidence eventually becomes part of our mainstream worldview. "Meta-analysis requires explicit details of how the analysis was performed, thus allowing independent analysts to confirm evaluation, when we see all the relevant studies in the analysis rather than just the good studies, most of the problems related to reviewer bias are prevented."[191]

In 1989 Radin and colleague Diane Ferrari did a meta-analysis to assess the mind-matter interaction effects in tossed dice experiments. Their literature search on this topic uncovered seventy-three publications representing investigations by fifty-two researchers from 1935 to 1987. It was found over this period 2,569 people had attempted to influence 2.6 million dice throws in 148 experiments, and there were 150,000 dice throws in thirty-one control studies where no mental influence was applied to the dice. Statistically it was concluded from this analysis that the odds against chance producing the results were more than one billion to one.[192] "Our meta-analysis findings led us to conclude that a genuine mind matter interaction did exist with experiments testing tossed dice. The effect had been successfully replicated in more than 100 experiments by more than 50 investigators for more than half a century."[193]

Radin felt that if this was so, there should be corroborating evidence using other types of physical targets; and in 1987, together with Roger Nelson from Princeton University, he undertook another meta-analysis. This analysis investigated the experiments with electronic random number generators (RNGs) from 1959 to 1987 and was based on 832 studies by sixty-eight different investigators, including 597 experimental studies and 235 control studies. All experiments in the analysis asked the same question: Is the output of an electronic RNG related to an observer's mental intention in accordance with prespecified instructions? The overall results produced a positive result, with odds against chance beyond a trillion to one.[194]

The PEAR (Princeton Engineering Anomalies Research) data for seven years to 1996 was reported by York Dobyns, a Princeton University mathematician, as closely replicating the results of the Radin/Nelson analysis.[195] Some other interesting information came out of these studies: It was found that on average the effects were larger for pairs than individuals working alone. Opposite-sex pairs produced twice the effect of individuals, and pairs that were related either by marriage or birth produced results four times greater than individuals. Finally, the results of local and remote experiments were indistinguishable. Distance was not a factor.

In summary Radin says, "After sixty years of experiments using tossed dice and their modern progeny RNG's, researchers have produced persuasive, consistent, and replicated evidence that mental intention is associated with the behaviour of these physical systems."[196] In 1993 Helmut Schmidt confirmed a successful RNG study that introduced a third-party observer into the experimental design.[197] Of this he says, "The present study confirms the psi effect under particularly well controlled conditions where the participation of an independent observer precludes experimental error or fraud."[198]

One of Radin's more recent experiments was to validate the work of the Japanese author Masaru Emoto, who claimed human consciousness had an effect on the molecular structure of water. Radin has provided us with evidence that positive intentions have an effect on the formation of ice crystals of water and in 2006 published the paper "Double Blind Test of the Effects of Distant Intention on Water Crystal Formation."[199] The results are consistent with the idea that positive intentions tend to produce symmetric, well-formed, and aesthetically pleasing crystals and negative intentions tend to produce asymmetric, poorly formed, and unattractive crystals. In 2008 a triple blind replication was performed with similar findings to the first experiment. Both experiments confirm the claims of Emoto, who has been severely criticized for his lack of training in scientific method and not conducting his earlier experiments with full scientific rigor. This may have been the case; however, Radin has now replicated the work with his usual flawless approach.[200]

There is also a remarkable history of extensive experiments sponsored by the US government in psychokinesis and other phenomena such as remote viewing and teleportation, exploring the influence of human consciousness on physical and biological systems and processes. These have been subject to rigorous research and documentation over an extended period of time. Some of these programs have been ongoing for the past twenty-five years and are now released for public scrutiny. Hal Puthoff, physicist in electrical engineering and parapsychologist, directed these investigations in the 1970s and eighties in collaboration with Russel Targ, also a physicist and parapsychologist, under the name of the Stargate project. Puthoff is founder and currently CEO of Earth Tech International, a privately funded company dedicated to research of the new physics of spaceflight energy and propulsion, investigating the energy of the zero-point field and over-unity devices. These devices can extract more energy from the zero-point field than they consume.[201]

Group Consciousness

Roger Nelson went on to develop the Global Consciousness Project. "Coherent consciousness creates order in the world. Subtle interactions link us with each other and the Earth."[202] This project is an international collaboration of scientists and engineers of various disciplines who are busy collecting information from a global network of RNG in seventy sites all over the world. Their information bank now has fifteen years of random data that enable the researcher to determine if there are correlations that reflect the activity of consciousness in the world. Their hypothesis is that there should be a pattern in random data associated with major global events that engage our hearts and minds. Peaks of order are commonly recorded during moments of shared attention and emotions. RNGs had the largest effects ever recorded by the Global Consciousness Project during major world events, such as the Twin Tower attacks. Other large recordings have occurred on presidential inaugurations, tsunamis, and the deaths of public figures. The positive results can be found on Nelson's website and speak for themselves. The overall data analysis reveals "the odds against chance of this mean shift over a database this size are about a hundred billion to one."[203]

Effects of Focused Group Consciousness

A study published in 1996 in the *British Journal of Psychology, Crime and Law* revealed that in 1988 the crime rate in Merseyside was significantly reduced from 1987 and previous years as a direct result of a group of people in Liverpool practicing Transcendental Meditation® and the TM® Sidhi program of Maharishi Mahesh Yogi. In each of the years 1989 to 1993, the Merseyside crime rate was significantly lower than the national norm. In 1987 Merseyside had the third highest crime rate in the United Kingdom. In 1993 by the end of the six-year study, it had the lowest crime rate of the eleven metropolitan boroughs. Overall crime fell by 15 percent, while the crime rate of the rest of the country rose by 45 percent. The author of the study, Guy Hatchard, was able to establish a clear relationship between the presence of this group and the resultant drop in crime. He used a powerful statistic technique of time series analysis, showing that TM® was the key factor in crime reduction, not factors such as unemployment, police practices, population trends, or drug rehabilitation initiatives. Hatchard stated, "Much crime is known to be related to high levels of stress and disorder in society. Transcendental Meditation® has proved effective at lowering crime because it reduces the overall levels of stress. Each individual contributes to the quality of life in a city. The scientific research shows that a small proportion of the population practicing Transcendental Meditation® to reduce their own stress produces an influence of increased orderliness in the whole collective consciousness of a city, thereby reducing collective stress and lowering crime rate."[204] Professor of Criminology and advisor to the British Home Office, Kenneth Pease, backed up these findings and recommended to British scientists and policymakers they learn more about the mechanism and application of what is known as the Maharishi Effect.

Summary

A human being lives in an encoded light projection of his or her own thoughts, emotions, intentions, belief systems, memories, and attitudes, manifested into material form. Because of the connection to the morphogenetic and morphic fields, all beings are constantly contributing to and receiving from the collective consciousness and together producing all that is perceived to be happening in our outside world. All realities lie within us as individuals and collectively and are mirrored in the matter we produce. We are indeed magnificent creators. Depending on our lens or perspective, the manifested form in the hologram can be changed. The ability to coalesce and concretize energy into its densest form demonstrates our fantastic ability to cocreate and affect matter. It is perhaps ironic that science itself, with its purpose of explaining the physical and material world, is leading us back to that which is nonphysical and nonmaterial as we see that energy, matter, consciousness, and mind are intertwined and inseparable.

CHAPTER 10

Emergence

Mae-Wan Ho wrote, "Reality is thus a shimmering presence of infinite planes, a luminous labyrinth of the active Now, connecting 'past' and 'future', 'real' with 'ideal', where potential unfolds into actual and actual enfolds to further potential through the free action and intention of the organism."[205]

Something wonderful is arising. Our voyage of exploration and appreciation of the various energy systems associated with observable reality is revealing the miracle of life: the subatomic wild world of quanta and the atom, the incredible bodies we inhabit, the beautiful planet that supports us, the life-giving sun and its system of planets, the dark galactic center, and farther on into deep cosmic space. There is still so much for us to learn, and yet our journey so far has birthed a momentous realization. What is emerging is a picture of continuity and cooperation throughout all these structures, from the smallest to the largest. The common denominator appears to be electric energy in all its various forms, densities, and frequencies. The electric universe is full of waves and fields of electromagnetic energy, powerful electric charges, coherent light and sound, mathematically coded and geometrically formed, making possible the greatest show on earth, you and me. Everything is a form of energy vibrating at a certain frequency, wavelike until it interacts with other energy, either by friction, collision, magnetism, or repulsion, collapsing the wave into particles of matter. The electromagnetic field of our DNA holds the holographic blueprint for our physical existence, together with text and instructions of how to build the organism made available from the morphogenetic field. This information is held in the form of scalar waves and used by the genetic apparatus to create our bioenergy field template and finally the physical body. All biological processes are a result of electromagnetic field interactions. These fields are the connecting link between physical matter and resonant geometric patterns, which hold the information of biochemical and bioelectronic actions, and thus our atoms and molecules become informed by energy. Our DNA can be adjusted by coherent light, sound, speech, thoughts, intention, and feelings that in turn affect the biochemistry of the body. This means balances and distortions can be adjusted and corrected at this level, leading to a harmonization of all the cells in our bodies and optimal physical functioning. Each cell holds consciousness of the microcosm and the macrocosm in its energy field.

Science itself is revealing to us that all life systems work on the same principle and is providing more and more evidence that supports the genius and magnificence of the creation that is us. Through conscientious, scientific method, we are learning to understand who we truly are and where we fit into this universe of teeming life energy. What once was science fiction is becoming science fact. Onward!

PART 2

The Keys to the Kingdom

You have sight now, Neo. You are looking at the world without time.

—The Oracle in *The Matrix*

There is a kind of love where burning passion knows no repose, where galaxies dance & restless lovemaking gives birth to universes.

—Rumi

CHAPTER **11**

Introduction to Part 2

In part 2 we will study energy from the perspective of energy consciousness and its significance in our daily lives. We now have the awareness that all manifest objects in the cosmos are waves, particles, and fields of pure energy vibrating as bands of frequencies of different velocity. In part 1 we have seen evidence that thoughts, feelings, intentions, and beliefs held in the consciousness of our vibrating electromagnetic bioenergy field can not only change our own matter but also affect inanimate objects and, more importantly, other living beings. In part 2 we will take a deep dive into the nature of energy consciousness and how this defines who we believe ourselves to be.

Throughout part 2 there are links to the relevant practice in part 3, "The Energetic Highway." There you will find a summary of the practices that connect you to your own energy system and practical guidance on how to begin your own personal energy management. It must be stated that these practices are an introduction only to this vast subject. There are many more practices, skills, and techniques available. These would fill another book. For now I have selected what I consider the most important to expand your awareness of the subject matter outlined in part 2 and to facilitate a process of ongoing self-inquiry.

The Absolute

In the beginning is unity, from which all energies emanate. It is a void of nonexistence and is equated with universal consciousness and the absolute condition of being. In unity there is no differentiation or relativity. There is no subject and no object. There is nothing to be or do or to relate to. It is absolute reality. There is just infinity without time. Then there is a movement, like a giant heart beating and a giant breath breathing. There is pulse and flow outward, as well as an eventual drawing inward. This is the creative impulse and rhythm of infinity.

Unity has both a potential and a kinetic aspect. The potential is intelligent infinity or space, and the kinetic aspect is intelligent energy or substance. Will is a particular focus of intelligent energy. Unity can only become activated or potentiated space by the catalyst of Will. From this undistorted whole there is a potential, a vast potential, to be tapped into by the focus of intelligent energy. Through this substance or matter, Unity gets to experience itself. All experience of the cosmos is actually the creator experiencing itself.

Intelligent energy is the primordial fundamental energy of substance. Its various manifestations lie along a spectrum and encompass all known forms of energy. In this context, energy is defined as a measurement of activity, a form of motion on any and all levels. It comprises motion, sound, light, color, heat, cohesion, electricity, magnetism, repulsion, nuclear energy, and other energies possibly still unknown to us. Spirit and soul may therefore be described as energies of varying frequencies.

Love is also a focus and a frequency of substance. This is the energy far beyond that which we know and experience in the three-dimensional world as romanticized love and emotional reaction. It is not merely a sensual, personal emotion, although this is one aspect of its power and a pathway to its ultimate realization. In Unity, the triune of Love, Will and Intelligence coexist simultaneously as potential. They are all aspects of Unity that manifest into being through movement in space. Love is a vibrational frequency of Unity. Omnipresent, omnipotent, omniscient, it underlies all. All is vibration. Vibration produces sound waves, no form or density levels, just the sounding of the eternal, rhythmic motion of space. Love causes intelligent substance to awaken within space consciousness, with the Will to manifest itself through creation. Love is the great activator and primal cocreator, together with Will, of all the various creations.

The first product of this vibration (sounding) is the photon, a wave of light that is pulsating at a frequency and thereby creating its own sound. Love infuses light and is able to direct it by adding vibrations and rotations, forming geometrical patterns of illusions and densities that condense into the multidimensions of universes, galaxies, solar systems, planets, humans, animals, plants, and minerals that consciousness experiences. It shapes, electrifies, informs, and thereby forms matter. The unfolding of the one into the many occurs according to harmonic, fractal, principles whereby one becomes two, then three, and eventuates into a sevenfold order so that the creator can satisfy its own knowing of itself. Those energies located closest to the creator source are less affected or constricted by confinement in dense matter, and they are therefore freer and more potent. This principle allows higher energies (spirit and soul energy) to impress themselves upon, and thus transform or vivify, the lower energies associated with physical matter.

The universe in which we live is a recapitulation in each part of infinity. A fractal configuration, therefore the same patterns of creation, recur in both the physical and metaphysical areas of life. The process by which the three aspects Will, Love and Intelligence converge to create physical manifestation takes place in space but without time. Time only comes into being once the process has been completed and the physical universe has coalesced. Time is the device that allows for relativity, separation of subject and object, here and there, you and me. It is a concept only. Love is the prime creative principle in this solar system. By cocreating and vitalizing physical substance, it impels an evolutionary process ever onward to form ever-increasing levels of complexity according to its will to experience. Everything that exists evolves, from the lowest form of life at its densest point of concretion to the highest and most etheric. Hierarchical patterns are formed as some portions of consciousness or awareness learn through experience in a more efficient manner. Love is the power that drives the higher energies (spirit and soul) to incarnate into physical form with the purpose of experiencing itself and evolving. The purpose of all life in this solar system is to gain experience of perfected unconditional and unsentimental love. By achieving mastery and control of the lower energies of the personality self, the being makes conscious contact with the soul, under whose guidance it develops full self-knowledge through expanding consciousness to connect with spirit. Thereby it attains cosmic adulthood.

The urge for union once more with its source dissolves all separation and impels the being back toward Unity. Love has experienced itself in action and perfected itself as unconditional through the creative process. The return of each individual to Unity brings more of this back to the whole system of which it is a part. This in turn begins the next stage of its evolution. It is the same for all systems, whether mineral, animal, vegetable, human, planetary, solar, galactic, or universal within the cosmos of being. The circle closes again as the many become one, and yet the cycle of life is infinite and the creative pulse eternal.[206,207]

Eckhart Tolle expressed it well when he wrote, "Now is the only thing. It is all there is. The eternal present is the space within which your whole life enfolds, the factor that remains constant. Life is now. There was never a time when your life was not now, nor will there ever be. The Now is the only point that can take you beyond the confines of your mind. It is the only point of access to the timeless and formless realm of being."[208]

Manifest your magnificence. What does that *really* mean? At the macrocosmic level, science space probes inform us our universe is still in a state of escalating expansion, accelerating at the speed of light. The standard orthodox view of the final outcome of this acceleration is that the universe will ultimately either just collapse or, alternatively, keep on expanding forever and end in heat death. If this is true, there is no meaningful purpose to our being.

However, our overview of energy and matter has clearly demonstrated an incredible story of evolution from one to many to one to many to one, leading to an increasing complexity of structures that include our magnificent selves. In this pattern of emergence, there is clearly a phase of expansion and activity, followed by a period of consolidation and rest. This can be seen in the very rhythm of nature itself—the passing of the seasons, the ebb and flow of tides. The fractals of nature reveal an ongoing flow of movement of everything toward order and symmetry, powered by an active intelligence guiding this movement. The accelerating expansion of the universe can be viewed from a different perspective. The universe appears to be moving forward through the construct of time from the one to the many to the one, not to an ending in heat death, but to the ending of time only, as all matter and antimatter eventually meet at zero—complete symmetry, complete wholeness. This very ending of time means there is a goal. All creation is brought back in the great inbreathing of the universe to the realm of the absolute. The field of quantum potential holds all possible configurations, all possible states, which exist timelessly because all are parts of a physically real zero.[209] But zero is not no thing. Zero means everything. Matter exists because there is an antimatter particle.

$$+ 1 - 1 = 0 = unity$$

The two together cancel each other out to zero. This is the point of balance in the space of all possible states; the ground of being that always is, was, and will be. There is no past, present, and future. It is all here now.

The realization that there is nothing to evolve to, that everything is already here in the now, is our magnificence. All that is necessary is to become aware of this. This is called mastery. Time is only a construct to help us realize this. The entire universe is conspiring to bring us to this realization. But can you see? What will you choose to manifest? The universe mirrors all our creations back to us. The voyage of discovery has taken us out into the far reaches of deep space to find all of creation before us, into a universe that is teeming with energy fields of information that we may know ourselves more and more deeply. It is our playground, a canvas upon which to paint the picture, using all the gorgeous colors of our incredible bioenergy field, a world full of sound and vibration in which we create and sing the song, a play in which each one of us appears and is continually writing the next act.

CHAPTER 12

Energy and Consciousness

Energy can be described as the strength, vitality, and power derived from resources required to create an effect or outcome by informing, deforming, reforming, and transforming matter. This term can be applied to all life and all its aspects: physical, emotional, mental, and spiritual.

Our voyage of discovery into the world of science has clearly revealed what energy is and what it does. If mind can have an effect on matter, as is clearly indicated by the mountain of scientific evidence available, and energy is defined as above, then:

Consciousness (mind) is energy.

They are interchangeable. Equally, based on the discoveries of science,

Energy = mass = information = consciousness.

The Macrocosm

The universe arises out of the consciousness (cosmic mind) of intelligent infinity. It is a construct or illusion, not in the sense of being nonexistent, but in the sense of being impermanent and finite, constantly changing. Everything in the universe is conscious but has its own form of consciousness on its own plane of existence, guided, controlled, and animated from within outward by a series of hierarchical energies. These energies construct the cosmos using intelligent power and forces that bring the creation of universal mind into manifestation.[210]

When viewed from this perspective, the vast network of energies to which we are connected is staggering, and rather than perceiving the self as the smallest part of this matrix, it serves us to understand our energetic connection to all there is and the support to be gained from this knowing. Human consciousness plays a vital role in the scheme of the whole matrix.

The Seven Planes of Consciousness

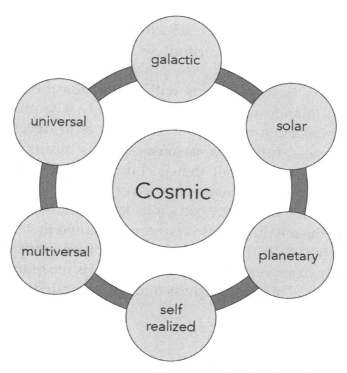

Figure 12.1 The Seven planes of consciousness hold all the scalar wave frequency bands more commonly known as dimensions

The Microcosm

The human being arises out of the consciousness of his or her own higher aspect, which is in turn a part of the whole; the monad or spiritual self, directed from within outward and mediated by the power and forces within the causal body (soul), interacts with matter that becomes the vehicle of manifestation, the physical body. The purpose of our manifestation into a physical body is to develop self-consciousness, full self-consciousness. This means knowing the self as one with all that is. Like the universe, it is a construct made from matter that gives us the opportunity of self-realization and unity consciousness by addressing those places in the self that are as yet unconscious and therefore split off from the whole. These are the aspects of consciousness that believe themselves to be separate. The goal is the reunification of every piece of consciousness that has separated itself from the whole.

Laws of the Manifest Universe

Consciousness

All outward manifestation seen as the objective world is consciousness working on its own plane. Everything has consciousness, from the rock to the cosmos, and represents the total of source mind experiencing itself in each aspect. Everything is connected to everything. What we think, feel, say, and do has an effect on all, whether we are conscious of this or not.

Correspondence

The law of correspondence means as above so below; as below so above. This principle enables humankind to reason intelligently, in different frequency bands and develop understanding and knowledge of the unknown through what is known.

Vibration

All matter is in constant motion. All substance vibrates, constantly creating its own sound; nothing rests. The different manifestations are a result of variance in vibrational frequency, and that which vibrates at a higher frequency has the ability to transmute a lower frequency.

Duality

In the objective world everything has an opposite. There is only one stream of life energy. Like and unlike are the same energy, opposite in name, only different by degree; therefore in the manifested world, all truth is only half-truth, and all paradoxes can be reconciled in the unity of the absolute.

Movement

In accordance with duality, there are two poles between all things that create movement: action and reaction, advance and retreat, in-breath and out-breath, rising and sinking, ebbing and flowing.

Cause and Effect

There is no such thing as chance. There is a cause for every effect and an effect from every cause. Reciprocity is an extension of this law and refers to giving and taking mutually and equally by accepting a positive action and returning with another positive action.

Magnetism and Repulsion

This could also be termed the law of gender or attraction. All matter consists of positively charged protons and negatively charged electrons held together by the field of energy they create together. This works in the creative process as generation, regeneration, and creation. Everything is either a masculine or a feminine principle. This mechanism is the same for atoms, humans, planets, and solar systems.

The Electrical Nature of Human Consciousness

Consciousness is the relationship between spirit and matter. It is the blending of the two energies of higher will and active intelligent substance through the influence of a third, unconditional love/love wisdom that produces the objective manifestation of physical form. Thus begins an evolutionary cycle using time and space so that the resulting form/matter becomes adapted and becomes an adequate vessel for the demonstration of the higher spiritual nature. Energetic etheric substances underlie all tangible form. Through the process of evolution, all creation is transmuting matter into finer and finer substances of higher and higher frequency on each turn of the spiral.

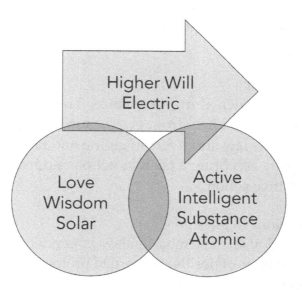

Figure 12.2. Three types of electrical energy movement in the cosmic system.

Everything in physical manifestation is electrical in nature. The origin of electric energy demonstrates as the forward or progressive movement in the abstract nature of the will-to-be, originating in unity. Electric energy (higher will) manifests as a vibrating impulse and through the direction and influence of spiraling solar energy (the love/wisdom principle) enables the sound of this vibration to awaken atomic matter into activity. All manifestation is electrified from a higher plane than our solar system (cosmic).

Electric energy then manifests as light, causing the creation of the spheroidal energy fields of atoms and all manifested physical phenomena, including the human bioenergy fields, each of which is synonymous with different aspects of consciousness. Electromagnetism holds the electrons (negative charge) of the atomic bodies revolving around a central unit of force, the nucleus (positive charge). This energy is rotary in its motion and creates heat and differentiation. These energy bodies manifest their different vibrations as colors on the electromagnetic spectrum.

Electrical energy emanates from groups of atoms and through radiation and/or magnetic interaction (law of magnetism and repulsion) with other atoms synthesizes form. Units of different polarity seek unity, balance, equilibrium, and synthesis. This electrical interplay between different electrical units causes all the energetic interactions of the various expressions of energy until eventually there is the synthesis known as at-one-ment. This is an ongoing activity of the evolution of material and etheric substance.[211]

A Map of Human Consciousness

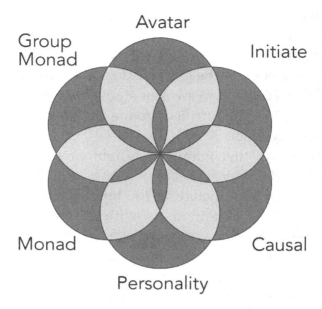

Figure 12.3. A Map of Consciousness

Avatar	Master
Initiate	Path of Service
Group Monad	Group Consciousness
Monad- Higher Self- Spirit	Higher Mind
	Higher Will
	Unconditional Love
Causal Body –Transpersonal Self-Soul	Conscious Mind
	Conscious Will
	Conscious Love
	Sets the course for each lifetime and receives imprints from Monadic vibrations
Personality- Form Self	Linear/Lower Mind
	Emotional Body
	Physical Body and Etheric Template
	Receives imprints from Causal vibrations and eventually directly from Monadic vibrations

Figure 12.4. Dimensions of Consciousness

The Territory

Unity represents the absolute of being, intelligent infinity where no separation exists and all is one. Matter and antimatter are in perfect equilibrium. The three aspects will, love/wisdom, and active intelligence are in perfect balance. Based on the map of consciousness, the task ahead for us is to connect with the higher vibrations of our being. This book concerns itself with connection to the monadic (spiritual) self through contact with the transpersonal self (soul). This eventually brings us into awareness of our group (the morphogenetic field) and onward through various initiations and a path of service to full mastery as an avatar. Although there are many other levels of consciousness in the cosmos, this book is concerned with the human being on earth.

The monadic vibrations are the highest frequency vibrations of active intelligence, unconditional love, and higher will. These are the higher etheric planes and are composed of etheric substance of the highest vibration on the seventh, eighth and ninth domains of dimensional space. There is no time on these planes and they lead the way to dimensions 10,11 and 12 bringing forth awareness of the group monad, the initiate path and the realized avatar self.

The causal vibration is the human soul and transpersonal mind that mediates the higher vibrations of the monad and sets the course for each lifetime, taking into account all karmic considerations of previous existences on the time line. This is also composed of etheric substance and carries lower (4th dimension) as well as higher vibrations (5th and 6th dimension) from all previous existences along the timeline in fourth-dimensional space-time.

The personality vibration consists of the lower mental energy body, the emotional body, and the physical and etheric template of the physical body; the physical body is a projection of our total consciousness. The human physical being is a coherent field of light energy drawn together by information from the electrical signals present in the unique energy field of our individual being. This manifests in accordance with how we are interpreting and defining reality through our senses. What we see, hear, touch, taste, smell, feel, intuit, and know informs our consciousness. These are the densest levels of matter and are in three-dimensional space-time.

Figures 12.5 and 12.6 recall the description of the anatomy of this coherent field of light energy in part 1. They demonstrate the interface between the energy, consciousness, and psychological aspects of the physical body and the personal energy field. The diagram and table show the seven main centers nourishing the physical body. In reality our bioenergy field is a swirling mass of all shades and variations, with energy vortices nesting one inside the other in the seven locations, connecting into the main power channel at the spine, back and front, and separated one from the other by seals that are either open or closed depending on the level of consciousness and the overall condition of the energy field. Our light bodies are dynamic, moving fields of energy, evolving as we continually expand our conscious awareness. It is impossible to draw their beauty in two dimensions. The diagrams are simply an aid to comprehension.

The Multidimensional Being

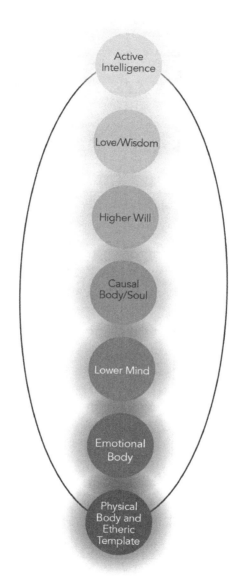

Figure 12.5. The stages of human awareness drawn in linear form, but in fact each human being is a combination of these stages, ranging from awareness incorporating all to only identifying with the lower three, depending on his or her stage of monadic and causal connection and integration.

Character	1st centre masculine	2nd centre feminine	3rd centre masculine	4th centre feminine	5th centre masculine	6th centre feminine	7th centre integrated
Colour	Red	Orange	Yellow	Green	Blue	Indigo	Violet
Location	Perineum Base of tailbone	Pelvis Sacrum	Solar Plexus	Heart	Throat	Centre Brow	Crown
Vortices	4	6	10	12	16	96	972
Endocrine Gland	Adrenals	Gonads	Pancreas	Thymus	Thyroid	Pituitary	Pineal
Supplies energy to:	Spinal column, kidneys and immune system	Reproductive system	Stomach, liver, gall bladder, digestive system	Heart, blood, circulatory system	Lungs, bronchial and vocal apparatus, alimentary canal, throat and jaw, respiratory system	Ears, nose, sinuses, nervous system, left eye and lower brain	Upper brain and right eye, nervous system
Element	Earth	Water	Fire	Air	Sound	Light	Thought
Sense	Touching	Feeling	Sensing	Loving	Hearing	Seeing	Knowing
Access to energy consciousness field	Cellular and physical body function and template	Emotional feeling	Lower Mind-Thoughts	Relational and Transpersonal	Higher Will	Love/Wisdom	Higher Mind
Birthright	To exist	To feel	To think	To love	To express	To perceive	To know
Psychological focus	Physical existence	Emotions and intimacy	Power and identity	Relational love and connection	Self expression and life purpose	Clear perspective	Connection to Higher Self and integration with personality
Positive associated aspects	Stability, vitality, abundance	Pleasure (physical, emotional, mental and spiritual), sensuality	Power, confidence, mental clarity, leadership	Love, compassion, connection, equanimity, healing	Truth, purpose/ service, expression, creativity, communication, surrender	Vision, intuition, insight, perception, clear seeing, wisdom	Unity, awareness, intelligence, understanding, miracles, bliss
Psychological dysfunction	Chronic fear, anxiety, materialism, instability	Low self esteem, anger, rage, jealousy, hate, envy	Low motivation, depression, laziness, limiting beliefs, domination	Lonely, antisocial, rigid, cruel, isolated	Fear of speaking, untruthfulness, lack of purpose and creativity	Nightmares, hallucinations, lack of insight	Over intellectualisation, confusion, apathy
Phsyical dysfunction	Bowel, blood or bone disorder, obesity, anorexia, kidney problems, auto immune disorders	Genital issues, sexual or fertility problems, hip or sacroiliac joint problems	Digestion issues, liver problems, diabetes, ulcers, chronic fatigue	Heart disease, high blood pressure, thymus issues, immune deficiency disorders	Lung disease, chest problems, teeth or gum issues, thyroid issues, throat, neck and shoulder issues	Hearing problems, migraines, sleep disorders, eye infections, neurological disorders	Alzheimers, mental illness, learning disabilities

Figure 12.6. Description of the human energy centers and their focus. These seven energy centers feed the physical body via the endocrine system and are each a gateway to a different and higher dimensional frequency field of energy comprising the overall energy body. Each field has its own seven vortices, thus making a total of forty-nine centers allowing communication between the various levels. The vortices nest

into each other back and front of the physical body, separated by seals and connecting into a vertical energy current running parallel with the spine. As the energy field is cleared of all that hinders the full flow of energy through the system, these seals or energy webs are broken and conscious awareness expands to connect with earth, galactic and cosmic aspects of love, will and intelligence.

Discernment

At the level of the personality self, our consciousness allows us to distinguish between the self and all other forms of existence. It distinguishes human from the animal kingdom. It is termed individualization or self-realization and is a necessary part of our evolution in order to develop our full potential strengths so they may be used for the benefit of the group (humanity) purpose eventually. Individualization is currently evolved to a very high degree on earth.

At the causal level, our consciousness enables us to differentiate between the transpersonal self or soul and the lower personality self. This is much less widely developed, as most cannot yet distinguish between themselves as the thinker in time and space and the vehicle through which they think, the transpersonal mind. However, once this stage is discerned, there is realization of the part the being plays in the group of which he or she is a part. In this case the group is the group consciousness of humanity.

At the monadic level of consciousness, the being has merged with the higher aspects and realizes his or her position in the whole scheme of creation and yet can still distinguish between his or her own personal identity and the soul, but also recognizes the differential between spiritual essence, soul, and his or her form in matter. There is a peace of beingness and a knowing there are even vaster levels of beingness to explore. There are potentially many other stages and groups of consciousness in an ever-ascending hierarchy of energies, at higher and higher vibratory frequencies, to which we are connected.

Good Vibrations

Our earlier review of the science of energetics shows higher frequency energy is emanating from the sun and the galactic center and disseminating throughout the solar system. NASA has given us evidence of these high frequency particles and some of the effects. They contain information encoded in the particles of light and bring in vibrations that can activate our bodies at the DNA and atomic levels and by harmonic resonance lift our atoms to a faster spin rate. This means all can increase their vibratory level and therefore access the higher aspects of the spiritual nature. Earth is intimately connected with the sun and solar energy, for without the sun, earth and her inhabitants cannot exist. We are literally the children of the sun, and it is powerfully and consciously helping us evolve in space-time. However, this cannot take effect if we are not in coherence. It is impossible to resonate fully with these new vibrations if our energy system is not attuned.

Raising Your Frequency

Why is it necessary to increase your frequency vibratory level? Possessing a fully integrated biofield of energy consciousness means that the human being is operating with full awareness and connection to all his or her aspects. Many people on the planet are operating from only a very small portion of their potential because they are disconnected from the main driver of the system, source energy. This means they are cut off from the higher frequencies of their own being and their access through those aspects to source energy. It is impossible to have a highly ordered coherent system, which is optimal for all living systems, if one is disconnected from part of it. It is impossible to be truly connected to another when one is disconnected within the self. Of course, this beloved planet cannot be perceived as a living, breathing entity if there is disconnection in the individual. Our purpose is to experience ourselves fully as the higher frequency beings we are and ultimately to know ourselves as one with intelligent infinity—to be part of the one, while still experiencing our unique individuality. Part of our higher aspect has descended into matter, stepped down through the frequencies, so that it may use matter to know itself experientially. This has meant being in the dimension of space and time, where there is relativity or duality; immersion in such dense frequencies has caused most of the human race to forget their origin.

However, it is intended that we should experience the magnificence of our being through matter and then bring back this learning to the whole. We and the source are one. Free will enables us to choose our path; in doing so we have made choices that have created the havoc, disease, and distress we experience in ourselves and our world/hologram, stuck in the lower densities of matter through fear, limitation, and faulty belief systems. The outer world is only a reflection of our collective inner world. The individual experience of reality is only a reflection of who the being believes itself to be. The fact still remains that human beings are the magnificent creations of the source mind, and just as we have collectively created havoc through our disconnection, it is equally possible to create a peaceful and abundant world for all by raising our frequency so that we can reconnect to each other and all that is. It is as simple as that. This is effected by literally bringing in more light energy, building coherence and wholeness back into our energetic systems. By doing this, pain, disease, suffering, limitations, erroneous belief systems, misqualified energy imprints—all are eliminated, and the being operates from the higher light frequencies of love, peace, and unity consciousness. The creative faculty becomes fully activated and consciously aligned with universal law and will. From this place creation becomes effortless and instant. Remember resonance? It is how energy works. If we are a coherent and harmonic system of life energy, this resonates out to all we meet and touch, to all we think and feel, to all we are being, to all we are with and even those we are not with, for there is only one of us. We are all entangled particles. And when we infuse this with our intention and will, we create unconditional love and peace and more light to radiate out and out and out, as the starlight we truly are. We are here to shine.

This starts with paying attention and making a commitment. There has never been a more auspicious time to do this work. The entire solar system is being subjected to intensely powerful cosmic energies, and all of physical life is being affected. There is an opportunity now, when all the energies of the cosmos are converging, to support and aid this passage into the higher vibrations of existence. However, it will demand cooperation and attention on your part. It will stretch you right out of your comfort zone and place you fairly and squarely sometimes into places you would rather not be. But here the golden nuggets are hiding. In these places there are incredible amounts of energy just waiting to be released into your life. Dissolving old paradigms, old images, thoughts and beliefs that have been hardwired into the system at the cellular level by environmental conditioning, childhood wounds, and misperceptions of reality, you will do nothing less than reform, literally. By creating new ways of being, new ways of seeing, new ways of perceiving, you will discover your magnificence and cocreate with source energy a new reality aligned with your true purpose. This energy can be used to transform all and any aspect of your life that is currently "not working" for you.

It will require deep trust, ongoing surrender, and a relinquishing of much you think you hold dear, particularly outdated beliefs about yourself and who you think you are. If you are still reading this book, you can be sure your soul has called you to do this—and now. What is sure, if you persevere, your life will change beyond your wildest imagination. So let us now begin the journey inward of opening our vision and awareness to the miracle of life, the genius of the plan, and the surprise that awaits us in the now.

CHAPTER 13

Building Coherence in the Physical Body

> In your investigation of the world, never allow
> the mind to desert the body. Examine its nature;
> see the elements that comprise it. When its true
> nature is seen fully and lucidly by the heart, the
> wonders of the world will become clear.
> —Ajahn Mun Bhurridatta Thera

Coherence in our energy consciousness system requires a thorough and honest exploration of the personality aspect of our being. This comprises the physical, emotional, and mental nature. These three are inextricably intertwined and form the densest matter and the lowest vibrations of our being. Blockages here prevent connection with our higher aspects. As we move through each aspect, there are energetic exercises accompanying each section that can be found in part 3 of this book, "The Energetic Highway." The description and sequence for the appropriate exercise is clearly indicated throughout, although you will find they can be used as and when required once you have mastered the skill. Each individual is a multidimensional being and not a linear format.

Prescencing, Grounding and Centering

There are three incredible energetic tools that form the foundation of your energetic exploration of self. These three practices are fundamental to managing your energy and support and accelerate the process of expanding your perception, raising your vibration, and increasing your coherence. All three encompass physical, psychological, and energetic components. A daily practice can achieve remarkable results.

Tasting Mindfulness

Have you ever had the experience of stopping so completely,
Of being in your body so completely,
Of being in your life so completely,
That what you know and what you didn't know,
That what had been and what was yet to come,
And the way things are right now
No longer held even the slightest hint of anxiety or discord?
It would be a moment of complete presence, beyond striving,
Beyond mere acceptance,
Beyond the desire to escape or fix anything or plunge ahead,
A moment of pure being, no longer in time,
A moment of pure seeing, pure feeling,
A moment in which life simply is,
And that "is-ness" grabs you by all your senses,
All your memories, by your very genes,
By your loves, and
Welcomes you home.

—John Kabat-Zinn[212]

Presence

> To be present in our body is a form of awareness,
> and it is a first step toward being kind to ourselves
> and others.
>
> —Linda Hartley[213]

Presence is to be here now in your body—literally, to be present. Here in the mind and in the body in the moment. Not in the stories of yesterday and the what-ifs of tomorrow, but right here in this moment of now in your physical body. Believe it or not, most people are not "here" most of the time. This is a fundamental part of transformation and creation. To presence the self requires a slowing down, a stopping of the rush and panic to do, do, do; stopping thoughts about what happened yesterday, last week, last month, last year. Similarly, we project into the future; while in the act of doing one thing, the mind is occupied thinking about the next and the next and the next. What will happen tomorrow, next week, next year; what will happen if? Life is spent … yes, *spent*, gone, wasted, thinking about a past that is gone and a future that is not yet in manifestation. Very little attention is given to being here in this moment connected to the body. Our thoughts dwell on the past and rush into the future, and valuable conscious creation opportunities are missed. Being in the body is bringing to our conscious awareness every thought, feeling, sensation, and energy, running through the miraculous physical body form from moment to moment. It is having a full experience of self in the moment. Slowing down is essential, allowing time and space to become aware of the movement of energies within the body; to become acquainted with our bodies intimately, not just the outside but inside at the cellular level; to become aware that our bodies hold all the answers to all our questions. They are an infinite fountain of wisdom and knowledge if we can just slow down for long enough and quiet the mind long enough to hear them speak to us.

Cellular Intelligence

> When the body is experienced from within, the body is not separated from the mind but experienced as a whole.
> —Bonnie Bainbridge Cohen[214]

Our cells each possess their own living intelligence. Each has its own consciousness and can initiate action and connection with other cells. Each cell exists as a separate entity and yet is part of a whole at the same time. They form the ground of our being before awareness of our conditioning sets in, and from our embodied cellular awareness arises knowledge of the physical, psychological, and spiritual self. The fundamental physical life of a cell clearly demonstrates its consciousness, intentionality, and will-to-be in its own individuation and the active intelligence that causes it to join with other cells to make its contribution to the development and maintenance of the physical body. Our cells form the template of our evolutionary process. Cellular memory holds the information of our entire existence, both in and out of the time construct, yet very rarely, if ever, do we open our conscious awareness to this.[215]

The condition of the physical body gives us many clues to where our work lies. Our energetic system at all levels interpenetrates the physical body. Our emotions and thoughts are constantly affecting all our body systems. We have created such busy lives; they are so demanding and stress filled. Not enough time, must do this, must do that. There is a constant flow of input to the senses with the arrival of instant communication via the Internet and cell phone; a virtual bombardment of the senses with information from the media. We are a species overloaded and overwhelmed with external information and stimulation; we rarely stop to listen in to the wisdom that resides within. Completely out of contact with self, perhaps we listen in to the body when there is no choice, when it is sick or diseased, and only then. This of course is very often the wake-up call, the two–by-four needed to get us to pay attention. Disease occurs first in our energy field as a result of blocked or stagnant energy caused by our emotional reactions and our ruminating thoughts and belief systems. These habitual, unhealthy ways of being cause us to create over and over again circumstances that cause stress, anxiety, depression, and pain, until ultimately the body breaks down and stops functioning correctly. Proper care and attention to the physical body takes time and effort and is imperative to manifesting your magnificence. It is a commitment to health and transformation.

❖ **See "The Energetic Highway," Practice 1: Presence.**

Golden Key

We do not make contact with self. Contact is a sensate experience, a process of knowing and feeling the self. It is essential to have contact with self to have authentic contact with another and the outside world.

Ground

Grounding is a direct physical connection to the earth. Grounding is essentially a balancing mechanism that brings our conscious awareness to the body and its connection to physical existence. It is an invaluable tool to use daily and particularly when faced with circumstances that cause our energetic system to be challenged in some way. This can be an emotional trigger, a looping thought mechanism, or a perceived/actual trauma or threat event. Any of these can create strong emotions or sensations, difficult and/or powerful experiences, or alternatively, thoughts can become so expanded that the sense of balance is completely lost.

Grounding keeps us connected to earth. It causes us to be here in the now moment, connected to our self and the planet.

It is a physical, psychological, and energetic process. Physically, the feet are firmly anchored on the ground, and the body's weight is pushing downward into gravity. Psychologically, it is the knowing our being is supported in a mutually reciprocating relationship by its own downward-moving energy meeting the upward flow of earth energy. Energetically, this process causes our energy field, energy centers, and boundaries to reconfigure immediately. By grounding the body, it becomes possible to hold more energetic charge and handle difficult feelings that arise. It also prepares us to hold the higher frequencies.

❖ **See "The Energetic Highway," Practice 2: Grounding.**

Center

Centering is coming back to the self. When the focus is constantly outside the self, either forward or backward on the time line or projected outward into the "out there" of the objective world, we lose equilibrium and the sense of self-awareness. The system is incoherent, out of balance. Somatically, our center is the brain, the spinal cord, the face and viscera, the endocrine glands extending down to the pelvic floor. When there is flow through our center, this radiates out from the center to the periphery of the body. Any breaks in this flow through breath, posture, or movement limits our known sense of self in that moment. Energetically, the point of gravity or *tan-tien* (*hara* in Japanese) as referred to in Chinese martial arts, located five centimeters below the navel, is the point of central balance in the body. Bringing attention to this immediately focuses the mind inward. Psychologically, centering is the balance of active intelligence, will, and emotion. In terms of energy consciousness, it is being fully present in the physical body while holding all the multidimensional aspects of human consciousness in balance at the same time. Being "fully centered," then, means holding the higher frequencies of the monadic dimensions in the body while simultaneously holding the denser earth frequencies. This is achieved through the gateway of the heart. This literally means that the consciousness is not withdrawn from the physical dimension into the abstract higher dimensions; neither is it focused at the denser levels, contemplating the future or ruminating on the past. It represents a still point of perfect balance in the present moment. Actions from this place are in perfect balance with higher will and aligned with your higher purpose. From this place there is perfect coherence in the physical body and the entire bioenergy field. There are no emotional reactions or outbursts because love, compassion, and forgiveness have created the bridge to a higher understanding. There are no recriminations about the past because the lessons are understood. There is no fear about the future because the outcome is known. This is the balance and harmony we are working toward in our physical system.

❖ **See "The Energetic Highway," Practice 3: Centering.**

A powerful practice, this energetic exercise creates your template for magnificence.

Golden Key

These three practices are extremely powerful and form the basis for all future work, but like any skills, they require your focus, attention, and commitment. They are called practices because that is what they are. This means they are to be performed over and over to become proficient, so commit and practice, please.

Physical Body Care

The physical body is the vessel for the higher aspects of being. Physical body care includes joyful physical movement, conscious breathing, nourishment and hydration from real food and pure water, and deep relaxation and rest.

Movement

All of life is moving energy. From the atom to the galaxy, all is in motion. Movement in its various forms is an expression of the life force within. There is cyclic movement of rhythm, rest, and renewal that occurs at all levels of physical life—from the life of a cell, in the flow of our breath, in the activities of living and sleeping. There is rhythmic movement present in all life, in all energy. In the movement of energy consciousness itself, there is the first vibrational impulse of purposed dynamic will, the radiating and spiraling quality of the heart energy, and the rotary movement of active intelligence in matter at the atomic level. Motion is an integral part of our existence.

There is a profound connection between consciousness and the movement of the physical body. Many of us have been conditioned from an early age to inhibit the natural feeling and expressiveness of the body; there may be certain body parts tensed, restrained, inhibited, or blocked that cannot move. As a result we have become disassociated from the body's innate knowledge and wisdom. The body needs movement to function optimally, and through the gift of physical exercise and movement, it is possible to access and process both positive and negative energy constellations embedded deep in its cells, tissues, and structures. It is a way to make contact with the self again. It helps us to enable our presence in the now moment. It focuses the mind, and the attention and consistent practice create metabolic fitness, strength, and flexibility, as well as psychological health. A consistent and daily discipline not only keeps the physical body fit and healthy but also focuses the mind and attention and can be a meditation of glorious motion, a great celebration of life.

A weekly combination of cardio (walking, cycling, running, swimming), resistance training (exercise with weights), and flexibility training (stretching, Pilates, yoga) keeps the body strong, flexible, and structurally aligned; encourages proper function of all body systems; creates mental stability; and reduces stress.

Recommendation: Move any way you like to; listen to your body and what movement it needs in the moment. Dance, jump, run, have fun. Lie down, wriggle, crawl, slide, rock. Just listen in to the wisdom of your body calling; surrender to its cry for your love and attention. Give yourself the gift and delight of joyous physical movement.

The Transforming Power of Breath

Breath is vital to life. Good breathing practice can lead to equilibrium in the physical and subtle energies of the body and purification of the nervous system. It can help us respond to the higher will of our being and gain control of the lower energies. It also enables the mental processes to become more sensitive to the evolutionary urge of the higher aspects of the true self. However, breathing can easily be taken for granted as an autonomous action of the body: inhaling oxygen from the atmosphere, utilizing this in the production of energy for the physical body, and then exhaling the waste product of carbon dioxide back into the air. It is a simple, involuntary controlling mechanism keeping our bodies alive and healthy. Most of the time respiration occurs without our acknowledgment or awareness. Even when in fear or shock sometimes, there is no awareness of holding the breath. Most assume because breathing is automatic and reflexes are instinctive, they are beyond our control. And yet, breath can be a very powerful tool if it is approached with conscious awareness.

Physics has shown us energy is permeating the space around us at all times. Inhalation can be an act of receiving energy in the form of breath. Retention or holding of that breath can savor the energy drawn in, and exhalation can become the emptying of all thoughts and all emotions with the outbreath. In the moment of suspension before the next inhalation, while the lungs are empty, the individual can surrender to his or her higher will and purpose of being. This describes the powerful practice of pranayama. This is the conscious prolongation of inhalation, retention, exhalation, and suspension. The techniques of pranayama encourage the respiratory organs to expand intentionally, rhythmically, and intensively by long sustained flow in each section of the breathing. Mind and body are connected. The movement includes horizontal expansion, vertical uplift, and circumferential extension of the lungs and rib cage. As a consequence, more oxygen becomes available to the system, and chemical changes take place in the body. The movement of the organs removes any obstruction that could impede the flow. The subtle bodies and energy centers are cleansed. The rate, depth, and quality of our breathing are under our own control.

Four Types of Breathing

- ❖ High—Muscles in the neck activate the top of the lungs only.
- ❖ Mid—The central part of the lung is activated.
- ❖ Low—The lower portion of the lung is activated, but the top and midsections remain less active.
- ❖ Total—The entire lungs are used to full capacity.

Using and filling the entire lungs is the goal of total breathing and is part of the practice of pranayama.[216]

Recommendation: Bring attention to your breath. Inhale consciously, filling the entire lungs. Exhale consciously. Practice breathing in a peaceful way, an accepting way, a trusting way, a loving way, a grateful way, a forgiving way, an inviting way, a surrendering way[217]; when you breathe consciously with a specific quality, these attributes manifest effortlessly in your life because you are aligning your bioenergy field with that particular vibration and magnetize more of that to yourself.

❖ **See "The Energetic Highway," Practice 4: Breath Awareness**

Nourishment

Blessed with this food and this life
We offer thanks
Thanks to the earth, to the sun, to the moon and the stars;
Thanks to the streams of water, to the pools, to the springs,
To the lakes, to the oceans,
Thanks to the mountains, to the forests,
To the meadows, to the valleys;
Thanks to the grasses, to the vegetables, to the fruit,
To the seeds, to the medicinal herbs
Thanks to the wind, to the clouds, to the rain,
Thanks to the great one at the source of all things
Who is the giver of breath and of health and of life
May this meal be taken in gratitude
May our lives be lived in gratitude.

—John Robbins[218]

Overfed but Undernourished

Physical nourishment from *real* food is also a must. Food is a controversial topic these days. World obesity is a real threat to human health. There are so many fad diets and eating regimens being presented for public consumption, and this, together with constantly changing reports of what is and isn't harmful for us, makes nutrition a confusing and difficult arena to navigate. A few simple facts may help. A large percentage of the western world is actually malnourished. This may seem unlikely as much of the western world is not short of food and is, in fact, obese. Here are the facts from the World Health Organization[219]:

❖ *Worldwide obesity has nearly doubled since 1980.*
❖ *In 2008, more than 1.4 billion adults, aged twenty and older, were overweight. Of these over 200 million men and nearly 300 million women were obese.*
❖ *Thirty-five percent of adults aged twenty and over were overweight in 2008, and 11 percent were obese.*
❖ *Sixty-five percent of the world's population live in countries where overweight and obesity kills more people than underweight.*
❖ *Forty-two million children under the age of five were overweight or obese in 2013.*
❖ *Obesity is preventable.*

Malnourishment means the body is not receiving the correct nutrients. This is one of the reasons that people eat more and more and obesity is the result. When the body does not receive the correct nutrients, it will simply register hunger and send out a call for more food. Obesity stems from emotional and psychological need, unconscious and therefore unknown. Yet also at the physical level, a typical western eating pattern that comprises lots of processed foods and red meats results in the body systems' lack of vital nutrients. Hence it keeps calling for more and more. It is a vicious cycle. At the most fundamental level of being, the body is being starved, and its wisdom knows that. Whatever emotional needs are being masked by food intake, they most certainly cannot be fulfilled by junk food.

Nutritionist Caroline Marie Dupont makes an interesting analogy:[220] "When we eat fake foods we become less authentic; when our foods are fractured we become less centered; when we eat chemical residues designed to kill life, we die a little; when we eat food grown or raised with an element of human or animal suffering, we become hardened to our natural compassion for all life; when we choose foods only because of speed or convenience, we perpetuate the madness that rules our days."

Not only do our air, soils, and water contain chemicals, pesticides, and toxins, but all processed foods do too, and many unprocessed foods are grown using nutrient-depleted soils and are treated with pesticides and chemically treated water supplies that are toxic in nature. Our bodies are made from energy and light and have a unique communication system of information flowing electromagnetically through the various energy fields associated with life. These cannot function properly in a toxic environment. Any recalibration of the body must include a complete review of how it is being nourished in all forms. Food affects all our cells, our energy field, and our thoughts and emotions through our body chemistry. Harmful toxins are stored in our body fat. In order to recalibrate the body and prepare it to receive an imprint of higher frequency energy, cleansing and detoxification are paramount.

The Big Balancing Act

pH stands for the power of hydrogen and denotes the amount of hydrogen ions present in any fluid. On a scale of 1 to 14, 7 is considered neutral; below this is acidic, and above this is alkaline. Our bodies work to maintain our blood pH between 7.35 and 7.45, which is slightly more alkaline than pure water. If the blood pH falls below 7.35, this leads to acidosis, causing a depression in the central nervous system and eventually coma and possibly even death. A pH above the level of 7.45 leads to alkalosis. This causes the nerves to become ultrasensitive and overexcitable and can result in spasm, nervousness, and convulsions. Balance is key to optimal health. The two main forces that can disrupt the balance are the acid- and alkaline-forming foods ingested and the body's own acid-generating mechanism. This comes about through the energy generation performed by cells regularly, resulting in acids being released into the body fluids. This is normal and unavoidable. However, what is ingested can be controlled. The body has three main mechanisms that work to balance the pH level in the blood:

- ❖ Chemical—carbonic acid/carbonates buffer system; protein buffer system; phosphate buffer system
- ❖ Breath—exhalation of carbon dioxide
- ❖ Elimination—hydrogen ions released from kidneys

These three mechanisms keep the balance. However, if any of these balancing mechanisms are disrupted, then the body has a problem. If the diet is low in nutrients or high in acid-forming foods, then these three systems become overworked, which leads to negative health consequences. For example, the phosphate buffer system uses phosphate ions to neutralize strong acids. Most phosphate ions come from calcium phosphate in the bones and teeth. If the body system constantly has to neutralize large quantities of acid, it will draw on its natural reserves found in these sources. This ultimately leads to weakness in the bones and teeth.[221]

The body is a design miracle. It already has systems in place for balance and harmony to maintain optimum physical health. All we need to do is keep that balance. So, an optimal eating pattern would be a good mix of nutrient-dense, alkaline- and acid-forming foods, with a higher percentage intake of alkaline-forming food. Most vegetables and fruit have an alkaline-forming effect, and most grains, animal foods, and highly processed foods have a high acid-forming effect.

Most Alkaline	Alkaline	Lowest Alkaline	Food Category	Lowest Acid	Acid	Most Acid
		Raw Honey, Raw Sugar	Sweetners	Processed Honey, Molasses	White Sugar, Brown Sugar	NutraSweet, Equal, Aspartame, Sweet 'N Low
Lemons, Limes Watermelon, Grapefruit, Mangoes, Papaya	Dates, Figs, Melons, Grapes, Kiwi, Berries, Apples, Pears, Raisins	Oranges, Bananas, Cherries, Pineapple, Peaches, Avocados	Fruits	Plums, Processed Fruit Juices	Sour Cherries, Rhubarb	Blueberries, Cranberries, Prunes
Asparagus, Onions, Vegetable Juice, Parsley, Garlic, Raw Spinach, Broccoli	Okra, Squash, Green Beans, Beets, Celery, Lettuce, Zucchini, Carob, Sweet Potato	Carrots, Tomatoes, Fresh Corn, Mushrooms, Peas, Cabbage, Olives, Potato Skin, Tofu, Soybeans	Beans, Vegetables & Legumes	Cooked Spinach, Kidney Beans, String Beans	Potatoes (without skin), Pinto Beans, Navy Beans, Lima Beans	Chocolate
	Almonds	Chestnuts	Nuts & Seeds	Pumpkin Seeds, Sunflower Seeds	Pecans, Cashews	Peanuts, Walnuts
Olive Oil	Flax Seed Oil	Canola Oil	Oils	Corn Oil		
		Amaranth, Millet, Wild Rice, Quinoa	Grains & Cereals	Sprouted Wheat Bread, Spelt, Brown Rice	White Rice, Corn, Buckwheat, Oats, Rye	Wheat, White Flour, Pastries, Pasta
			Meats	Venison, Cold Water Fish	Turkey, Chicken, Lamb	Beef, Pork, Shellfish
	Breast Milk	Soy Cheese, Soy Milk, Goat Milk, Goat Cheese, Whey	Eggs & Dairy	Eggs, Butter, Yoghurt, Buttermilk, Cottage Cheese	Raw Milk	Cheese, Homog-enized Milk, Ice Cream
Herb Teas, Lemon Water	Green Tea	Ginger Tea	Beverages	Tea	Coffee	Beer, Soft Drinks

Figure 13.1. Nutrition table of alkaline and acidic foods

As we are beings made of energy, it may also serve us to consider the energy and information that are available to us in and from our food. Raw, fresh produce contains the maximum amount of phytonutrients and more direct light energy from the sun through photosynthesis, all of which protects the body from harmful toxins and increases coherence so energy and information can be passed easily throughout the body and the bioenergy field. Energy and consciousness are interchangeable. If an animal has been raised and slaughtered in an inhumane way to provide food, there is no doubt that the residual fear held in the cells of its flesh will be ingested in human consumption. Everything is inextricably linked.

Consider then adding the following high vibrational food to your daily intake[222]:

❖ Live or raw
❖ Fresh
❖ Organic or biodynamic
❖ Plant-based: vegetables, fruit, nuts, seeds, whole grains, pulses
❖ Grown, picked, and prepared by conscious people
❖ Know the source of the produce and that animals have been treated with compassion and respect if eating animal products.

This is not a diet but a way of living in balance and harmony within the body and with the other kingdoms of nature. As a rule of thumb, it is a good idea to eliminate totally:

❖ Wheat and gluten
❖ Red meat
❖ Dairy except eggs and yogurt
❖ Alcohol
❖ Sugar
❖ All processed food
❖ Caffeine
❖ Low-fat products (usually high in sugars when low in fat)

Another good tip is to eat little and often; this keeps the metabolism working optimally. Also, rethinking your eating pattern does not mean that you must never have a treat. The occasional cake and chocolate become extra scrumptious when you don't have them daily. The occasional glass of wine helps celebrations be celebrations. But it is recommended to eat clean and consciously for most of the time. It is your choice like everything else, but if you can change your nutrition pattern to a higher frequency input, you will be amazed at the energy you have and what you can accomplish. The food we eat becomes our affirmation of life. Every meal can be an opportunity to affirm the desire to be more alive and energized at all levels. For more information see figure 13.2.

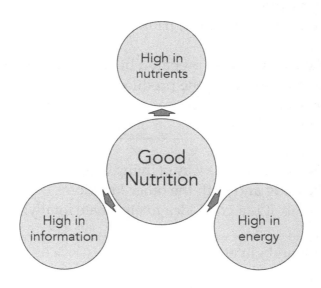

Figure 13.2. Good Nutrition

Hydrate

Water is essential for life. It forms the liquid crystalline structure of the living matrix though which life-supporting energy is transported at the molecular level to power the cells and the living organism. It is central to the metabolism and transfer of energy that powers all living processes. It also plays a leading role in many of our physiological functions: lubricating joints and cartilage, aiding digestive and other body processes. It regulates body temperature by transporting the blood to and from the surface of the skin. Blood plasma (92% water) also regulates the pH, circulates antibodies, and regulates osmotic balance (transfer of water through cell membranes) to maintain body temperature. It removes harmful toxins from the body through perspiration and urination and reduces the burden on the kidneys and the liver by flushing out waste products. It keeps the elimination process effective by reducing constipation and ensuring waste products are eliminated quickly from the body. Water also transports vital nutrients around the body.

Our total body content of water is on average 65 percent. The brain consists of 95 percent water, lungs 92 percent, and blood 82 percent. Mild dehydration is a very common cause of daytime fatigue, and unless you are drinking at least two liters a day (women) or three liters a day (men), you are mildly dehydrated. If you are athletic or highly energetic or are at the opposite end of the scale suffering from any kind of disorder such as diarrhea or constipation, it is likely your body will require even more water intake than this. As water is such a crucial component to life, the quality of the supply becomes as important as the quantity. In part 1 the subject of water was discussed extensively, and for optimal health and cellular functioning we need H3O2. The best water to drink is clean, pure, and full of naturally occurring minerals, such as: well water, springwater, artesian water, or mineral water that can be spring or artesian, comes from an underground source, and contains 250 parts per million dissolved solids of minerals and trace elements. If these are not available, you might want to consider a water purification/ionization system.[223]

❖ **See "The Energetic Highway," Practice 5: Nourishment**

Sleep Easy

Rest is a priority for your physical well-being. It is not something to be done after everything else is finished. It requires conscious choice to follow the good sleep tips recommended by experts,[224] some of which are listed below. Together with physical movement and real nutrition, addressing your need for relaxation and rest is a priority for optimizing your energy levels and preparing your system for energetic recalibration.

❖ *Establish consistent sleep and wake schedules, even on weekends.*

❖ *Create a regular, relaxing bedtime routine, such as soaking in a hot bath or listening to soothing music; begin an hour or more before the time you expect to fall asleep.*

❖ *Create a sleep-conducive environment that is dark, quiet, comfortable, and cool.*

❖ *Sleep on a comfortable mattress and pillows.*

❖ *Use your bedroom only for sleep (no TV or computer).*

❖ *Finish eating at least two or three hours before your regular bedtime.*

❖ *Exercise regularly.*

❖ *Avoid caffeine and alcohol products close to bedtime and give up smoking.*

❖ **See "The Energetic Highway," Practice 6: Movement and Rest.**

Golden Key

How we care for the self directly correlates to how we care for others. Self-neglect in order to care or do for another does not serve the individual or the collective. There is a vast difference between caregiving and caretaking. We have been conditioned to believe that taking good care of the self is selfish and that our energy "should" be spent on others. Caretaking is a form of control over others and presumes they cannot do for themselves. It exhausts the "giver," whose need to control is fear-based, and disempowers the "receiver." In the end, neither is served. Caregiving stems from a completely different intention, based on love and compassion for others when they truly cannot help themselves. Caregiving starts with the self. The degree to which we can care for our self is the degree to which we can care for another.

CHAPTER 14

The Creative Process

The Pulse of Creation

> To everything there is a season and a time to
> every purpose under heaven.
>
> —Ecclesiastes 3:1
> (King James Bible)

Our voyage of discovery has shown that there is a rhythm and pulse to all of creation. In the vast ocean of energy in which we experience our being, there is an ebb and flow of life. A beautiful metaphor for this is the tides of the great bodies of water on the planet, which rise and fall in regular rhythms and the waves continue rolling to the shores in such a variety of endless and varied patterns. In our own breathing, there is an inflowing, a halting, and then an outflow. In nature, the seasons clearly reflect energy as dormant or static in winter, life force moving and awakening in spring, expansion and growth in the summer, and then a withdrawing of life energy and contraction in the autumn. And so it is with all physical manifestation, from the cosmic to our individual self. Each individual life has a rhythmic pulse beat. There are three distinct phases that govern all creation: expansion, equilibrium, and contraction. These principles work in harmony together so that they can support, amplify, and enhance each other. It is important to be aware that all life has this life pulse, with its own timing, perfection, and reason for being. Nothing can be created without these three principles.

Expansion

An outgoing, forward movement of energy; creating; searching; learning; growing; discovering; reaching out; giving; building; passionate; active.

Negative aspects: aggressive, hostile, creates separation.

Equilibrium

A place of nonmovement; preservation of energy; halting; resting; a collecting of energy for the next outward movement; passive.

Negative aspects: stagnation, inertia, lifeless; stuck.

Contraction

Inward movement bringing back to self; introspection; assimilating all that has been discovered; self-searching; restrictive; restricts the outward movement in order to allow the fruits gathered during the expansion to be manifested in the next outward movement.

Negative aspects: regression; going backward in the wrong direction; holding up progress, separation.

In all that we do, these phases exist. In all that we are, these phases exist. In everything we wish to manifest, there are these phases. Therefore, it supports our progress to know and recognize these attributes of the creative cycle so that we can work in harmony with them. The negative aspects are just as important to be aware of so that we can check in to witness what is going on in our own process of life and can be curious, explore, and question.[225]

* **See "The Energetic Highway," Practice 7: Creative Life Pulse.**

Golden Key

Whether aware or not, human beings are constantly creating their reality individually and collectively. Our task is to develop mastery over the lower densities of matter and create by becoming aware of and using consciously the creative pulse of our lives. The greatest creative act is to bring all that has been learned during our individualization in physical life on earth back to the whole of the one consciousness that we are. This aids the evolutionary process of all people, our planet, and the entire cosmos.

Purpose and Intention

Purpose can be defined as the true intention held behind any thought, word, or action. It is a very powerful concept in the creative process and very little understood. Intentionality starts the process of creation. It defines the purpose of that which is required to be manifested. Quantum physics has confirmed that we live in an ocean of all possibilities, where everything exists as potential. Because of the dual nature of particles, they can be either particles or waves of energy but not both at the same time. The movement of energy is random, with unlimited potential, but becomes ordered by human intention and thought. The waves of energy are collapsed into matter based on our intention. However, what is projected onto our hologram of reality consists of thoughts, beliefs, attitudes, feelings, and memories. All consciousness is energy. These aspects of our consciousness all create energy fields called "attractors."[226] The laws of magnetism and harmonic resonance cause the attractor energy fields to disrupt the creative process if what we are thinking, feeling, and being are not in alignment with the original intention. There are four different types of intention: constructive, destructive, dualistic, and adept.

Constructive

Constructive or affirmative intention arises from your higher aspect and is aligned with love, appreciation, and gratitude. It is made from the place of unified consciousness, even when there is present a very strong urge to do otherwise.

Example: I am guided to give up my job, change continents, and write a book. It is my intention to write a book, but I am afraid to give up my job and change continents. I give up the job anyway, change continents, and write a book. This is positive intention.

Destructive

Destructive or negative intention originates from the lower aspect of the self and is aligned with negating the flow of life and self, choosing separation and isolation. It is made from the place of fear. This is not an unconscious state, nor is it a deeply repressed state. It is *known* to the being but denied. It is very difficult to admit feelings of spite, hatred, envy, and jealousy. These become masked by denial even to the self. When we constantly ignore an aspect of our self because it is unpalatable, its origin is forgotten, and this way of being becomes the norm.

Example: Every time my partner looks at a pretty girl I am jealous because I am afraid she is better, prettier, smarter than me and he will choose her. I feel insecure and this creates more negative feelings of spite. This causes separation all round. First within me from my higher self; then between me and my partner; and finally between me and the pretty girl. Alternatively, I consciously wish a negative outcome for another in some way and feel pleasure when I hear of this.

Dualistic

This type of intention occurs when the mind is split. The conscious mind wishes to manifest something from a place of positivity. The unconscious mind is fearful due to limiting belief systems that are *unknown* to it, and therefore the intention is not fully aligned with either positive or negative energy.

An example of this would be I wish to attract a loving relationship into my life for the purpose of love and mutual growth. At the deepest level I am really afraid to share myself with another because I am afraid of betrayal or rejection. Rejection is the pattern of all my previous relationships. This is not yet in my conscious awareness, because I believe I really want the relationship. I am sending dual energetic signals out to the universe and create accordingly. The chances are I will create the relationship, but it will be one of betrayal or rejection due to my unconscious belief and because of the attractor patterns I am sending out to the universe.

Another type of dualistic intention is where we are just not clear about what we intend. We start with one intention and keep changing to another. Be crystal clear in your intention. This requires direction, focus, patience, and dedication. Be firm in your purpose. Stop changing your mind.

Adept

This intention is fully aligned with higher will and true purpose. It is associated with feelings of great pleasure. The whole of the being is lifted and infused with love and feels supported and loved by all around. This is because the being is fully aligned with the higher frequency energies of unity consciousness and connected to the real self. Intention is fully aligned to the cosmic plan and purpose and manifestation becomes totally effortless and almost instant.

It is through working with our intentionality that our life tasks are revealed to us. When we align with our higher aspects and create with effortless intention through feelings of joy, love, and gratitude, we are in the flow of universal energy, and the universe conspires to bring all that is required to fulfill the creation. When aligned with higher will and purpose, the feelings that arise are ecstatic, and we know our path. Things fall into place without struggle

Example: When your intention is fully aligned without impediment to your higher aspects you can set an intention to manifest something in your life and opportunities to fulfill that are created immediately. Guidance becomes clear knowing.

Something as small as just thinking about someone can bring them into immediate contact with you. An intention to significantly increase your bank balance can provide an immediate opportunity to do so. A key part of this is not to be attached to the "how" but rather keep open to all possibility and be discerning with what comes forth. The opportunity also requires action on your part; the action of making a choice to follow or ignore it. This is where discernment and clear knowing are vital.

Golden Key

Intention is a conscious act and a deliberate choice to do, act, be, or create something. It is important to differentiate between will and intention. *Patience, acceptance, and understanding of the flow of life are essential life tools and play a large part in intention and manifestation. This does not mean we do not focus our intentionality, but it does mean there is no forcing current of energy behind it. Effortless intention springs from the place of deep pleasure and knowing one is fully aligned with the self and its purpose.*

Fear is most certainly present when we lock ourselves into imaginary time frames instead of allowing the natural flow of attraction and synchronicity that brings to us all that we envision when all aspects of the self are in full alignment. This is why we need to explore our inner being and become aware of any destructive or dualistic intentionality. The practices of centering and setting our intentions engage us with our deepest longings and desires and meaningful purposes in our lives. Even if we are not yet sure of that purpose, these practices will help us align to the imprints from our causal and monadic bodies, and our path forward will clarify. Be open to the process; practice and use discernment with what manifests.

❖ **See "The Energetic Highway," Practice 8: Setting Intention.**

The Process

Creation starts with your intention. This provides direction for the movement of energy. This is different from a goal, where there are specific outcomes required. It is interesting to note that goal setting actually limits the outcome of the creative process. A goal is a fixed outcome. Yet our power to create is unlimited.

Using our intention requires surrender, trust, and equanimity. This means there is no attachment to the how or the outcome or even the when. If we are aligned to the creative pulse of our lives, this determines the when of our creations. This also means there is no limit to what can be created, and very often that which we wish to create shows up in ways that are most unexpected. If we limit this process, we are not open to the possibilities of how our intention is manifested by the interaction of our bioenergy field with the photons of light in the quantum field. This is why it is important to always qualify your intention for the highest good of all concerned, invoke the higher frequencies, and be open to what shows up. It is also so important to do our inner work. If there is no awareness of the lower frequency energy emanating from our bioenergy field due to our DNA coding, energy blockages, faulty belief systems, and misqualified energy patterns, then no matter what the intention, we will never create the desired outcome until our energy matrix is transformed. Due to harmonic resonance, our unique energetic signature will continue to attract similar energy.

Golden Key

When our bioenergy field is in coherence and is resonating at a high frequency, our recalibrated energetic signature allows the attractor fields to resonate with energies of similar frequency in the quantum potential field of the superposition state, collapsing the energy wave into the manifestation of that which is intended.

Balancing the Masculine and the Feminine Energies

In order to build a coherent bioenergy field and energy signature, it is necessary for our energy to be balanced. The requirement of balance and harmony is a prerequisite for all creative processes and for creating and sustaining life itself. From the life pulse to the breath, from creation of galaxies to babies, it requires input from both masculine and feminine energy. In physics this would be called positive and negative charge. Particles with more protons than electrons are positively charged. Particles with more electrons than protons are negatively charged. This is the basis of the attraction between particles of matter, consciousness, and energy. This has nothing to do with gender, as both sexes hold these frequencies. However, most do not hold them in balance. Figure 14.1 lists the main attributes of each.

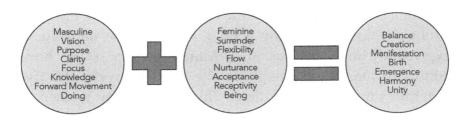

Figure 14.1. Balancing the energies.

The feminine energy of being is where creative ideas are conceived and birthed and then passed to the masculine aspect to make them real on the material plane. The masculine energy of doing informs the being of when it is necessary to act and assert the self. It gives the confidence, clarity, knowledge, and ability to move things forward in the physical world. Nothing happens without both working together. This supports the expansion, contraction, and equilibrium phases of the creative pulse.

Negative Aspects

The negative aspects of either energy are equally damaging. The negative aspect of masculine energy results in aggression, hostility, dominance, hardness of heart, selfishness, and wrong use of power. The negative aspect of feminine energy produces stagnation, depression, laziness, caretaking, lack of purpose, lack of structure, and unhealthy boundaries.

Both positive and negative aspects of the two energies pertain to the cosmic and collective consciousness as well as the personal. In the collective consciousness, the imbalance of these two energies over millennia has produced unhealthy, unbalanced patterns of abuse and victimization sexually, culturally, and spiritually and continues to play out today in patriarchal societies, where power is taken by the male to dominate women and children. This is an outpicturing of the imbalance of the energies. And it must be stressed that this is not only determined by gender, although the imbalances express through gender also. Many women today have dominant masculine energy. In the western world, the rise of feminism in popular culture "liberated" many women to develop their potential in ways never before experienced, resulting in masculine energy imbalance. Equally, through the influence of feminism in western culture, many men have sought to reconnect with their inner feminine energy, and though commendable, in some this has resulted in cases of overpassivity. There can be no judgment and no victims; all are responsible individually and collectively for rebalancing these energies. In a balanced individual, there is a balanced flow between the two: being and doing, active and passive, masculine and feminine. Our ability to manifest and express these energies depends on our inner alignment and intentionality, not on our gender. Our own inner balance becomes reflected in the external world of our relationships as our ability to create and maintain harmonious relationships with all other beings.

Cosmic Magnetism and Human Sexuality

Science demonstrates a magnetic field is established wherever electrical charges are in motion, and we now know ourselves to be a force field of electrical energy in motion. Magnetism is in reality the law of attraction, and the plan of evolution is to ultimately unite all individual consciousness through this law. This law of attraction is the inherent energy that moves individuals toward one another, pulling us out of seclusion and isolation and encouraging us to be with one another in relationships. It is through the medium of relationship that we are able to develop the conditions for the ultimate union of consciousness with all creation. The cosmic plan of life moves all humankind toward contact, pleasure, and oneness. Physical life itself is created through union in relationship. At this level human beings create life, and yet deep within the collective psyche is the misconception that unity will bring annihilation of the self. This keeps us in separation and isolated in our consciousness even though we may join with another physically. This is a split in the collective psyche that denies life while literally creating it. This is a duality in our lives at a most fundamental level that most are unaware of. The other great dualistic misconception is the development of negative force associated with the pleasure principle. For some, the basic natural instincts toward life, pleasure, and union have been misjudged, denied, and split off into duality, which sees them as "bad" and opposite to our higher "spiritual" nature. This actually means the life principle is held in consciousness as "bad." Because of this, human sexuality is very often disconnected from feeling. Rather than feeling "bad," feeling is suppressed, and sex is reduced to a physical action rather than a full union at all levels.

Cosmic magnetism is a primary energy force that cannot be eliminated and is always encouraging all nature toward unity. However, because pleasure becomes associated with guilt, shame, anxiety, and tension, the two become intertwined, and because we believe it is "bad," we come to fear this pull. Where there is fear, there cannot be love in our contact with another. This in turn causes pain. So, fear-producing pain, hurt, anger, and various protective strategies all become linked to pleasure and our most natural urge toward unity. This huge conflict is deeply held in the collective psyche and is responsible for much misuse of the sexual nature of man and woman. It becomes apparent that we cannot balance the energies of masculine and feminine without investigating and addressing these deep distortions to the life flow created by fundamental misconceptions and attitudes toward our sexual nature.[227]

❖ See "The Energetic Highway," Practice 9: Balance of the Masculine and Feminine Energies.

Golden Key

You are a magnificent creator. You have the tools of creation within you. By connecting to the heart while being in a balanced energetic state of doing and being, overcoming all ideas of limitation, you are free to create anything.

CHAPTER 15

Emotional and Mental Stability

> Your true nature is something never lost to you, even in moments of delusion, nor is it gained at the moment of enlightenment. It is the nature of your own mind, the source of all things; your original luminous brilliance. You, the richest person in the world, have been going around laboring and begging, when all the while the treasure you seek is within you. It is who you are.
>
> —Huang Po

To build coherence in our bioenergy field, it is essential to have emotional and mental stability. These two states are inextricably intertwined. Thoughts, feelings, emotions, faulty belief systems, and intentions can all limit our progress of alignment with the innate nature of our being. These keep us stuck in looping cycles in the lower frequencies.

Feelings versus Emotions

This is often a confusing concept, but there is a distinct and important difference between a feeling and an emotion. A feeling is an internal biological response to an outside stimulus. It is a sensate experience, that is, felt in the body. I feel warm. I feel cold. I feel excited. I feel fear. Certain feelings are based on our evolutionary biological programming and are instinctive. Our physical nature has evolved from primal states that have been imprinted by the morphogenetic fields of our species. The amygdala in the brain of all human beings holds the old biological responses based on seeking, rage, fear, panic, lust, care, and play. Jaak Pankskepp in 1998[228] identified these innate psychobehavioral processes to be present in all mammals and constitute the basic survival reflexes.

However, we also *feel* our emotions.

An emotion is a state of consciousness, which also displays a physiological response to a stimulus but is based on our perception and how it has been *rationalized by the mind and then felt.* So it could be said our emotional response to a stimulus results in a feeling. Our consciousness informs our feelings. This is not only brought about by external stimuli but can also be brought on by our internal thoughts, beliefs, memories, images, attitudes, and environmental conditioning. We respond based on how we have learned to respond to a stimulus. It is not our feelings that are conditioned by the mind—they are events that arise naturally within our bodies—but *our response* to the outside or internal stimuli creates an emotional reaction that drives a cascade of hormonal and chemical changes in the body. This results in a feeling in the body. The limbic system in the brain regulates the body via chemicals, hormones, and temperature, and the cerebral cortex of the brain is where thinking, reasoning, and planning take place. This is the region where holographic data are stored. Our bioenergy field and physical senses are taking in information constantly, even when there is no awareness of this.

And so it is that our emotional and three lower mindstates all affect the development of consciousness. Emotional and mental stability become intertwined.

Environmental Conditioning

Parental, peer, school, church, societal, and cultural conditioning all influence our thoughts and perceptions about our self and the nature of reality. From an energetic perspective, the energy fields that surround us in utero, both internally and externally, initiate our environmental conditioning. Our DNA is informed by the morphogenetic fields of information. Our earliest conditioning starts at this level and is built in from birth; imprinting of new life experience starts here.

Science has shown us that our environment, not our genes, controls our physical health and well-being, and our emotional and mental balance is affected by our care environment in childhood. There are several basic needs that must be satisfied for every child to enable healthy development. In order to develop emotional and mental stability, it is useful to understand the requirements for balanced psychological development.

A child needs physical and emotional contact and an environment that allows the free expression of the child's needs and impulses. There must be an adequate satisfaction of those needs and supportive mirroring by the caregiver. There is also a delicate balance required between indulgence and deprivation in order that the child can eventually individuate and become independent. This concerns something called "optimal frustration." This is the amount of frustration an infant can tolerate between the extremes of overindulgence and deprivation in relation to the infant's demands for mirroring. That is, when a child repeatedly experiences a parent not responding to his or her requests for instant gratification and soothing, the child internalizes that he or she must find inner sources to soothe and comfort the self. This is essential for mature development and individuation. However, for healthy development there must be balance between positive and negative response on the part of the caregiver. If the child's overall needs are not met in the first three years of existence, the child's security, self-esteem, independence, personal power, and relational skills are affected throughout his or her life.[229,230,231]

Foundations for Psychological Health

There are seven psychological life issues that are common to *all* human existence that create an energetic signature in the bioenergy field. There are also seven common patterns by which a dysfunction due to the energetic imprint of the faulty belief mechanism associated with these issues expresses itself. These cause predictable behavioral strategies to navigate the issue and "protect" the being.[232] Indecisiveness, inconclusiveness, obsessive doubt, and procrastination mask the underlying anxiety of imperfection and fear of error. Unfortunately, these strategies lead to a disconnection within and to repression, suppression, ignoring, demonizing, and avoidance of the associated emotions. In effect, we become someone else. We use these protective mechanisms to navigate through life masking the underlying disconnection. This strategy becomes a habitual way of living and being and denies the magnificence of who we are. Our understanding of these patterns helps to develop awareness, compassion, forgiveness, acceptance, and love for our self and all others caught in the recycling of behaviors that do not serve them.

These patterns exist in *all human beings*, who may consider themselves normal and healthy to lesser or greater degrees. A seemingly competent and well-integrated adult may easily regress into dysfunction under stress or a perceived threat of discovery of his or her key issues. It is important to note that dysfunction can be caused by the *perception* of the infant/child as well as an actual event. The mind does not differentiate between actual and perceived. While these issues may appear as a catalogue of deliberate abuse, equally they can be initiated by well-meaning parents who held good intentions and did the best they could but were parented in a similar pattern. You cannot give what you have not experienced, and children model themselves on their parents or first caregivers. Please also bear in mind these issues can also be held, in many people, in the blueprint of the personal bioenergy field and the DNA before physical manifestation in order that during this particular life cycle misqualified energy may be transmuted into a higher frequency.

Life Issue 1—Existence and Safety

The infant experiences his or her environment as cold, hostile, and threatening. This can occur even in utero because the child is unwanted. The caregiver is not attuned to the child's needs. Caregivers are distant, detached, rejecting, and unwelcoming. The feeling in the infant is terror and rage, and yet this cannot be safely expressed. These natural responses are suppressed and turned against the self. The child negates his or her own life.

Energetic Imprint
An unwanted child receives an energetic imprint that informs him or her: "I have no right to exist." "There is something wrong with me." "To be here and live threatens my life."

Energetic Signature
Life issues that result are fear of living fully and inability to manifest on the physical plane; performance anxiety; feeling hated; feeling empty at the core; having difficulty in maintaining commitment; or having disconnection from life

processes such as his or her own body, feelings, intimacy, community, and in some cases food. Tries to win approval and acceptance by using cognitive abilities.

Behavioral Protection Pattern

Their protective measure is to withhold themselves or to avoid and withdraw; they develop their cognitive abilities at the expense of feeling.

Life Issue 2—Need and Loss

The environmental response to the child's request for attention and nurturance is ignored, causing the child to feel uncomfortable expressing his or her needs for nurturance and intimacy. The child is wanted, but erratic nurturing results in repetitive emotional abandonment. Therefore the infant suppresses his or her neediness to avoid repetitive negative experiences and painful disappointments. The child abandons his or her own needs.

Energetic Imprint

An abandoned child receives an energetic imprint that informs him or her: "I cannot need. I will not need. I dare not need. I don't need you. I can do everything myself. If I express my needs, I will be abandoned and disappointed. If I keep giving and loving, I will get what I need."

Energetic Signature

There is an unfulfilled need for nurturance, sustenance, and touch. The being needs to be able to find and have what is nourishing to the self. The external experience of being abandoned is coupled with the internal experience of feeling weak, resigned, empty, and collapsed. There is wishful thinking and a sense that the being can never have real confidence in his or her expectations being fulfilled.

Behavioral Protection Pattern

The abandoned child's protective measures are to retreat into an attitude of passivity and dependency. There can be depressive moods, muscular weakness, and a collapsed state of being. The body usually has a low energy level, and the person feels shame at being needy, while at the same time he or she has feelings of helplessness and victimhood. Such people often enter relationships to get love.

Life Issue 3—Identity and Agency

The environment requires the child maintain his or her contact with the caregiver and continue his or her dependency and entanglement even when he or she needs to individuate. The initiative to see what one can do and be as an individual is either blocked, causes parental anxiety, or is punished, and the child must restrain the impulse for adventure and independent exploration. Eventually identity is found in the relationship with others and living through others rather than an individuated self. The child submits and loses his or her own power.

Energetic Imprint

An owned child receives an energetic imprint that informs him or her: "I don't want to separate. I will be loyal. I will live through another. I will be safe as long as I hold onto you. If I let go, I will be helpless."

Energetic Signature

The main issue is the being experiences aggression, assertion, and opposition as dangerous. The assertive impulse to individuate has been discouraged and, at worst, punished. The child has extreme difficulty in self-activation and motivation. He or she could be described as lazy. The needs of others are necessary to initiate activity. The self feels empty without entanglement with another.

Behavioral Protection Pattern

Such beings protect the status quo by merging. They can be people pleasers, molding the self to others' interests and tastes, and can only feel a sense of self in losing the self in another. They absorb the other's negative state and take responsibility for it, while at the same time deeply resenting the other for causing their negative feelings; these people have trouble saying no. Rather than separate, they use passive-aggressive resistance and avoidance of confrontation rather than assertiveness and self-expression.

Life Issue 4—Self-Concept and Self-Esteem

Here the environment fails completely to mirror the child. Children are objectified and required to be something other than themselves. The message becomes "If you become what I want, I will love you." "Who you actually are is not enough or too much …" The child can never truly realize the self and develops a pattern of self-betrayal when he or she continually satisfies the expectation of the parent (and any authority in later life), feeling special and confusing this positive objectification as love. Such children hide from themselves and others what is rejected by the caregiver. The child betrays the self each time he or she conforms.

Energetic Imprint

A used child receives an energetic imprint that informs him or her: "I am bad." "I must never be wrong. If I am wrong, I will be humiliated." "I must control and manipulate others to need me and get what I need." "I must never surrender; if I surrender I will be helpless and die." "I must be perfect and never fail."

Energetic Signature

Used people can show neither their magnificence nor their vulnerability. They have unbearable feelings of worthlessness and feel "bad." They must be perceived as competent, knowing, and right. They have intense fear of being controlled, humiliated, and defeated. They confuse ordinariness with worthlessness and therefore need to be special. They use others to bolster, fortify, and aggrandize the false self. They rely on achievement to bolster self-esteem.

Behavioral Protection Pattern

They are strong-willed and want to dominate others. Grandiosity compensates for feelings of badness. This results in lack of humility, inability to accept failure, inability to accept criticism, a sense of entitlement, manipulation, and a constant drive for power and control.

Life Issue 5—Control and Freedom

This occurs when the child has locomotion, memory, and language. The child needs to and is ready to determine and sustain his or her own self-expression. The environment takes over and completely crushes and defeats the natural autonomous functioning of the child. The child's will is persistently, intrusively, and possibly even sadistically thwarted and beaten into submission. Because of the power differential between the child and the caregiver, the only way to get even is for the child to display his or her own self-defeat. Self-sabotage becomes the pattern. The child victimizes the self.

Energetic Imprint

A controlled child receives an energetic imprint that informs him or her: "Life is a burden; it is so hard, but I must bear it." "I must sacrifice myself. Pleasure is wrong and sinful." "I must always be 'good.'" "Yes, but ..." "If I express myself, I will be humiliated." "I must hide what is inside."

Energetic Signature

This is about sustaining one's own will. Underneath the pattern of self-defeat is deep rage and spite and a desire to get even. The only way this is perceived to be possible is through the pattern of self-defeat, which manifests in constant self -sabotage and frustrates all attempts of help, eventually becoming defeating and abusive to others; these beings are extremely resistant to change. The pleasure in self-degradation is not conscious. These beings indulge in chronic stalemating of others, breeding hopelessness, pessimism, and despair. They are chronically dissatisfied with everything in life and complain bitterly.

Behavioral Protection Pattern

These controlled people protect themselves through self-victimization. They learn to enjoy their own defeat. This becomes their only way of getting back and having power over others. They obtain negative pleasure in displaying forbearance and sacrifice to the world and will resist attempts to change such behavior.

Life Issue 6—Love, Sexuality, and Competition

Here the caregivers either exploit or compete with the child's natural sexuality. The child has a natural and innocent early sexual curiosity and the need for physical contact and contact pleasure; the child requires nurturance and attention and has a certain jealousy of the exclusive aspects of the parental relationship. Exploitation of these needs range from unwanted and intrusive sexual abuse to a seductive and sexually motivated environment, where one parent is warm and sexually collusive with the child and the other parent is cold, neglectful, and in competition for affection and attention, but there is no physical contact or requirement for secrecy. The latter situation typically involves the female child, where the family pattern includes a seductive father and the presence of rivalry between the mother and daughter for attention. Cases of male sexual abuse within the family setting are relatively fewer.

Energetic Imprint

Victims of incest believe they are "irredeemably evil." Other beliefs held are, "I am contemptible." "If I reveal the secret, I will be blamed." "It is my fault." "I am the seducer/seductress, and I have hurt the mother/father I love."

Daughters of a seductive father try to be the "good" Daddy's girl but believe there is a contemptible person beneath their façade. "I am bad.""I am guilty." "I am incompetent and insubstantial." "I cannot solve problems." "I am not responsible."

Energetic Signature

Sexually exploited children long for safe relationships with the opposite sex but elicit relationships of intrigue and concomitant exploitation. They harbor unconscious hostility toward the opposite sex for exploitation and conscious hostility toward men who are weak and unable to rescue them.

They have lots of relationships so they can keep cycling through the problem, but there is no completion, resolution, or integration. Dramatic outbursts keeping the system from overwhelm are experienced by others as inappropriate in context and intensity and are seen as phony and inauthentic.

Behavioral Protection Pattern

The incest victim usually submits to the self-victimization protection stance of the controlled child. The daughter/son of the seductive father/mother adopts the position of a winner and imposes upon herself or himself impossible standards of achievement. They disassociate from the threatening topic. They use repression of thought and feelings. They delete and block information. They disassociate thoughts from feelings. For example, they may act provocatively but are unaware of sexual thoughts and feelings. Emotional outbursts provide a distraction from real feelings of overwhelm.

Life Issue 7—Will and Authenticity

The child uses will to adapt to a disciplined and controlled environment rather than be his or her authentic self. Caregivers are dutiful, conscientious, and competent. They rely on authority rather than attuning to the spontaneous needs of the child. The environment is rigid and rule-bound with no flexibility and no play or emotion. Anything passionate, sensual, or self-indulgent must be kept under control, with high restriction of all spontaneous expression. There is pursuit of perfection and avoidance of mistakes, and the child is expected to follow these exacting standards. Such children cut themselves off from all feelings.

Energetic Imprint

A disciplined child receives an energetic imprint that informs him or her: "If I show my feelings, I will be rejected." "I must be appropriate." "I must have and keep control."

Energetic Signature

Hostility, rebellion, and deep resentment at suppression of self are repressed and expressed as obstinacy, stubbornness, persistence, and passive-aggressive behavior. Such children are aloof, distant, cold, and authoritarian with those perceived to be beneath them. They crave order and precision and do not have a good sense of priority. Indecisiveness, inconclusiveness, obsessive doubt, and procrastination mask their underlying anxiety of imperfection and fear of error.

Behavioral Protection Pattern

All feelings are kept at arm's length. These disciplined children are rational, reasonable, and correct but stay in the periphery of circumstances, deal in abstractions, and remain in continual conflict and vacillation so deeper feelings do not emerge.

The Child Consciousness Within

All human beings carry these early developmental injuries to some degree. It must be stressed they can be either perceived or actual injuries to the psyche. The mind does not recognize the difference, but the outcome is the same. For example, an infant may perceive himself or herself as being unwanted as a baby; this may be the truth, or it may be that the mother just did not know how to cope and the child was truly wanted. These injuries to the developing child in most cases are not conscious on the part of the caregiver. They are hereditary patterns of behavior, passed from father to son, mother to daughter, down the generations. It is important to note that most of the difficulties encountered in our childhood as well as the limitations taught and modeled to us by our caregivers were already brought forward by us from other time lines of our existence. We bring them forward into this lifetime as an opportunity to bring these pieces of consciousness back into unity.

These injuries, actual and perceived, are extremely well hidden by the variety of protective measures conceived by the developing being in order to navigate a way through life and reject and repress any painful feelings. This results in parts of consciousness being separated off, hidden, and denied, and ultimately becoming unconscious. Through adaptive measures the child has become an adult, carrying the same familial injuries as his or her own caregivers, and so the cycle perpetuates. The parts have separated and remain as "undeveloped or child consciousness," frozen, never allowed to surface through fear of an outcome that is perceived as losing that which is most longed for, love. This part of the consciousness becomes the "child within."

These thoughts and images become embedded in our energy matrix, and depending on the protective measures taken to adapt to the original issue, create energy blocks and disruptive patterns in the flow of energy in our personal bioenergy field that can and do eventually affect the development of the physical body structure. We have seen the evidence that thought affects matter. This is true even if the thought is not conscious. From this unconscious place within, due to the harmonic resonance of energy and the attractor pattern being sent out from our energetic signature, we continue to recreate, over and over, the same familial pattern in all our relationships with others, whether personal, at school, in the workplace, or in the boardroom, and will continue to use the same habitual protective devices anytime another triggers this original issue in any way.

But this is not who we are! It is just a construct to protect us from experiencing painful and inconvenient feelings. These patterns of being govern our behavior and limit our opportunity to achieve all that is possible in our lives.

Energetic Patterns of the "Child Within"

Child consciousness	Habitual pattern
Unwanted	Withdrawing
Abandoned	Collapsing or passive aggressive pulling
Owned	Merging
Used	Dominating
Controlled	Resisting
Exploited	Exploding
Disciplined	Holding

Figure 15.1. Child consciousness and its habitual pattern

The table above is a simple generalization and to be used as a guide only. This can be useful as a map to the self to enable a rapprochement of the separated consciousness within each of us and allows for deep compassion and understanding of those parts of self that may still remain in separation and isolation.

Golden Key

The human psyche is complex and multifaceted, and the bioenergy field holds the information for the complete time line of our existence, not only this life in space-time. We have all played the roles of perpetrator and victim at some point. It is to be remembered that time is only a construct to draw attention to the focus of our task in this particular time frame. The task is none other than to reconcile these fragmented pieces of consciousness with the whole of our being through acceptance, self-love, and forgiveness.

❖ **See "The Energetic Highway," Practice 10: The Child Consciousness Within.**

CHAPTER **16**

Mind Games

How much longer will you go on letting your energy sleep? How much longer are you going to stay oblivious of the immensity of yourself?
                    —Bhagwhan Shree Rajneesh[233]

The limited mind must transcend itself in order to realize its unlimited power and scope. The path therefore constantly requires that the mind bridge the gap of its own limitations by considering new possibilities for other alternatives for the self, for life, for expressing the self in life.
                    —Eva Pierrakos[234]

Many are operating at the lower mind level of the personality. Our goal is to connect with and integrate the higher levels of our being. Most important to remember is that our objective reality is caused by our consciousness. What is "out there" is individual and collective manifestation and interpreted and defined through our senses. Once we think we know the way "things are" through our conditioned learning, we behave and act in agreement with the "truth" as we perceive it. This does not make it the truth, but our thoughts are powerful energy and create accordingly based on our belief system. Thus our environment will reflect our beliefs about it back to us.

The Lower Mind of the Personality Self

The lower mind of the personality can be subdivided into three categories.

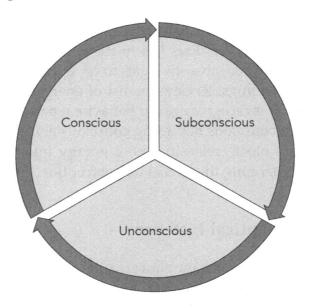

Figure 16.1. The three minds of the personality.

Conscious Mind

This is the awareness in the present moment of environment, breath, what you are doing or being.

Subconscious Mind

This consists of information that is readily accessible once the attention is directed to it. This is really memory recall. It is possible to do certain actions without having full conscious awareness in the moment. For example, you walk to the store while calling your friend on your cell phone. It is easy to bring to your conscious awareness the path to the store and also the telephone number of your friend, but you are not consciously alert to either of these in the moment.

Unconscious Mind

This holds information not easily accessible and contains the limiting beliefs, patterns, and maps of reality that inform our consciousness but of which we are unaware. The road map to what is unconscious lies in the energetic patterns of behavior that are adaptive strategies to cope with difficult and unintegrated feelings. Review the list of energetic signatures for guidance. It is recognizing our behavioral patterns that can lead to the unconscious becoming conscious and the removal of the energy block, releasing more energy into the overall system and changing the lens of our perception.[235]

Become a Skeptical Listener

Self-talk is the constant conversation that we have with ourselves in the mind. This can be a wonderful asset when it is used to enhance self-esteem and performance because it can influence our feelings and behavior. Confident people believe they can and act accordingly. They concentrate on mastering new challenges rather than anxiously worrying about imaginary setbacks. However, our truth is built on our own thoughts about ourselves and by listening to what others tell us is the truth about ourselves. To this day I remember when I was little girl, a teacher at school told me I could not paint. It took me fifty-five years to pick up a brush and create a painting.

Become a skeptical listener. If your perception is you cannot do or be something, you will subconsciously remember and creatively avoid what you believe you are not good at doing or being. Much of our identity or self-image is based on what has happened in the past. This is the now! Today, by using positive thoughts about yourself and changing your self-talk habit to reflect positive opinions and beliefs about the self, it is possible to build self-confidence and self-esteem. This does not mean other people around you will suddenly cease to be negative and destructive. It means you reject and dispute their negativity. Maybe that is their reality. It does not have to be yours. You are what you believe yourself to be.

Golden Key

An image is a limiting belief about life and about who we are and the resulting constricted emotions and protective strategies used to support it.

The Language of Crazy Making[236]

Practice	Description	Example
Selective Filtering	Picking out a single negative detail and dwelling on it exclusively	I didn't perform well today, I missed that one note
Rigid boundaries	Everything is black and white. Less than perfect is failure.	I'm useless because ...
Generalizing	Seeing a single negative event as a never ending pattern of defeat	I always.....
Making it up	Mind reading: you think you know how people are thinking and what their motives are.	He looks so serious, he must be mad at me.
	Fortune telling: you think something will turn out badly and consider the prediction an established fact	I am going to miss my train
Magnification and Minimization	Exaggerating the importance of things (your own error)	I made a mess of that presentation and I 'll never get the order.
	Making things insignificant (your own achievement)	Even though I am a great receptionist, I'll never get the job
Faulty Control Issues	Internal: I am the cause of collective success and failure.	If they only gave me the job, we would win the contract.
	External: It is fate, its out of my hands	Don't give me the position, I'll only lose the contract
Paranoia	Everything people say and do is a reaction to you. Assuming you are the cause of a negative event out of your control.	He said it was a team weakness, but I know it was meant for me.
	Always comparing self to others.	I'll never be as good as her
Non- accountability	Always putting the blame on others. Having a victim mentality.	He forced me to say that because of his poor introduction.
Downgrading the positive	Rejecting a positive experience by insisting it doesn't count for some reason or another	It doesn't matter if I write well. I'm still a poor speaker.
Should statements and judgments	Hearing the collective voices of perceived authorities ... (mother, father, teacher, professor, peers, priest) coming through you, saying you should do this do this or you should be that. (Guilt)	I should be able to..... I should be more......
	Directing should statements to others (anger and frustration projection)	They should be able to ..... They should be more ....

Figure 16.2 The voices in our head that create our negative reality.

The Compassionate Observer

> The ability to observe without evaluating is the
> highest form of intelligence.
> —Jiddu Krishnamurti

Our inner voice becomes our guiding principle for life. Depending on how we have been parented and supported in our younger life, this inner voice can be negative, harsh, and critical or even benign with reasonable shoulds and shouldn'ts that keep us appropriate, disallowing our impulses, not rocking the boat, keeping us in our comfort zone. It is never more present than when we come to try something new and follow our passion and longing. As we move further and further into the unknown, this voice gets louder and larger, and this "threshold guardian" will try to keep us in perceived safety. This is a good sign, for it usually means we are right on track and getting nearer to our objective. The nearer we get, the louder it shouts. If we listen this can result in paralyzing fear that halts onward progress. Sometimes it is extremely hard to hear anything except this critical internalized voice, and yet each of us also possesses a compassionate objective observer self. How do we contact this observer self? Through the practice of centering, finding the still point within and exploring even more deeply our inner landscape. This enables us to push past those limiting boundaries of distorted thought processes and internalized voices of the past.

Golden Key

There is an image present wherever we see a negative pattern in our lives, whenever and wherever we seem stuck and unable to change. If we are attracting troublesome people or certain types of negative events into our lives, an image always underlies this.

❖ **See "The Energetic Highway," Practice 11: Identity and Images.**

Dissolution of the Ego

As we begin the process of change and challenge our long-held beliefs and thoughts about the nature of reality, fear inevitably arrives. It is the fear of the ego that the persona we believe ourselves to be will be annihilated. This is the same fear that comes when we experience a job loss, a bereavement, the end of a relationship, the prospect of death—anything that challenges our status quo and leaves us feeling out of control, anything that threatens our perceived safety in any area of our lives. This is then usually projected onto the outside environment as blame for whatever and whomever it is perceived caused the event wave. Our defense strategies become heightened, and we adopt a masking persona to hide behind.

This mask is the image that we present to others when our sense of identity is threatened in any way. It is inauthentic and unreal, concerned with putting on a show rather than being in the present moment. It does not allow our vulnerability, humility, or even our authentic feelings to show up. We pretend everything is fine as the reality created by our dualistic intentions begins to shatter and fade. We wear our disguise because this is how we have navigated our way through life and we believe this is how we are supposed to be in order to be accepted and have our needs met. We all know people whose low self-esteem causes them to pump' themselves up in the façade of power, people who use a disguise of love and through constant submission allow their own exploitation, superior beings that withdraw because they cannot accept their own negative traits as they are reflected back in the mirror of life.

These masks can be difficult for us to recognize without the reflective mirror of the objective world. We believe our identity is totally the roles we play in material life and the disguises we wear. We become so buried in this identity that when its dissolution occurs, usually through a crisis of some kind, we feel lost and alone. As the old identity starts to dissolve, there is, for a period, a vacuum where we no longer know who we are.

Sadness can arise as the ego starts its deconstruction. The emerging realization of the true nature of reality and the feeling of having wasted valuable parts of living investing in an illusory world can cause a deep sadness, as well as a grief process for the sense of loss we feel as the shattering of the personality self occurs—particularly when we start to see more clearly how we have caused our own separation from our own higher aspects. The realization of how we have clearly given our power away and annihilated, abandoned, betrayed, repressed, rejected, used, and exploited ourselves can often result in a mourning process. It is important to allow this to upwell and pass through our bodies and energy fields. Eventually the vacuum gives way to a more stabilized physical expression, balance of the emotions, and clarity of mind as our consciousness begins to open more fully to the influence of the soul expression.

When fear arises breathe deeply and bring your conscious awareness to your heart space. Bring the fear to this space and allow it to just dissolve. It may help to visualize your fear in whatever form it emerges for you, and in bringing this to the heart center, see, hear, and feel it being enveloped by rose-white light radiating from your heart until the form disintegrates. It does.

"I Am" Affirmations as Tools for Change

"I am" is one of the most powerful phrases in our language. Language and sound are vibrating energy, and what follows *"I am"* creates our reality. As we think, write, see, and speak our affirmation, we trigger experiential imagery and create a new vibrational signature in our personal bioenergy field that will register and resonate with like vibrational energy patterns in the field of quantum potential. Use this phrase well and wisely to reveal your magnificent self as cocreator with the universe.

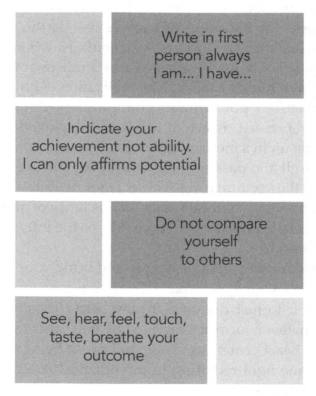

Figure 16.3. Affirmations.

Affirmation Tips

Be personal	You cannot do this for another. Use personal pronoun I always
Be in the Now	Describe yourself as you wish to be. "I have the job". "I have graduated from college." "I AM intelligent." "I AM grateful."
Balance your affirmations	Review all areas of your life and see which is important or lacking: relationship; work; rest; play; personal development; studies
Be realistic	If you can envisage doing; having; being; project your vision as far as you can at this stage. If you set something so far ahead that you cannot see it, then it is not realistic at this stage. We create in incremental stages; step by step; not always knowing the total picture but intuiting the next step.
Indicate achievement	I CAN equals you have the potential. I AM means you are it.
Use action and emotion	Life is a moving picture. Use words that cause your picture to move.
Visualize the future in the present	Use powerful words of feeling in the present tense. I forgive myself. I AM forgiveness. I trust myself. I AM trusting. I AM wise. I AM wisdom. I AM peace. I AM abundant. I AM grateful. I AM safe.

Figure 16.4.

❖ See "The Energetic Highway," Practice 12: *"I Am"* Affirmations.

Meditation and Mindfulness

Through meditation, contact with the higher aspects of our consciousness is deepened and strengthened and gradually brings about the infusion of the causal (soul) and monadic (spirit) qualities to the personality self. The practice of centering is a perfect tool to use for initiating longer periods of meditation. Once the still point has been reached and the mind is quiet and peaceful, practice just sitting in this state. If thoughts or feelings come in, let them pass through, using the breath to return to the still point of alignment—no judgment, just acceptance and letting go.

Our purpose is to build a fully coherent personal energetic system in order to allow a synchronized fusion of the personality self with the higher frequencies of consciousness. Regular meditative practice enables higher consciousness to use the human mind to initiate action in accordance with the individual's higher purpose. In effect, contact with our higher aspects allows stimulation of the receptive mind and opens the heart center. It accelerates and implements the process by which the individual begins to identify with unity consciousness, and personal needs/desires eventually become transmuted into unconditional being. In order for this to happen, the lower self must relinquish its hold on the personality through mastery of the emotional and mental functions and become subservient to the "supervision" of the soul and the spirit.

Common Elements of Meditative Practice

> ❖ Focus of attention
> ❖ Relaxed breathing
> ❖ Quiet setting
> ❖ Comfortable position

Meditation has been practiced for thousands of years, originally to deepen the understanding of the sacred and mystical forces of life; and even though nowadays it is more commonly used for relaxation and stress reduction, regular practice is key to quieting the mind and allowing the higher vibrations of consciousness to work within the lower bioenergy fields. It is an incredible tool for focusing the attention and eliminating "monkey mind"—the jumble of never-ending thoughts streaming through our mind. It gives rise to a sense of calm, peace, and balance, helping manage stressful situations and negative emotions by increasing self-awareness and focusing on the present moment. These benefits continue throughout the day and night, long after we finish our practice. There is also a mounting body of scientific research to demonstrate the positive effect meditation has on managing health conditions such as anxiety, asthma, cancer, depression, heart disease, high blood pressure, pain, and sleep problems.[237]

There are a variety of different ways to meditate, and it pays to try them all to find which method suits you. It may be that you will use a combination of styles in your practice.

Mindfulness Meditation

The practice of mindfulness meditation develops an increased awareness and acceptance of living in the present. It encourages the meditator to bring attention inward to focusing on what is being experienced in the moment. The meditator observes thoughts and emotions that arise, letting them pass through without judgment or condemnation—just noticing, bringing the attention and focus inward rather than outward and then letting go.

Guided Meditation

This is usually done either with a live facilitator or an audio transmission and uses imagery and visualization techniques of relaxing places and situations. It very often calls upon all the senses, using sight, sound, texture, fragrance, and taste to bring the meditator into deep relaxation and altered consciousness.

Mantra Meditation

This technique uses the silent repetition of a word, thought, or phrase to focus the mind and prevent activating the thought process.

Transcendental Meditation

This is similar to the mantra meditation except a personal mantra is assigned by a teacher and this is repeated in a specific way. It allows the body to settle into profound rest and relaxation, and the mind achieves peace.

Qi Gong Meditation

This is an ancient Chinese practice, meaning literally the cultivation of life energy, and uses the alignment of physical body exercises with breath and mind. It is a moving meditation, using slow flowing movement with deep rhythmic breathing, and is characterized by a calm and meditative mind-set.

Tai Chi Meditation

Similar in character to Qi Gong and derived from Chinese martial arts, this uses slow, graceful movements together with breath work to calm the mind.

Yoga Meditation

Asanas (postures) and controlled breathing promote flexibility of the body and a calm mind. The asanas require balance and concentration and therefore focus of the mind in the present moment. Combined with controlled breath work, they create a powerful moving meditation.

Meditation can be done in many ways: lying, sitting, standing, walking, moving, even lovemaking. As our consciousness expands and we begin to achieve mastery of our thoughts and emotions, eventually our whole life becomes a mindful meditation, a practice of being present in the now moment, fully connected to the self and our environment. Being in nature is a wonderful way to connect with one's feelings and essence. Everything is connected, and all creation conspires to support that connection. Nature calms the mind and relaxes the body. We are all part of nature and cannot survive without a healthy environment. Gratitude, appreciation, and recognition of the self and our oneness with planet earth deepens our connection to the self, mother earth, and all that is.

❖ **See "The Energetic Highway," Practice 13: Meditation.**

CHAPTER 17

The Power and Intelligence of the Heart

Love is the most healing force in the world, nothing goes deeper than Love. It heals not only the body, not only the mind but also the soul. If one can Love then all one's wounds disappear. The innermost core of one's being can be healed only through Love.

Those who know the secret of Love know the greatest secret of life.

—Osho

Come to the still spaciousness of your heart and breathe deeply. Acquaint yourself with the home of your soul. Hear the sounding of your great heart beating. It is powerful beyond measure.

Science has demonstrated the power and intelligence of the heart. The "intuitive" heart is the key regulatory organ in the physical body and continually communicates information to the brain and the body via its electromagnetic field. Remember, its energy field is far greater than the brain field, and its electrical component is sixty times higher in amplitude. It is our true power center. Science has confirmed it receives information *before* the brain from outside the normal physical time line. The "heart brain" then sends this information to the "head brain," where it is processed and sent out to the physical body. We are constantly connected to each other and to all life through the incredible energy fields of our hearts.

Science has also shown that positive feelings such as love, gratitude, and appreciation bring our bodies into coherence and allow access to the intelligence of the heart. Our lives and our perceptions have been conditioned by how we think and then translated into a feeling as a response to that thought. In order to live from the heart, it becomes necessary to leave the thinking, linear mind behind and listen in to the wisdom of our hearts. This is why it is so important to bring our awareness inward to our bodies: presence, ground, and center. Incoherence in our system reduces our possibility to connect and listen in to the voice of the heart and its wisdom. The lower mind can conceptually understand the idea of wholeness and unity, but we can only experience this through the heart mind.

Based on our map of consciousness, the heart is the gateway to the soul's longing and mediates the higher energies so that we can know and live our true purpose. When we are on purpose, we feel peace, joy, acceptance, and forgiveness. This creates a radiating energy in our energy field that radiates out to and affects all life. The body tells us when we are on purpose because this is experienced as a feeling in all the cells of the physical body. It is excitement, joy, aliveness, enthusiasm. The wonder and innocence of the child is reclaimed as we explore all the possibilities that open up for us. We feel liberated and empowered by openheartedness.

The heart has *fully* opened when the desire to help and serve others becomes the impelling urge and central purpose of our lives and its great wisdom has discerned the difference between caretaking and caregiving. The heart center creates a bridge between the lower densities of the matter of the physical objective world and the higher frequencies of the spiritual dimensions, where there is no longer time or duality. Connection, empowerment, inclusion, sharing, collaboration, supporting, caring, agreement, accommodation, creativity, and peace become our ways of being and feeling. Forgiveness, acceptance, equanimity, and love become our tools to navigate the way through all life's trials and challenges. Our behavior reflects understanding and wisdom as we experience our cocreations with others as opportunities to learn and show up in a different way than before. When the heart is fully open and in total coherence, it enables the formation of a powerful scalar field of healing energy that radiates out to all points in space at once and along the time line. When a wounding of the heart is healed in the now space, it is also healed in those we are connected to on all the time lines of our existence. When we forgive, love, and accept ourselves and forgive, love, and accept another, even though he or she may no longer be on the physical plane, we change the energy matrix, and everything in it changes. With that thought in mind, let us look at the true purpose of relationship.

The Transpersonal Self

The transpersonal self is the soul. The forward, progressive movement of the spiritual energy of higher will is the cause of the evolution of the transpersonal self. This energy is governed by the law of synthesis, purposed in blending the lower aspects of our nature with the higher aspects of our being and culminating in merging with the one unity consciousness. Imprinted by the will aspect of the spiritual self, the soul-self manifests as a spiraling energy. The path is not a straight line. It is a spiral, causing a continual revisitation to aspects of life and our reality we thought we understood and yet revealing even deeper truth on the turn of the upward spiral. The purpose of the soul is an expansion of its consciousness for the purpose of development and evolution and an eventual return to spirit, bringing back all that has been learned to the whole. The human spirit holds the projected personality self in objective manifestation in order that it may contact matter through the mediation of the soul. The rotary motion of the energy of matter creates the spherical form of the atoms and the energy bodies that comprise the lower bodies of the personality self (physical, emotional, mental, and etheric). In its movement it is a separating and outward movement of energy. An example of this is the movement of electrons within the atom. Energetically, the soul purpose is to enliven this separating energy and cause its upward spiraling movement through the consciousness centers of the human bioenergy body so that it may join with the higher frequencies of consciousness on the spiritual plane. The relationship among these three centers of energetic motion—rotary, spiral/cyclic, and progressive—creates the evolutionary pulse of each human being and is ultimately responsible for the synthesis of the personality self with the soul and the spiritual self.

Soul Purpose

* ❖ Gain experience of the lower planes of matter
* ❖ Allow spirit to contact matter
* ❖ Acquire deep self-knowledge
* ❖ Achieve mastery and control of matter
* ❖ Attain cosmic adulthood
* ❖ Expand consciousness

The energy of love is the vitalizing energy factor of the soul and all thought forms fabricated by the being. The energy of the heart center is invoked to create and manifest all on the physical plane. However, this works imperfectly when we create only from the lower personality self. Few people are adequately in touch with the higher frequency aspects of soul and spirit to build matter on the mental plane that reflects the expression of the thoughts, purpose, and desire of the soul.

The True Purpose of Relationship

The energy of the transpersonal body or soul is love/ wisdom and is the highest radiation of this solar system. Its energy is based on a spiral upward movement and is governed by magnetism and the laws of attraction and repulsion. It is therefore only through *relationship (that is, the attraction to and repulsion of other energetic beings)* that the soul evolves.[238] *This is the true purpose of all relationship.* Our objective world, through the agency of "other," mirrors back to us the thought-forms of our imperfect creations until we get the message and are propelled to explore the inner landscape that conditions the thinking mind. All our relationships, intimate and otherwise, are purposed to help us learn and grow that we may reveal the perfected manifestation of unconditional love. This love is not the personal, sentimental, romantic love that most people think of as love. This is usually based on conditions and attachments, and relationships are entered into to obtain what is believed to be needed to complete us or, worse still, because someone else needs us to be a certain way or do a certain thing.

The love/wisdom aspect underlies all of creation and is omnipresent in all manifested creation. We can never be separated from this, because we are made of it. We are it. The issues of early relationship, great or small, are the foundation of all other relationships in our lives. The protective strategies developed from these real and imagined issues are all based on adaptive measures to obtain love. All are based on need, want, and lack. The transpersonal self is already carrying the energetic signature of this at birth. Its higher purpose is to unify this separated consciousness with the whole being using the vehicle of the personality in the material world. Our relationships, including these earliest, are revealing only that which needs to be brought to our conscious awareness. The crises that occur in our lives are all gifts to wake us up and will keep coming in one form or another until we realize everything is a reflection of our own consciousness. There is nothing outside the self that we need to fulfill us, because we have never been separated from our source and with source energy can cocreate all that we need.

When this is finally realized, it is then we can view the entirety of creation with unconditional love and see the blessings and gifts each being brings to us. We can love without condition or attachment, knowing love is not something we get from another. *Love is something we are.* Until that point we continue to project our consciousness outward and stay in separation. Sometimes the challenges may seem very harsh and hard. This is what our higher being has contracted to do. Sometimes we need the two-by-four hit, orchestrated by the soul with other souls, to enable us to hear, see, and understand the message. This is not about an external God sending us lessons or punishment or demanding retribution.

Our life is our choice to realize our magnificence as cocreators with the source of love in every moment lived, regardless of the challenges. What will you choose? Everything in our lives is a reflection of our consciousness at some level. The creative universe reveals the good, the bad, and the ugly. What is not owned in our self is projected outward onto another. These can be positive qualities as well as not so positive. Someone we really admire mirrors the same in us that maybe is unacknowledged. Anytime there is a strong negative reaction to another, it must be asked, "What is he or she showing me about myself that maybe I am unaware of?" Very often this is a place held in shadow in our consciousness. These parts of self are unacceptable to us, hard to tolerate, or totally rejected and so they are projected outward, for example, judging someone as demanding or cruel rather than experiencing our own demands or cruelty. There may be unconscious attempts to provoke thoughts, feelings, or behaviors in others that are perceived as preserving a form of relationship, for example, "I am used to being in an abusive relationship, and therefore I unconsciously provoke anger in another to fulfill the known way to relate." Sounds crazy, but this is what human beings do. A repressed feeling or perceived threat may elicit a defense strategy evoking in others precisely that which has been projected and which causes the fear to arise. For example, one may be afraid of being abandoned or rejected and behave in a way that pushes the other away and causes the other to abandon or reject us. Our reality simply mirrors our own fears.

Transference

Due to early childhood relationships and subsequent life experience that repeatedly confirms our thoughts about how things are, about 95 percent of the time most human beings are in transferential relationship with each other. Transference happens when we experience a present-day circumstance through the construct of our past conditioning, and so we react to what is happening in the present as if it was the past. It is a projection of our unresolved thoughts and emotional reactions to the past situation. We relate to others based on our memories and expectations, rather than seeing them for who they are and being in the now moment. It is a reactive state of being, where we actually reenact a response to mother, father, and/or numerous other authority figures. It feels very real because it engenders thoughts and emotional reactions and is felt in the body as a physical sensate experience, causing us to believe it is reality. It can be positive as well as negative. Someone kind and caring may remind us of our dear grandmother, and everything the person does is experienced as highly positive; we relate to her from that place. Either way, we are in a transferential relationship with another when reacting from past circumstances, positive or negative, and not seeing or relating to the *real* being in front of us.

Example: A friend makes an innocuous comment about my appearance. I react with intense and exaggerated anger, as if this is a criticism. I am reacting to this comment in a totally disproportionate way. I am relating to what is said from the unconscious conditioning of an upbringing of rigid discipline that required I look appropriate and perfect always, but in the moment I am unaware of this. All I "know" is I am feeling judged and afraid I will lose the relationship because something about me is not perfect. I am feeling and expressing the repressed anger of the past that has been triggered by this new moment in the present. I am not even aware at this stage that my anger is because I am not loved for who I am, as I am, by parents with exactly the same issues. Unfortunately neither I, nor my friend, are aware of this in the moment, and so this has an effect on our relationship in the now.

This is just one example of countless ways we transfer and project our unconscious and habitual patterns that will be played out over and over again. We can spend most of our time in all our relationships, whether intimate, social, or business, acting out these patterns until they are recognized and transformed.

Projection

This is an unconscious defense reaction to experiencing our own repressed and disowned qualities. It could be feelings, fears, fantasies, or desires that are attributed to the other person that have been denied in the self. We become highly judgmental of the other person and have no empathy for him or her, wishing to totally disassociate from the person we are projecting onto. The other person is not conscious of this. Anytime we feel highly critical of another should alert us to the fact that something is going on. The other person is exhibiting something about ourselves that we are not owning. This is a sure sign we need to dig deep into our inner psyche and ask, "What is he or she showing me about me?"

Remember, no one can make you feel anything. We often hear the saying, "Oh, he makes me feel this way; she makes me feel that way." You, and only you, are responsible for the way you feel about anything. It is a choice. We so easily and often blame others "out there" for what we believe is happening to us and how they are making us feel and, of course, may even encourage this because it satisfies our need to be in relationship at any cost. Remember that others have their own issues too and will be unaware of any manipulation because it is satisfying their need to stay in relationship also. It must be emphasized that these strategies are typical human interactions across all types of relationship. Figure 17.1 shows some of the unhealthy ways we maintain relationships.

Issue	Relational attitude	Implicit communication	Induces in other feelings of
Dependency	Helplessness	I can't do this without you	I must look after her/him
Power	Control	You can't do this without me	I'm useless
Ingratiation	Self Sacrifice, Helpfulness	You owe me. If I do this for you, you will do something for me.	I must pay this back in some way. I really appreciate this.
Hostility	Passive-Aggressive	It's your problem	I feel really angry (not usual)
Victim	Provoking	It's not my fault	I feel like its my fault
Sex	Eroticism /Seduction	I'll make you a real man/woman	I feel aroused all the time

Figure 17.1. Unhealthy ways of maintaining relationships.

Beneath all the maneuvers and manipulations of the unconscious mind is the fear of isolation and separation. We act in ways we think will maintain the relationship. These strategies have kept us in relationship with others in the past, and this is how we think we must be and who we think we are. The fear present in any of these adaptive strategies can only be dissolved by looking deeply and honestly within, acknowledging our fears, and risking a new way. This way we take back our responsibility and power in relationship. Whatever issues are underlying the behavior of the other will cease being played out when we stop feeding them with our projection.

Golden Key

Whatever has been rejected or denied in the self creates judgment and anger in the self when it is displayed in another.

❖ **See "The Energetic Highway," Practice 14: Transference and Projection.**

Acts of Connection

"I know you think you know what I said, but are you sure you heard what I meant?"

Our relationship with others is the key to our development and evolutionary growth on the material plane. The physical world of relativity enables us to discover the truth of who we are. Communication (from the Latin *communicare*, meaning to share) is an act of connection and fundamental to all relationship. Exchange of information and meaning is the connecting principle that makes all life possible. From the constant information exchange between our personal bioenergy field and the sea of energy fields in which we live to the complex physical networks that coordinate our cultures and societies, our communications networks are the nervous system that connect us all energetically and physically.

Our work to develop deep contact with the self is crucial for our development of genuine and authentic relationship with another. Contact is a state of opening our awareness and meeting another while also being connected with our self. It does not mean just focusing on the other; neither does it mean physical touch. It is a state of being that reflects our awareness of self and where we are at. The more open and undefended we are, the more deeply we can connect to another, even if the other is in a place of separation. It creates space for the other to be where he or she is at without judgment on our part. It also recognizes our own places of separation and yet we still have the ability to remain in relationship with the other.

Similarly, real listening to another requires being present and open and in receiving mode, not necessarily agreeing with everything you are hearing but allowing the other to be heard and allowing him or her to feel and know he or she is heard. This can be the greatest of gifts. Experience this and give this. When we are fully present within our own being, it is possible to "hear" what is not said; we are able to perceive others in their struggle of separation and "see and experience" them as the greater beings they are in their fullest potential and essence. Energetically, this full presence of self, with a focus of intention to really hear and create an allowing environment for whatever arises, can have a remarkable effect on others, encouraging them to drop their own strategies of protection and risk opening to receive us. Of course, our early conditioning determines how we are in contact and receive others, and through this we may not always hear what is being communicated. It pays to check in by repeating back what you believe you have heard. This can always be confirmed or not by the other and opens the way for our greater understanding. However, the more we understand and are able to listen deeply to the self, the greater our capacity becomes to hear others.

The power of these acts of connection and willingness to stay in relationship with each other even when others may not be fully in relationship with themselves should not be underestimated. Our way of being with another can have a radical effect on the relationship. Whatever we are thinking and feeling is reflected always in our energy field, even if we are not consciously aware of this, and affects the relational field no matter what is being said or heard. When we are in a state of centered stillness and acceptance, with no demand on another to change, it creates a potential space in the relational energy field for transformative energy to engage and unify and may offer the other a new experience. The experience of true connection and communion can be a very beautiful occurrence for both and is a powerful way to create balance and harmony.

Forgiveness

> The real voyage of discovery consists not in seeking new landscapes but in having new eyes.
> —Marcel Proust

Human behavior is a complex issue. However, as the light of understanding pierces through the veils of the past, we can begin to see the self and others in a new way. Introspection leads invariably to new insights and expands our consciousness so that the personality self is transcended and we begin to identify more fully with the group consciousness. We are able to see past the illusory and limiting confines of personal love—its desires, needs, and wants. This does not mean we give up family, friends, and other loved ones, but rather expand our love to include all.

With this comes a deep compassion and forgiveness for all perceived and actual injuries. This does not mean bad behavior is condoned or accepted; it means we no longer carry the burden of pain around the issue, and instead of blaming and shaming, we offer our love to the perceived perpetrator, knowing that throughout time we have all played many roles for each other. We know that all is an illusion and all is one. As our consciousness expands, we come to know we are responsible for all that shows up in our lives through our own thoughts and intentions, urged on by the soul purpose to evolve and grow. In forgiveness, all is released, and through the transforming power of love, both parties have an opportunity to make another choice.

Personal Love

Our entire descent into material form throughout the evolutionary cycles of the soul is purposed to be in duality so that through relationship we can discover and experience perfect, unconditional love. This is what duality means. There is a you and a me, a here and a there, an up and a down. It is through our personal relationships that we get to experience who we are and who we are not. By the choices we make, one way or another, we start to learn about the incredible energy of love. This is what we have come to perfect. We all want to love and be loved. However, for many it is difficult to understand love unless it is manifesting through the human personality. We express the love we know to our intimate partners, family, and friends. Our affection or the feeling of loving becomes centered on a select few. This brings harmony and comfort to us as they fulfill our needs of loving and being loved. However, this is only the training ground for a much greater and grander version of love.

As our consciousness continues to expand through the heart mind, we come into contact with the energy at the root of all existence, the higher frequency of love/wisdom, where there is no separation between us and our fellow human and the love we feel for certain individuals only is experienced unconditionally for all humanity and all life. There is total balance in our energy system, and the personality self, with its desires, needs, and wants, is subjugated to the higher aspects of our being. Love is not limited, as we are not. It is a dichotomy that in order to contact this higher aspect, it is a necessary experience for us to love individuals first, so that we may come to know that the love of a personality self is an illusion. The love sought in one is shining through all. We no longer search or need or desire anything other than to radiate this immense transformational force for good and behold the true quality of love in all we meet. This awareness does not negate our personal relationships, but rather it enhances them. Relationships are no longer based on self-interest nor self-denial of either party. The child consciousness of need is no longer at work to secure emotional comfort. Our full and complete self seeks only to bring and share the love that we are to all.

❖ **See "The Energetic Highway," Practice 15: The Transforming Power of Love.**

CHAPTER 18

Express Your Magnificence

Higher Will

Our soul longs to share its immeasurable and unique aspect of the love/wisdom principle with all creation. The soul expressing through the intuitive heart is the bridge between the lower dimensions of the personality and the higher dimensions of consciousness, which are constantly pouring their gifts forth to humanity in accordance with the overall evolutionary plan. Only through the transpersonal self/soul's mediation do these higher frequencies reach our physical, emotional, and mental energy bodies and ultimately the physical self. However, once this has occurred and the twelve energy vortices of the heart are fully opened, the higher frequencies of will, unconditional love, and higher mind are able to greatly accelerate the connection to universal consciousness so that the individual, earth, and humanity can experience love, peace, harmony, and joy as a daily living experience. This requires the surrender of the personal will to the higher will aspect by aligning our intention, actions, and behavior for the highest good of all in accordance with the higher principles of unconditional love and higher mind. This surrender means letting go of our need to personally control our lives and handing this directly over to the guiding power of our higher will aspect. It means adopting an attitude of acceptance and gratitude, knowing that all our experiences on earth are designed to accelerate our growth. It means giving our self time, space, patience, and love.

As we begin the relationship with these higher aspects of our being, this demands trust in the support and guidance we receive. This is why mastery of the emotional and mental faculties is paramount. This dissolves fear, worry, and anxiety about the future and allows us to clearly receive the guidance and follow it unwaveringly in order for us to be in the flow of our own creative life pulse, without resistance. The more our lower personality will becomes aligned with our higher will aspect, our true creative purpose begins to unfold, and our next steps become clearer and clearer. The urge to express our magnificence and our gifts for the benefit of all our brothers and sisters becomes an impelling force. Every single one of us has a gift that longs for expression. This is always connected to that which brings us the most joy. Our deepest passion that burns within may have been spurned and denied because of our limiting thought forms, our preoccupation with the practicalities of physical living and of how we perceive our lives are supposed to be based on preconditioning.

Once connected to our higher aspects, anything and everything is possible. It may be service through culture: music, art, literature, theater, film, dance, sport. It may be education and teaching. It could be the sciences and scientific discovery. It could be building a conscious business or a new world spirituality that encompasses all faiths and beliefs. It may be parenting, caregiving, or social service. It could be a passion for health care, well-being, and fitness. It may lie in governance and developing social structures that are sustainable for all. It may be care for the environment, nature, the animal kingdom. Whatever is your passion and ignites your enthusiasm and joy is undoubtedly the key to your purpose, and every human being, without exception, has incredible and undeniable magnificence to share with humanity.

Handing over our lives to higher will is a step-by-step process of trust, surrender, acceptance, and deep knowing that we are supported and held by a magnificent universal intelligence that can be accessed instantly, constantly, and without fail. It takes time and practice, and there are many acts of surrendering required to enable the imprinting of higher will energy to fully engage the totality of our being. The best news is we also have incredible help and support always available to us through our guidance system. We are never, ever alone. Our daily practices of centering and meditation become vital in shifting the energy and the emphasis and really aid in the development of the willpower to keep exploring our consciousness at these deeper levels.

Guidance

Guidance is always available to us no matter where we are in our development. We are never separate from this or alone. It is up to us to pay attention. As children many of us had senses that were very highly developed, only to be shut down as our perceptions of reality altered due to our environmental conditioning. All through our development as a human being, we have been receiving guidance, initially through what we know as conscience, the inner sense of what is right and wrong based on our beliefs, assumptions, thoughts, and value system—all of which have been influenced by how we perceive the universe. However, at any time we can open to receive from the higher dimensions of the holographic field in which we are immersed.

Science has now shown us the evidence of the knowing of the intuitive heart. This powerful energy field is receiving information before the brain and the rationalizing mind and innately "knows" before we become conscious that we know something. This we can trust. This is the higher aspect's knowing directing the lower personality self and is the first form of guidance. This knowing of the heart is felt in the body as it relays the messaging to the brain that subsequently informs the body. This is the origination of the gut feeling that most have experienced at some time or other. It usually is a feeling of discomfort when we perceive something or someone as being out of integrity. Our study of the various energy fields of the universe has demonstrated our personal bioenergy field is in constant communication with all other fields of existence. As our awareness of higher energy frequencies expands, so do the five senses through which reality is perceived.

The five physical senses through which the objective world is perceived become heightened as we clear away the psychic energy debris from our energy fields and the higher aspect's vibration becomes more influential. Our boundaries expand to encompass more and more of all that is. The entire universe conspires to bring us guidance and confirmation to all our questions through all our senses and all our being. All we need do is open our awareness to what is showing up in our bodies, in our minds, and in our lives. All is the mirror of our consciousness.

- ❖ **Hearing:** becomes clear hearing (clairaudience), eventually telepathy.
- ❖ **Seeing:** becomes clear seeing and highly developed insight (clairvoyance).
- ❖ **Touch:** becomes sensitive to the finer vibrations we are now able to resonate with.
- ❖ **Taste:** becomes more sensitive and refined. We no longer have an appetite for lower vibrational energy foods.
- ❖ **Olfaction:** may become more sensitive.
- ❖ **Intuition:** strengthens; it is clear and infallible.
- ❖ **Knowing:** (clairsentience); when this occurs there is no longer need for a reliance on the other senses.

If we require specific guidance, information can become available through the dream state. There may be visions of perceived past time lines, in or out of dream state, if this is helpful for the progression of the soul. Very often information is downloaded during meditative practice or after practice. Development and refinement of the senses is a normal part of an expansion of consciousness and yet should not become the goal. Each being is unique and will receive guidance in his or her own unique way. Psychic development is not our goal. It is only an effect as we expand our consciousness. There may be good reasons that a specific sense may not expand as fully as another or at the same rate. This is when nonattachment and acceptance become a necessary way of being. These may be the very qualities the transpersonal self is developing, so do not be attached to how you receive your guidance or compare yourself with others. Trust that all is perfect in its unfolding for you.

It is possible to receive guidance from your higher self, a guide, the devic kingdom (angelic beings who have not taken the human evolutionary path), a master (one who has trodden the path before us), solar and galactic light beings, or even cosmic mind. There is an entire hierarchy of beings who are able to transmit and impress our minds with information. They are all part of the hologram we are. In each tiny part exists the whole. All that is required is that we open our awareness to this. Books, art, music, film, and particularly nature—plant, animal, and mineral—are frequently used as tools for imparting information. Being clear about what you want to know is a good practice. Receiving without any preconception and being open to what shows up, not being attached to the method or making comparisons with others—such practices ensure a respectful attitude to our questioning. We can certainly call upon the masters who have trodden the path ahead of us and invoke the devic realms for support and help on the journey of unfolding and information transfer. Our overall purpose is to synthesize our lower being with the higher part of ourselves. The more we call upon the wisdom of our own higher self and the higher dimensions of consciousness and *practice* tuning in to their frequencies, the faster this bridging will be accomplished. Like any relationship, the more we honor the practice, the more fruitful it becomes.

Golden Key

You hold all the answers within. Trust yourself and your inner knowing. Your intuitive heart holds the key. In order to develop and strengthen our trust and surrender to higher will, we are often shown only the next step rather than the whole plan. We may receive guidance that does not make sense to the linear mind. Sometimes it will demand from us what may seem incredulous and outlandish action that may not fit in with what our linear mind "thinks" it knows or the direction in which we "think" we are heading. However, if we trust, accept, and surrender, we are inevitably led to that which is perfect for our growth and development.

❖ **See "The Energetic Highway," Practice 16: Receiving Guidance.**

The Nature of Pleasure

The child experiences an intense flow of energy and pleasure simply by being alive.
—Susan Thesenga

Suffer little children to come unto me, for such is the Kingdom of Heaven.
—Master Jesus

Pleasure is our birthright. It is simultaneously a physiological experience, an awakening of consciousness, an opening of the heart, surrender to the creative flow of life, and an expression of our innate magnificent self. Physiologically and energetically, pleasure is the felt sensation of the energy of the life force running unobstructed through the physical body. There is only one life force that energizes all expressions of life, and this can flow in a positive and life-affirming manner or can be turned into a destructive, negative current. However, it is all the same energy. The energy itself is not polarized. This living, energetic flow produces pleasurable sensations for all perceiving consciousness in all living organisms; all move toward realizing this potential in nature. The more fully the consciousness is developed, the greater the pleasure is experienced as the flow of energy. When this natural flow is impeded in any way, either by inner or outer conditions, the energy current is halted and diverted and attaches itself to whatever condition is being expressed. This is important to note, as the energy itself is intrinsically the same; it is the *expression* that changes.[239]

If a child meets with conditions in his or her outer environment that stop the natural flow of his or her pleasure current, the extent of the damage depends on how free the energy system is from existing inner blockages. There may be none. Where there is no previous block, there will only be a temporary disturbance in the flow. However, there may be existing blockages lying dormant because they have not been eliminated in previous time lines. A problem or unhelpful way of being that persistently shows up in life is based on such an energy block. If this is the case, then the outer negative condition in the current life experience is not totally responsible for the block but acts as a trigger to bring the dormant condition into the forefront of our conscious awareness. Each life occurrence that is experienced as unpleasant, problematic, or anxiety-producing is a result of the original event distortion.

These energy blocks present in the energetic system start to shift as exploration of the psyche opens our awareness to our issues, our behavioral strategies, our faulty beliefs and images, our self-talk and imagined voices of authority, our transference, and our destructive, dualistic intentionality. This investigation leads us to uncover the separated consciousness that longs for unity, and yet still there is struggle to manifest the pleasure and fulfillment of our magnificence. There may be frustration when, after all our attempts to transform our lives, we still are attracting relationships and events that seem to validate the old way of being. It feels like there is still a block to bringing our longing and passion to the world. This is a sure sign that there is a negativity payoff at work.

Beware the Negativity Payoff

Our emotional experiences are a result of how we interpret an experience. Our experiences of pain and pleasure are personal interpretations based on our perspective at the time. Research by Dr. David Borsook at Harvard Medical School[240] has shown that pain and pleasure activate the same circuits in the brain. Very often a child who grows up with inadequate or unconscious caregiving adapts to any real or perceived lack of love or healthy attachment. As yet, the small child is unable to perceive the difference between positive and negative life circumstances. Life is experienced as one continuous flow of energy and pleasure. The child loves his or her parents and wants and needs to be in their presence to feel safe and secure however they behave. The child can attach the energy of the love and pleasure currents he or she naturally feels to being in their presence, even if this is inadequate or negative, and comes to equate this lack of fulfillment and negativity with the feelings of pleasure and the giving and receiving of love.

This distortion is imprinted energetically into the energy matrix and becomes part of the energy signature, particularly if there is already an existing prenatal energy constellation. This then creates a potent inertia in the energy system and holds the negative attachment in place. Because the painful experience comes to be associated with pleasure, it is carried forward into adulthood and is perpetuated throughout life with very little incentive to change. Stagnation of this type actually requires a lot of unconscious effort to sustain resistance against the natural inclination for growth. This distortion can demonstrate in a variety of ways, all of which inhibit our ability to access and feel the true and real pleasure principle that is our birthright and flows from the harmonious experience of life.

In relationship adults recreate the way they were related to as a child. They reprise their childhood role in the family configuration, not only because it is a familiar pattern but also because they feel the pleasure of the child in full energetic flow. The payoff is the adult now derives pleasure from operating in this familiar negative family distortion. It is safe and comforting and upholds the family "values," even though they are negative. Or the adult now adopts the old parental behavior and role as a way to avoid and compensate for unresolved painful feelings in childhood. The payoff is the pleasure of the revenge of possibly controlling or punishing others as this adult may have been treated as a child. This is unconscious and is transferential. In the adult life, the other becomes the parent substitute and receives the punishment. Or there can be pleasure derived from keeping a state of victimhood going. The payoff becomes feeling the distorted pleasure of the victim rather than the shame, guilt, and fear that now have come to be associated with the positive energy of the real pleasure current.

It is an extremely powerful energy distortion and can keep us fixed in our old patterns of behavior even when we are fully aware of them. It also severely limits our development until it is addressed.[241]

Examples of the Negativity Payoff

Circumstance	Familiar expression	Compensatory expression
Felt love on earning approval	Suppresses needs and longings, pleasure in struggling to prove self and earning acceptance from others	Demands others perform, prove they are worthy
Felt judged and controlled	Pursues partners or employers who are judgmental, controlling	Judges and controls others OR withholds love in the face of judgment and control
Emotionally or physically abused	Derives pleasure from abusive adult relationships; victim experiencing cruelty, humiliation, power over	Is a cruel perpetrator of abuse
Contradicted, invaded or emasculated by a smother mother or authoritarian father, Not allowed to individuate	Derives pleasure from dependency and caretaking roles	Attempts to punish and have control over others OR pushes others away

Figure 18.1.

Even though we may be aware of the negativity in our intention or action, the pleasure derived from the behavior prevents the motivation or inspiration to change. The connection between pleasure and destructive negativity is the reason that many humans feel guilt about the experience of pleasure, and yet the desire for the original constructive and life-affirming experience keeps them locked in a destructive expression of this. Life and pleasure are one and the same; even if it is linked to destructiveness, it cannot be given up. The destructive current needs to unfold, express, and reconnect to its original expression.

Exercises for identifying and addressing the destructive behaviors of negative pleasure require even deeper exploration of what is working and what is not working, as well as *absolute honesty*, to be effective. They require a drastic change in self-perception and a deep inquiry into the circumstances of our lives. This engenders a high resistance. However, this resistance shows us we are very close to the golden treasure hidden in our negativity. It is then possible for us to reframe the old imprinting and effortlessly anchor in new ways of being that allow us to be in the creative flow of our lives and experience the greatest true pleasure and joy in this.

❖ See "The Energetic Highway," Practice 17: Addressing the Negative.
❖ See "The Energetic Highway," Practice 18: Anchoring the Positive.

The Creative Power of Sound

By harmony all phenomena are formed and sustained. There is a scientific statement to the effect that this earth is a vast harmonic wave system that is built and sustained by unheard music.

—Corinne Heline (1882–1975)

Each celestial body, in fact each and every atom, produces a particular sound on account of its movement, its rhythm or vibration. All these sounds and vibrations form a universal harmony in which each element, while having its own function and character, contributes to the whole.

—Pythagoras (569–475 BC)

Electric energy first manifests as vibration. It is the vibrating impulse or first sound that awakens matter into activity by creating photons of light and thereby all that is perceived in physical manifestation. Science has shown us sound has the power to activate, manipulate, and affect matter. Research has shown that DNA responds to sound and the human voice. Not only the content of our speech but also the energy with which this is expressed has a profound effect on our own bioenergy field and all other energy fields to which we are connected. All speech is sounding energy that creates energetic forms that reverberate through time and space. Words create an energy signature that is a blueprint and design expressing the entirety of our consciousness at any given moment and an energizing force for the manifestation of all that is known, experienced, and felt. Words can express our knowledge, plans, opinions, feelings, attitudes, intentions, thoughts, and desires. In the process of creation, first there is thought, then word, then action. These three reveal our will in any situation, whether it is the lower will or the higher will aspect, unconscious or conscious.

Speech is yet another very powerful aspect of our creative abilities, and therefore it serves us to be mindful when speaking and to use this wisely, graciously, and consciously. We have explored the power of affirmation and looked at the language of crazy making. Figure 18.2 reflects both speech that limits our potential to manifest our gifts and be of service to the whole of creation and speech that enables our growth into our own magnificence.[242]

I won't	Using forcing personality will energy with a negative intention creates block to creation
It is hard	Is a command to any situation and that is what it will become - HARD.
I don't believe	Limiting Conditioning
I am a skeptic	Closes to possibility, negates energy flow
I don't like it	Will never learn, blocks opportunity for growth
I am trying, I will try, I can try	Stating you are trying to do something creates just that.... TRYING. It is never ending and non achieving
I can do it	This is a command to the self; what follows is achievement
I am	Creates your reality
I believe	Whatever you believe becomes your reality
I know	This is a body sensation of infallible, intuitive knowing
It is done	Unconditional knowing, acceptance and surrender to

Figure 18.2. Negative versus positive speech.

It is possible to infuse our words with great power. Through the agency of sound, we are able to build in matter more accurately, and our thought forms become more strongly vitalized and are therefore able to perform their function with a greater precision. Through speech we bring our intention and thought out of the abstract and into materialization. By using mantras, invocations, and decrees, it is possible to build outcomes in matter, for the laws of speech are the laws of matter. All is vibrating energy. Our words create an energetic frequency signature of our will and intent and set the building particles of form into motion. It is useful to remember that when we use invocation, we *call forth, entreat, or ask* substance and beings of a *higher vibration* and *summon and command* substance or beings of a *lower vibration*. This, of course, is dependent on our level of multidimensional awareness.

CHAPTER **19**

The Significance of the Head Energy Centers

Through the dedicated exploration of our inner landscape, there is a shift from a physical-based reality to a consciousness-based reality. A transformation and expansion of our perception occurs as we transcend the lower personality structures of limiting beliefs about the nature of the self, and we now identify with the higher aspects of our being. As this connection to the transpersonal self strengthens and develops, this allows for even deeper connection to the absolute inner core of our being, the monad/spiritual or higher self. We begin to contact our essential nature, and our consciousness experiences a further expansion.

The scientific studies in part 1 of this book have demonstrated the holographic nature of the brain and its role as an antenna and quantum processor of electromagnetic wave energies carrying information. There are energy centers in the head correspondent to each of the energy vortices present in the bioenergy field. As we move though our life processes and clear energy blockages and distortions, the corresponding head center becomes energized and activated. For those kinesthetically sensitive, these can be felt on the surface of the scalp as they come into fuller activation. Through the fusion of the transpersonal self with the personality self and the perfected alignment of our intentionality with, and unconditional surrender to, the monadic aspects of the higher will, love/wisdom, and active intelligence of the higher mind principles, we become clear and purified vessels that receive and integrate these higher frequency energies unimpeded. The head energy centers have reprogrammed, reconfigured, enlivened, and activated, reflecting the development of the bioenergy field centers as we move through the journey of transformation and transcendence to know and experience our full essence at transfiguration.

As the whole bioenergy field begins to reconfigure during the processes of transformation and transcendence, the vibrations of the higher frequency energies containing the new light language-encoded particles activate the pineal gland in the head. This tiny gland contains crystallized light receptors that act in the same way as the rods and cones in the physical eye retina in perceiving light. However, our physical eyes are limited to vision of the light frequencies in the spectrum between infrared and the ultraviolet light range. The receptors in the pineal gland are very small and have been found to be calcite microcrystals (calcium, carbon, and oxygen) with piezoelectric properties similar to those found in the ear.[243] The pineal allows us access to light frequencies above the normal range of the human eye. These receptors can process intensely higher vibrations of photons and provide the light and color in the higher dimensions of the inner world landscape and also in the outer world scape. Here objects glow iridescently from within rather than perceived as the reflected light of the physical eyes in the physical dimension. The higher frequencies of light activate the pineal and can also be perceived as high-pitch sound signals through the hearing mechanism of the body as information waves are downloaded into the brain processor through the now heightened senses. As we now access, receive, and integrate this higher frequency information, this activates our source memory, and we begin to perceive objective reality in a very different way.

Imagination as a Creative Tool

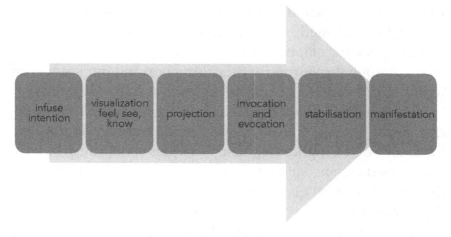

Figure 19.1. The creative process of visualization.

Use of the imagination is a powerful tool in the creative toolbox. It can also help to shift old patterns that no longer serve us. It can be used to create and recreate any experience we choose. It helps to build confidence in our positive traits and, using a multisensory approach, creates very vivid images that can help control anxiety, anger, and frustration. The example below shows how to use this tool after setting an intention to manifest a particular outcome. Once the intention is brought to the space of the heart and infused with the energy of love, at this point we can use our imagination to visualize the intention. For example, I *see* myself sitting at a desk, writing a book. Maybe I *see* the cover, the typeface, the illustrations. I *see and hear* myself talking on radio, on TV, on the web about my book. I *see and hear* myself teaching others from this book material. I *feel* in my body what this feels like—fulfillment, joy, excitement. I *know* this is happening. I project this vision onto my mind screen. I *ask* for the support of the higher energies that are aligned with my purpose. I *charge* the lower energies of active intelligent substance to create this form. I *stabilize* this vision by fully grounding my physical body. I am not attached to the how or where this will happen. I *open* myself to synchronicities of manifestation and wait and closely observe all opportunities that then present themselves. I use discernment to choose the opportunity that matches the vision. Taking action is an essential part of manifestation. So many brilliant ideas and dreams come to nothing because of our inability to ground the idea into the physical dimension. Presence, centering, and grounding once more are essential practices that enable us to take action when an opportunity presents itself. The more we practice conscious cocreation, the more we will perceive our place of resistance and create the means to deal with this. In a sense we cannot lose. If we are mindful and pay attention, either we can create exactly our desired outcome or what does manifest will show us exactly where we are in resistance, bringing in an opportunity to clear the blockage for good. As long as we have a map to recognize the territory, we can see that all is perfect in its unfolding. There are no wrong turns, as all outcomes eventually must lead back to unity. This is the nature and impulse of the evolutionary process, governed by universal law.

❖ See "The Energetic Highway," Practice 19: Visualization.

Dualism and Resistance

As we approach nearer and nearer to unity consciousness, the first experience of unity is an incredible and liberating experience. We may have had glimpses of this throughout life in moments that may be termed peak moments, where there is an experience of oneness with all creation and our source. These moments can be fleeting or can last for a while, but either way they change us forever. The state of unity exists partially at first, and we can experience this in many areas of our lives as our outer circumstances become joyful, vibrant, anxiety-free, and more aligned to our purposes. We are in the flow of life, and synchronicity and intuition lead us on. However, there may still be a misconception held around what unity consciousness actually is. This is usually because there is still a place in the psyche that is deeply affected in some way by fear, doubt, or lack of self-acceptance. These energetic patterns are so deeply ingrained and hidden within our energy system that more work is required to uproot and clear them. Even those who have undergone much personal development work mistake the meaning of unity. There is such a state as spiritual ego, an idealized image of how we think an evolved being should be; such a state is far more tricky to recognize and acknowledge in the self. We may consider ourselves to be further along in our development than we actually are as the dimensions open up to us in our more expanded states of consciousness. This can bring in spiritual pride, and what was an issue at the lower levels still manifests as a distortion in our consciousness and in our way of being.

Because we still exist on the material plane, with its dual nature, we have misconceived the idea of opposites. Everything is categorized as good or bad, right or wrong, black or white. All is classified depending on our value system. We think of unity as being the good in the good versus bad scenario. This is not the case. This is not unification. Unity consciousness means transcending opposites in the full awareness that everything is an illusion. To become polarized with only one side of the equation means there must be opposition to the other side. Polarizing with good and opposing bad is not unification. Our task is to reconcile both sides within the self.[244]

This necessitates a profound honesty and positive intentionality to uncover the ugliest and darkest parts in the psyche, for when these are *acknowledged, understood, accepted, and brought to the light of day,* they can then be *integrated and unified* in our conscious awareness. These negative parts of the self must be admitted into full conscious awareness. This is where our resistance will become its strongest. Resistance obstructs the flow of energy movement and therefore always obstructs the manifestation of the real self.

There are three major resistances:

❖ **Resistance to unity** will not accept the oneness of all, separating the self from others and elevating the self above others. It says, "I am right; you are wrong" or "I know better than you; I will fix you." "I am better/greater than you."

❖ **Resistance of lower will and negative intention:** the dogmatic, closed view that says, "It has to be my way. I resist any other way."

❖ **Resistance and fear as a vicious cycle:** The slowing down of the movement of energy created by resistance limits the vision and experience of life. Life is perceived as fearful, hostile, and frightening. This creates more resistance. Fear and resistance become intertwined, a vicious cycle each feeding the other.

Within the system are two streams of energy: one that longs to develop the self, expand its consciousness, raise its vibration, and manifest its magnificence; and another part that resists the truth that it carries negative feelings, attitudes, and beliefs. It says, "I want all of that but not at the price of exposing or admitting anything that might show me to be bad, inadequate, or afraid." If the will-to -good is stronger than the destructive element, the crisis in the life may be relatively minor. If the destructive element is the stronger, then major crisis may be avoided for quite some time and stagnation follows. However, if the will-to-good movement strengthens and the resistance continues, inevitably an accumulation of energy is created that explodes and destroys the negativity that created it. This is the nature of energy and consciousness. The energy movement of the soul destroys the old negative structure in order that it can be rebuilt in a purer form. The flow of life cannot be extinguished on its evolutionary path to union. This means the outer manifestation of life changes dramatically.[245] Thus we can come to understand and accept that every crisis becomes an integral part of creation. This greater awareness reveals the magnificence of creation, of the universe and our self; deconstruction of the old energy structure no longer serves, and awareness reveals the construction of the new.

The effects of this process can be diminished considerably if we sincerely commit to uncovering our destructive negative intentions and change them to positive, constructive, life-affirming intentionality. We no longer live lives of polarity and the resultant, projected reality, nor do we await crisis in our lives as an impetus for change. At this momentous time in our evolutionary cycle, humanity is being gifted incredible support to hasten our homeward journey.

It is up to each one of us how this affects life. If we have the courage to reach the depths, we have the opportunity to experience the heights. If we can go deep within with humility and sincerity, no matter where we think we are in our development, and really acknowledge our own negativity rather than running away from it, there is no need to create more crisis or drama in our lives. This is the key. What will you choose?

❖ **See "The Energetic Highway," Practice 20: Redirecting Resistance.**

CHAPTER **20**

Our Energetic DNA

DNA is the blueprint for all life. It holds all the coding for the physical body and energy field. Our physical DNA is formed by information transfer from the subtle energy template of the personal human field, which preexists the physical and the morphogenetic field of the species. From these information fields, all matter develops. Currently in the double helix there are two strands of DNA, coiled into a spiral in most human beings.

Scientists at Cambridge University have recently published a paper that confirms four-stranded quadruple-helix DNA structures— known as G-quadruplexes—also exist within the human genome.[246] Their study confirms DNA is dynamic, with structures constantly being formed and unformed. Geneticists claim that one day we will have twelve strands and we are undoubtedly mutating and evolving. Very recent research has also shown that extending the length of the protective ends of the chromosomes called telomeres reverses the aging process of the cell, turning back the internal clock programming.

What was one thought to be junk DNA (around 97 percent of the known existent DNA) is now realized to be a quantum microprocessor of information fields. In order to access our full human potential, the information stored in the dormant energetic DNA is just awaiting the correct multidimensional codes to be activated in order to materialize into form by the higher self mind. The more DNA that is activated, the greater our potential, and the greater the expansion of consciousness that can be realized.

Most humans have two physical strands of DNA, however our DNA has an energy field consisting of at least another ten energetic strands and in some cases many more, holding the dormant codes awaiting activation. The master cell held in the pineal gland, upon receiving the higher frequency information, activates all other cellular behaviors. As we move through our transformational work and are able to receive and metabolize the higher frequencies, this also changes our physical DNA. It is possible for us to do this work ourselves and activate the dormant information; the original blueprint before conditioning, energetic imprinting, and genetic meddling during our evolutionary process can be restored. It is not necessary to wait for mainstream science to catch up, and neither do we need any special equipment. We have the means within our own energetic system to activate these dormant codes, providing us with radiant health and abundance, halting and reversing the aging process, and accelerating the return to our original harmonized blueprint, synchronous with higher will.

We are in the process of changing from a carbon-based human to a more refined physical matter: a silica liquid crystalline being. Clearing more and more discordant energy from our DNA and our energy field enables the higher frequencies to alchemize the substance of the physical and energy bodies, increasing the spin and the frequency vibration of the atoms so that each level of our energy field becomes finer and finer. This includes the physical body. We literally transfigure. We achieve this through our intention, action, thought mastery, and energy work. It is a very exciting and possible prospect. What will you choose? Figure 20.1 shows the energetic blocks to dormant DNA activation.

Energetic Hindrances to DNA Activation

Energetic anatomy distortions	Thought forms
<ul><li>Blocked or torn energy centers</li><li>Mucus and tears in the matrix</li><li>Distortions in the energy channel parallel with spine –perineum to base of skull.</li><li>Broken meridians</li><li>Entangled streamers and relational chords</li><li>Stress webbing</li><li>Soul fragmentation</li><li>Disconnection from transpersonal dimension</li><li>Disconnection from spiritual essence and Higher dimensions</li><li>Distortions and blockages in energy field of organs, tissues, cells and DNA</li></ul>	<ul><li>Fear based discordant, polarized thought-forms (when constantly projected out attract like energy and eventually can develop into an entity)</li><li>Mis-qualified energy streams</li><li>Thought-forms held in the morphogenetic field</li><li>Jumbled and chaotic thought creations</li><li>Unfinished thought creations</li><li>Feelings, beliefs and speech creations</li></ul>
Contracts	**Energetic Implants**
<ul><li>Hereditary energetic signatures passed down the generations</li><li>Personal, familial, country, race, planetary and solar system karma</li><li>Vows, covenants and curses</li></ul>	<ul><li>Unnatural implants from historical planetary influences and previous solar system activities</li></ul>

Figure 20.1. DNA blocks

❖ See "The Energetic Highway," Practice 21: Repelling Negative Energy Field Forces.

CHAPTER 21

At-One-Ment and Integration

Forever is composed of nows.
                    —Emily Dickinson

In the unified state of the absolute, energy and consciousness are one. In the material world of duality, they are not. The dualistic mind creates the illusion that they are two separate manifestations. We divide our holographic world up into neat boxes of perception that do not threaten our comfortable status quo. Energy has been perceived as a mechanical force with very little to do with consciousness. Similarly our thoughts, beliefs, attitudes, feelings, and intentions all seem disconnected from the cause of our lived reality. This is because in our limited view, we have not appreciated or understood the connection between cause and effect nor the connection between energy and consciousness and that it requires focused attention, commitment, and awareness to open our minds sufficiently to comprehend this connection. We believe we know the way things are because that is what we experience with our five senses. Only when our consciousness expands can we have an appreciation of the connection between the incredible power of the mind and the energy it sets into motion.

There are those who perceive the universe as an energetic phenomenon and those who perceive it as pure consciousness. Both are correct, and yet both are very different philosophies and appear to be opposite. It is true both are correct, but each is incorrect when claiming there is only one view. Science, in its search for truth, is now supporting the fact that energy and consciousness cannot be separated.

Similarly in the unified state of the ultimate reality, there is no evil. All thought and intention is positive, constructive, pure, and in truth. Feelings are joyful, loving, and peaceful. Yet consciousness (mind) can change its thoughts, will, and intention into limiting belief systems accompanied by fear, hate, cruelty, and negativity, creating a new distorted version of itself. When this happens the energy changes its manifestation. On the one hand there is no evil, and yet on the level of human manifestation there is. Both statements are true. At the level of the present collective human consciousness, both polarities exist, and the only way to overcome this is to continue with further investigation into self. The mirror of the collective is only reflecting that which is deep within each one of us. When we honestly discover our own negative traits and truly understand the nature of cause and effect, we will never look at another human being in judgment or condemnation but only with the deepest compassion and love.

There is only one true cosmic life stream of energy, and in duality that life stream becomes distorted only by the thought, intention, belief, or feeling it attaches to. This is the magnitude of our ability to create. This is the true meaning of being made in the image and likeness of our source. This is the very genius of the plan for creation. This is the alchemical work of the creative universe, spiritualizing matter. This is what we are doing within our very being. We are alchemists.

As we move into at-one-ment, the frequencies of all the head energy centers are synthesized in the crown. This receives and emits the highest frequencies of integrated spiritual energy, and light can be "seen" emanating from the eyes and around the head and at the top of the head when all are fully activated.

This cohesive energy is our divine presence, our heritage, and our birthright. A deep knowing permeates our being. It has been there all along, just waiting for us to acknowledge and connect. There is a reflection of all that has passed on the journey and a deep understanding of the good and bad experiences that we are now able to evaluate in a totally different way. Everything is understood, even the most tragic conditions, the most sorrowful moments, the most painful events, the negativity that we have harbored within, the knowledge that we are the all of it ... the good, the bad, and the ugly. A deep security penetrates the entire being, knowing that it cannot be harmed or annihilated by suffering of any kind, including death, and that we have cocreated the all of it.

Our perspective changes radically. We realize the work we do on ourselves is done for all and that we are no greater than or lesser than any other. We are no longer afraid of pleasure, knowing we are born to experience joy and fulfillment. There is great clarity of purpose. We become aware of the divine plan for humanity and our place in the scheme of planetary evolution. We operate from our knowing and the active intelligence of the higher mind. All selfish considerations are put aside. All ego considerations are put aside. All judgment is put aside. Fear is gone, and unconditional love resides. Emotional nature and mental activity are in balance and stabilized. The desire nature and its perceived needs subside, and the lower density energies spiral upward, transmuting to higher vibrational creative energy. Our creativity and its expression surge and are irrepressible. We live in the creative pulse of life and *know and feel* its ebbs and flows in our physical bodies, at the cellular level, without the need to work out intellectually what we "should" be doing next.

Our DNA and physical bodies are transfigured and become radiantly healthy. All our thoughts, words, and deeds come under the conscious supervision of the soul and spirit nature. We are able to notice immediately when we are out of integrity in any way. We feel a liberation that brings exquisite feelings of joy, excitement, peace, and wonder. We live with the exuberance and innocence of a child, and we are guided infallibly to our responsibility and role of active service to humanity through the love/wisdom principle of the spiritual soul. There are no longer boundaries of separation, and our experience of time changes dramatically as our perspective reorients to our spiritual experience of the self, observing its physical projection in time and space. The now moment of all life becomes real and is no longer a concept. We are at one with all life. Dualistic conflicts subside. We are no longer separate from our greater self, others, or our world as we operate from a balanced central core of being. Our lives become full of miracles governed by embodied presence, intuition, and synchronicity. There is peace within and peace without.

This is our magnificence and our blessing.

❖ **See "The Energetic Highway," Practice 22: At-One-Ment and Integration.**

The end is the beginning.

PART 3

The Energetic Highway

CHAPTER 22

Introduction to Part 3

"The Energetic Highway" is a series of energetic practices to support and accelerate your journey to magnificence. Each practice is prefaced by a short commentary to remind you of its key purpose. The recommended frequency will be noted at the end of each exercise, and you are invited to keep a journal of anything that comes into your conscious awareness during your practice. This can be a remarkable tool for you to develop an understanding of the self, the body, and your unconscious mind. It aids the process of your unfolding magnificence, keeping you focused, dedicated, and mindful as the miracle of who you are is revealed. Through this deep process of self-reflection and inquiry, the mind and heart are further expanded each time we access an illusion, for unless our thought, word, or action is seeded in love, it is an illusion.

Commentary on Keeping a Journal

Recording what is going on in your process is a remarkable tool for self-discovery. Unraveling the conditioned mind and the associated reactive emotions can occur through spontaneous revelation, with no apparent ordered timing. This is because often the root cause of an erroneous belief system is based in another dimensional time frame. Every piece of information received is a signpost to integrating fragmented consciousness. If you do not record it, it can easily be forgotten by the conscious mind. I found that writing information down or drawing a symbol received visually helped the process of embedding a new perspective enormously. Because I love to write, I found I would awake sometimes in the middle of the night and be compelled to write something ... it could be a dream about my personal process, an inspiration to take action, a plan for the next day, or a fantastic idea to follow up. This can happen at any time of the day or night now, and so I always keep a notebook handy.

I personally found the act of journaling with pen to paper rather than just keying something into an electronic notebook, phone, or computer to be important. First, it is a conscious intention to stop what you are doing, become present to the moment, and acknowledge what is arising for expression. It is a form of contemplation and connects the kinesthetic energy of the body with the consciousness and the mind. It is a way of contacting the deeper self and maintaining that contact without any distraction of the next e-mail or text to ping through on an apparatus. Technology has its place and is vital to our lives, but now and then it's good to close everything down and flow in the moment. Words, images, and symbols may appear to you. Whatever is your way to express, make time to do this. You will find it is a surprising treasure chest of knowledge.

Keeping a Journal

As a supplement to your practice, you are encouraged to keep a personal journal of your journey. This is a wonderful way to reveal your magnificence. You will be amazed at how much you discover about yourself. Draw, write, collage ... use whatever creative tools you wish to record your information.

- ❖ Your successes
- ❖ Your setbacks
- ❖ Your aha moments!
- ❖ Life events
- ❖ Your beliefs
- ❖ Relevant information from this book, other great books to read, great people you meet
- ❖ Your feelings as they arise
- ❖ Information about your patterns
- ❖ Your intentions, goals, and affirmations
- ❖ Dialogue with yourself to encourage positivity when you feel discouraged.
- ❖ What is getting in the way of your highest potential?
- ❖ How do you stop yourself from manifesting your magnificence?

At the end of each day before retiring, ask yourself,

"What am I grateful for today?"

Commentary on Presence

This is really what the entire journey of transformation is about. To be fully present means you have full consciousness of your multidimensional self, just being in each moment in your physical body.

After years and years of conditioning and unconscious blocking of energy flow in my body to prevent acknowledgment of pain or inconvenient feeling, it took quite some time for me to actually feel my entire physical body and become aware of the energy flow there. Slowly as I unpeeled the layers, I found I would be able to feel another part of my physical self. The paradox is sometimes you are not aware of what you cannot feel until you feel it. I am talking from the perspective of a sensate experience in the body. The body is the vehicle used to develop our conscious awareness of mind, soul, and spirit. From the point of view of consciousness, to not live from the past and not worry about the future is a key element in creating a new reality for yourself. If you live in the past, it becomes a self-fulfilling prophecy; if you worry about the future, you push away the bright new moment. To be fully present and alive in the body in each moment becomes our goal.

Practice 1: Presence

Note: End points are face and head, hands, feet, and pelvic floor.

Find a space with room to move and an area where you can lie down comfortably.

- ❖ Bring your awareness to your body. How does it feel? What does it want to do? Move in whichever way it needs. Walk, dance, stretch, yawn—then lie down.
- ❖ Bring awareness to the breath. Allow this to come and go in its natural rhythm. On the next breath, inhale and then exhale with a prolonged sigh. If this feels fine, experiment with different volumes and pitches of your voice.
- ❖ Begin to bring your awareness to the body again. What sensations are there? Wherever your attention goes in the body, notice the sensation. As you feel it, give it permission to move, breathe, and sound however it wants to.
- ❖ Follow your attention wherever it takes you. It may go to a thought. Feel the sensation arise and let it move, breathe, and sound.
- ❖ Using the sensations as a guide, get a sense of how the energy in your body is moving and where it is not moving. Notice areas that have a lot of activity and those that have little, where there is flow and where there is congestion. Get to know how your energy moves and feels.
- ❖ Pay attention to the energy circulating through your face and head. Feel all the sensations in your face: your jaw, your mouth, your gums, your teeth, your ears, your lips. Give these sensations your permission to move and breathe and sound in their own way.

❖ Let your head and face awake and feel how that draws energy up from the throat and chest and the rest of the body. Allow the face and head to lead your body. And then give yourself permission to feel the whole body and move, breathe, and sound however it wishes to.

❖ Repeat this process with the other end points: the hands, the feet, and the pelvic floor. Allow each part to feel itself. Allow yourself to feel the emotional tone of the sensations that arise and the emotional tone of allowing them to sequence through your body and out to the end points.

❖ Allow your attention to focus on a particular sensation and then shift it out through all of you letting this happen in its own way and allowing it to move, breathe, and sound.

This practice* introduces you to the energy of the body and brings your conscious awareness inward to the self.

Practice as much as you want to but at least once a week until this becomes an integral part of your being. Learn to listen in to the body and follow its wisdom.

I am connected to my body. I feel my energy. I am here now.

Journal about whatever came up for you.

---

* Adapted from *Body-Mind Psychotherapy; Principles, Techniques and Practical Applications* by Susan Aposhyan. Copyright ©2004. Used by permission of W.W. Norton, New York.

Commentary on Grounding

Grounding is such an important skill. As more and more psychic debris is cleared from the system, vibrational frequency is increased as contact is made with the higher dimensional frequencies. More and more photons of light pour in, resulting in an enlightenment of the bioenergy field and light-headedness, literally. The challenge is to hold these frequencies in a physical body that is vibrating at a lower rate. Essentially there is a struggle to be in a 3-D reality. By this I mean actually grounding our thoughts and creations into the physical manifestation of life. Lack of grounding is usually a sign of fear being present and a forgetting of why we chose to be here on planet earth in the first place.

An example of this: when I moved back from Canada to the United Kingdom, I could not find a place to live for six months; in effect it took me six months to finally land. I could not get fully here, because my linear mind was in fear. I had completed a high-paying contract and knew from the higher mind that I had to come back to the United Kingdom. I was following a higher imperative. But when I got to the United Kingdom and could not find a place to live, this seemed to confirm my fear and I questioned the higher imperative instead of trusting the intuition that had proved itself time and time again. This in turn caused me to not be able to ground (literally live) in my new reality for some time. My thoughts had created a cycle of events that perpetuated the fear vibration of my linear mind (negative feedback loop), and this was reflected back in the physical reality. Immediately I moved through the fear, handed the outcome over to higher will, and grounded; *the very same evening*, the most beautiful and unexpected solution to my living arrangements occurred.

This energetic practice is a key skill to help you as you passage through the various dimensions. We are here to manifest a reality on the physical plane, bringing the higher vibrations through the denser physical body. This exercise really supports that process.

Practice 2: Grounding

❖ Stand tall, with a slight bend at the knees and feet just outside the hips, toes pointing slightly outward. Relax the upper body. Arms hang loose by your sides. Inhale and exhale deeply several times. Bring your conscious awareness to the feet and feel them firmly placed on the floor. Feel all four corners of the feet placed squarely on the ground. Feel each toe touching the floor. Stamp the feet, bend the knees, crouch, do whatever feels good to bring the energy down. Return to standing with knees slightly bent.

❖ Bring your awareness to the tan-tien. This is located four finger widths below the navel. When you have found this location externally, bring the four fingers of your right hand to the thumb and place all fingers on the tan-tien.

❖ Visualize a sphere of golden white light in the center of the body internally at the tan-tien; breathe deeply into this place. As you inhale see this light expanding and, on the exhale, send a line of energy from this sphere of light down into the crystalline core of the earth. Make this connection very strong.

❖ Feel your feet firmly on the ground. Imagine lines of energy coming down the legs and right through the feet into the earth like roots. Continue breathing deeply.

❖ Feel and see the energy in the lower body connecting with the earth below you. Feel the heaviness in your legs as you connect to the gravitational pull of the earth and her energy field.

I am safe and supported by the earth at all times.

In this practice you are grounding the energy into the earth to stabilize the bioenergy field. You are literally transferring excess electrons to the earth to stabilize your highly charged system. Practice as often as possible and use this technique whenever you feel ungrounded.

This is an important skill to master as it enables the body to hold the higher frequencies. Through this deep connection to the earth as we clear and transmute the lower frequencies, so we do for our beloved planet.

Commentary on Centering

Centering is a very powerful skill that requires practice to perfect. This practice is the key to how we manifest our reality in the physical dimension. Centering is building the energetic link between the higher and lower dimensions. In this practice you are creating a pathway for the higher vibrational frequencies to reach the lower density of matter within your multidimensional system. It takes you out of your feeling, emotional, reactive nature and your linear mind. There is no feeling, no thought, just the stillness and connection to higher mind. It is a shortcut to the stillness many search for through years of meditation. This also prepares your system for conscious creation as opposed to the unconscious creation that is going on every moment of your existence. By constant practice you build an energetic highway to the higher dimensional fields of being. The conscious creative process is a scientific process that can be mastered through practice and eventually becomes focused, conscious, and effortless. The ability to center is an integral part of this process.

Practice 3: Centering

- ❖ All steps as in practice 2: Grounding. Make this connection strong. You are connected to the earth's core. Hold the sphere of light at the tan-tien (four finger widths below the navel) with your four fingers and thumb of the left hand. Make this strong and bright.

- ❖ Once you have grounded, bring your conscious awareness to the heart region. At a point four finger widths down from the collarbone, visualize another sphere of golden white light. Breathe deeply into the tan-tien. Imagine a line of energy running up from the sphere of light in the tan-tien and passing right through the center of the body to meet the sphere of light at the high heart.

- ❖ Use the breath to make these connections strong.

- ❖ Once the connections are strong, visualize another sphere of golden white light originating three feet above the head. This is the monad. Visualize a line of golden white light running from this sphere through the center of the head to meet the sphere at the heart. Make this strong. Hold the sphere of light at the heart with the four fingers and thumb of the right hand. Breathe deeply into the heart.

- ❖ Once the line is complete and strong and all the points are joined, feel the calm, still point of center in the body. You are grounded and, at the same time, connected to the higher aspects of your being mediated by the heart. Continue breathing deeply.

This is the place of no thought and no emotion, just calm, centered stillness of being. The bioenergy field is completely balanced.

**I am connected to the earth and to the
source of all life through my heart.**

I am equilibrium.

Practice three times daily—on waking, at midday, and at
the end of the working day.

Start with three minutes for each, gradually increasing
this to twenty minutes for each period. This can form a daily
meditative practice.

Commentary on Breath Awareness

It is surprising how little attention is paid to the breath. Without bringing this energy into the body, physical life is impossible. It is also another amazing tool for well-being, relaxation, and transformation. You can use your breath to explore places in the body that are blocked, tight, or painful or simply places that you are currently unaware that you do not feel. You can explore your emotions using breath. By bringing attention to your breath, you can direct thought energy using breath as your guide. It can become an effective tool in dislodging energy blocks in your system when used mindfully or at the very least will bring your attention to those places. As you breathe in oxygen, you breathe in life; as you exhale you release toxic waste and that which is no longer useful. It is also a beautiful experience for your body when you begin to pay attention to your breath. You begin an intimate dialogue with the vehicle of your spirit.

Practice 4: Breath Awareness 1— Yin Breathing*

In breath work there are two types of practice: yin or passive breathing and yang or active breathing.

❖ Just bring your attention to your breath and notice it come and go.
❖ What is the quality of the breath?
❖ Is it long and smooth or short and disjointed?
❖ What feelings and sensations occur?
❖ Where do you observe those feelings and sensations in your body?
❖ Where does the breath go in you?
❖ What moves when you breathe?
❖ What does it touch?
❖ What else is coming up in the mind and in the body? Emotions, self-talk, habits, patterns, physical tensions, reactions?
❖ Just notice and accept. You are the observer witnessing the breath.
   If the mind wanders, just bring the attention back to the breath.

Have your journal at hand so you can record what came up for you during the session.

It is recommended to practice both types of breathing so there is balance between doing and being, between breathing and being breathed. Bring attention to your breathing daily.

---

* Adapted from Dan Brule, http://www.breathmastery.com/the-two-basics-aspects-of-breathwork/.

Practice 4: Breath Awareness 2— Yang Breathing**

This is conscious breathing, and in this format you are breathing the breath. The breath is given a certain quality or pattern created by your intention. You are controlling and directing the breath in some way, as in pranayama.

❖ Inhale slowly and deeply for a count of 7.
❖ Hold for a count of 1.
❖ Exhale slowly and deeply for a count of 7.
❖ Hold for a count of 1.

There are many different practices where we use conscious breathing.

❖ Breath and movement are combined as in yoga and other types of exercise.
❖ Breath and sound, allowing a sound to emerge from the body on the exhale.
❖ Breath can be used in visualization and affirmation work to deepen the process.
❖ A different way of inhaling and exhaling can be employed.

  • Inhale through the nose and exhale through the mouth.
  • Inhale through alternate nostrils.

I breathe in life, vitality, and radiant health. I breathe out all that no longer serves my highest purpose.

** Adapted from Dan Brule, http://www.breathmastery.com/the-two-basics-aspects-of-breathwork/.

Commentary on Nourishment

All foods taken into the body have an energetic component. If you wish to elevate the vibrational frequency of your cells, it becomes necessary to monitor what you are taking into your system. As a younger woman, my lifestyle was not healthy. For quite an extended period of my life, I drank more alcohol than I ate and I chain-smoked, initially to be what I thought was socially acceptable. Later, these substances became emotional props. As I moved through the transformational process, I noticed my eating habits began to change quite naturally, and I stopped drinking and smoking completely. As I began to care more about myself and pay attention to what was going on inside rather than outside, the proper nourishment of my body at all its levels mirrored this change in my consciousness.

Practice 5: Nourishment

❖ Bring your attention to what you are eating during the day for one week.
Make a note in your journal of what you eat and drink in an average day.

❖ How does this compare with the foods recommended in this book? Does your daily consumption include a lot of foods that are recommended to be excluded?
If so, how do you feel about this? Are you open to changing this?

❖ Check the table of alkaline and acid foods in the book. Is your weekly intake more acid than alkaline or more alkaline than acid? By what percentage is this out of balance? How do you feel about this? Are you open to changing this?

❖ How is your body being hydrated? Are you drinking enough water?

❖ What other substances are you taking into your body? Drugs, supplements, alcohol, cigarette smoke? How do you feel about this? Are you open to changing these habits?

❖ Are you dieting? If so, why? What are your expectations?

❖ What is your attitude to your nourishment in general? How do you care for yourself in other ways? How do you nourish your whole self?

**I am the balanced energy of the food I ingest.
I assimilate information from the highest
intelligence fields of light available to me.**

Commentary on Movement and Rest

Our bodies are designed to move. The sedentary nature of many occupations means that intention and effort are required to ensure you take adequate exercise to maintain a healthy body. Your body loves to move, but your mind may inhibit that movement. I am sixty-four years old. This is my chronological age, but it has nothing to do with my fitness level. I have a daily exercise routine of X-biking, strength training a specific muscle group each day, and stretching. I practice yoga. I run. My body is in peak health and fitter now than at the age of thirty. I take adequate rest and use energetic tools to eradicate stress from my life.

It is never too late to begin. The body is a mirror of the consciousness within. How it looks, feels, and behaves is a decision made by you, always. Through resonance the higher frequencies can transmute the lower frequencies of matter. You can reprogram your DNA to prevent disease and degeneration.

Practice 6: Movement and Rest

❖ Stand in front of a mirror for three minutes and take a long look at yourself. What does this bring up for you? Was this difficult for you? If so, why?

❖ How do you feel about your body?

❖ Did you move your body today? How does it want to move? Can you allow this?

❖ Do you exercise regularly? If not, why not?

❖ Are you able to incorporate any exercise into your weekly routine? If not, why not?

❖ What would need to change for you to exercise your body?

❖ Are you willing to make these changes? If not, why not?

❖ Are you getting adequate rest? If not, why not?

❖ What needs to change for you to have adequate rest?

❖ Are you willing to make these changes? If not, why not?

Some form of daily exercise is recommended. Most gyms can provide you with a tailor made program to suit your body.

I am the wisdom of the body moving.

I am the restoration of the vibrations of wholeness within me.

Commentary on the Creative Life Pulse

This is about joining the flow of creation rather than resisting. There are cycles in all manifested life creations. The creative life pulse is an inherent part of the evolutionary process and is part of your life too. Conditioning may have taught you to push and compete to be successful, or it may have left you with a lack of motivation or an inability to take action when required. Knowing there is a cycle to every manifestation of creation and where we are at any given time in our own life cycle is great to be aware of and understand. From this place trust, acceptance, and surrender of the lower will are developed. You begin to tune in to your life and its meaning at a deeper level, align with your purpose, and join the great evolutionary flow of creation.

Practice 7: Creative Life Pulse

Have your journal at hand and answer the following questions:

❖ Where am I on the creative life pulse?

> ➢ Expansion
> ➢ Equilibrium
> ➢ Contraction

❖ If you are unsure where you are, ask:

> ➢ Am I moving forward, in ward, or backward?
> ➢ Am I afraid of something? If so, what?
> ➢ What am I feeling?

❖ If you are in a negative contraction:

> ➢ What is inside me I am afraid of?
> ➢ What do I not trust within me?
> ➢ What do I think is bad within me?
> ➢ What do I think I need to hide within me?

We are creating every moment we live. Every manifestation is subject to this cycle. Ask these questions at any time to find where and when you are stuck or if you are just in the natural cycle.

I am a wave and a particle in the ocean of life, ebbing and flowing in the perfect rhythm of my creative life pulse.

Commentary on Setting Intention

This begins your conscious act of creation. You know you are accountable for all that manifests in your reality. Here you are using the tool of centeredness and the connection to the higher dimension of your being to create in accordance with the knowing of your transpersonal self (soul) and your higher aspects (spirit). This is a powerful skill but cannot be used successfully without having done the work to discover and remove any destructive or dualistic intentionality that you may initially be unaware of.

When your multidimensional system is resonating at its highest capability, you will attract people, events, circumstances, places, and opportunities that reflect your highest intention for your life.

Practice 8: Setting Intention

❖ Be very clear about what you intend. What do you wish to create?

❖ Ground and center (practices 2 and 3).

❖ Your physical body is grounded. You are energetically centered connecting the earth core with a line of energy to the golden, white sphere of the tan-tien and up to the golden, white sphere of energy at the heart. Use your breath to make these connections strong. Inhale, bringing a line of energy down from the sphere of golden, white ball of energy three feet above the head; exhale to connect with the heart.

❖ Use your breath to direct the energy. Make these connections strong. There is no emotion and no thought. Your active intelligence, will, and emotions are all in perfect balance. You are at a still point.

❖ Bring the attention to the heart, breathe deeply, and set your intention verbally. "In the name of my *I AM* presence, I set the intention to be … do … act … create … in accordance with the highest good for all concerned."

❖ Stay here for a few minutes, breathe deeply, and let this drop in.

Use your intention on a daily basis to create the reality you desire.

I set the intention …

Commentary on Balance of the Masculine and Feminine Energies

All beings carry both masculine and feminine energies. This has nothing to do with your gender. A balance of these energies is connected in to the creative life pulse that you can witness in all nature and in yourself. When these are perfectly blended and balanced, there is harmony in life and an intuitive knowing of when to act and when to acquiesce, of when to give and when to receive, of when to do and when to be. Through the harmonic flow of these two energies within your system, you can experience heaven on earth.

Practice 9: Balance of the Masculine and Feminine Energies

❖ Bring your attention inward and breathe deeply.
❖ Ground and center (practices 2 and 3).

Masculine Energy	Feminine Energy
Visionary	Imaginative
Determined	Intuitive
Clarity	Sensitive
Focus	Empathetic
Leadership	Compassionate
Knowledge	Open-hearted
Adventurous	Flexible
Strength	Receptive
Courage	Accepting
Integrity	Nurturing
Articulate	Allowing
Creative -Inspires	Creative -Births

Figure 22.1. Table of Masculine and Feminine qualities

❖ Reflect on these core qualities. Check each that applies to how you see yourself.
❖ Is there a balance?
❖ If not, what would you like to develop more in yourself?
❖ What is holding you back?

I am whole, complete, and in perfect balance.

I am the lover and the beloved.

Commentary on the Child Consciousness Within

The child consciousness within refers to those parts of the psyche that have been unable to develop naturally due to childhood environmental conditioning. This can cover the span of in utero to early adolescence. It is the delicate fragmented part of you that may not be initially in your conscious awareness. The developing child creates mechanisms to bypass feelings associated with perceived or actual trauma. It can take time and patience to access this part of the psyche, or it may be clear to you, but a destructive or negative intentionality keeps you from reaching this aspect of self. You may need help from others or a facilitator to do this.

Ultimately the knowing of the self as being the source of all this fragmented energy consciousness needs to blossom and grow and join the stream of adult consciousness in the being. The paradox is, when this occurs, life is viewed and lived through the innocent eyes of a child once more but also incorporates the wisdom of the learning.

Practice 10: The Child Consciousness Within

Review chapter 15, "Emotional and Mental Stability."

❖ Bring your attention inward and breathe deeply.
❖ Ground and center (practices 2 and 3).
❖ Set your intention to connect to the child consciousness within.
❖ Bring your awareness to the heart. Give yourself permission to release the layers of anger and fear that block the flow of your life force.
❖ What does your child within need in this moment?
❖ How does he or she feel?
❖ What would she or he like to do?
❖ Can you give your inner child whatever he or she needs now in this moment?
❖ Release any shame that has covered the truth of who you are.
❖ Remove the filter from your mind that inhibits the light and love of who you are coming forth.
❖ You are deeply loved. Love yourself deeply.

Practice whenever you have a negative emotional reaction and particularly after reading Chapter 15

I am the child within.
I see, feel, hear, and tenderly embrace the child within,
bringing her or him to the safety of my loving heart.

I relinquish my childish reactive ways,
while still viewing all life with the awe,
innocence, and exuberance of a child.

Commentary on Identity and Images

Who you think you are, who you are, and who you may wish to be are the subjects of this practice. Do you realize you are making your own identity up as you move through life? When you are not connected to the higher aspects of your being, you cannot be an authentic representation of those frequencies. You look outside the self for clues as to how you think you should be and act. I wanted to please my parents, so I became the good student. I thought to be accepted by my social group as a young woman, I needed to smoke and drink. In my working environment, I thought I had to be and act like a man in order to be accepted, liked, and respected by my predominantly male peers. When I first started to work in the field of energy management, I thought I had to be "holy" and ignore the shadow side of my being. Throughout my life I had created images of an idealized self of who I thought I should be, instead of being who I was, to such a large degree that I totally lost the true me and it took me quite some time to find the truth. I had different identities for different circumstances. I wore various masks of being to adapt to wherever I was and whomever I was with so I would fit in because I wanted to be accepted, liked, loved, and of course successful. On other occasions I became an aggressive and angry monster, pushing away all that I wanted most. Does any of this sound familiar to you?

This practice will help you identify how you deny your own magnificence and hide it behind masks and defenses through fear of not living up to your own self-created image.

Practice 11: Identity and Images*

*An image is a limiting belief about life and who we are and the resulting constricted emotions and protective strategies used to support it.

Review Chapter 16 Mind Games

Ask yourself the following questions and enlist the help of family and friends. Record your answers in your journal.

- ❖ Who are you? Who do you see yourself as?
- ❖ What impression of yourself do you wish to create and why?
- ❖ What demands to be "perfect" do you place on yourself? Where do these demands originate? Are you conforming to original demands placed on you from your mother, father, or both?
- ❖ How do others see you?

  - ➢ Ask a friend.
  - ➢ Ask a colleague.
  - ➢ Ask a significant other.

- ❖ Do you resonate with these descriptions? If not, why not? What do they reflect back to you?
- ❖ Can you identify your mask self? Can you identify this at work in your interaction with others? Give examples. What are your reactions when exposure of the mask self is threatened by others?
- ❖ Can you relate your mask self to an underlying image of the way you think life is?
- ❖ Create a time line from birth to the present, listing events that shaped your life and created meaning, your challenges, and your successes.
- ❖ Are there any significant repeating patterns? What do you wish to change in your life?

Commentary on "I Am" Affirmations

Affirmations are powerful practices only when combined with a process of self-inquiry and energetic clearing. You cannot change your energetic signature until you increase your vibration, and affirmations alone will not do this. You must do the work. Affirmations support the process of the transformation of consciousness by helping to create positive intentionality and aid in the reversal of faulty programming. They will help you to see yourself in a new way, past the image and false identity of who you think you are supposed to be.

Practice 12: *"I AM"* Affirmations

"I AM ..."

abundant	determined	knowing	self-confident
active	diligent	likeable	sensitive
adventurous	dynamic	limitless	successful
amazing	fearless	loving	strong
adaptable	feminine	a leader	social
articulate	forgiving	magnificent	sympathetic
assertive	fun	motivated	thankful
authentic	focused	nurturing	thriving
a shining star	friendly	original	tolerant
blessed	generous	open	truthful
brave	a genius	patient	unique
capable	giving	passionate	understanding
caring	grateful	peaceful	universal
comforting	growing	positive	visionary
complete	genuine	playful	vibrant
confident	happy	potential	worthwhile
conscientious	healthy	powerful	worthy
courageous	honest	radiant	wise
curious	helpful	reasonable	emerging
creative	important	reflective	unfolding
compassionate	infinite	responsible	energy
competent	intelligent	resourceful	love
considerate	intuitive	safe	light
a champion	kind	seeing	peace

Figure 22.2. Affirmations.

Commentary on Meditation

The benefits of a meditation practice should not be underestimated. All practice that focuses the being inward rather than looking outward to the illusion will foster the acceleration of the connection between the lower and higher frequencies of existence. This is our aim: to bring the two together so the lower frequencies may be transmuted into the higher vibration. Meditation allows us access to the higher mind, higher will, and unconditional love. As I am writing this section, I am reminded of an Oxford academic, a professor no less, who very recently suggested people should stop meditating because it was emptying their minds and stopping them thinking. Yes, I am afraid, dear professor, this is exactly what is required—to stop thinking with the linear lower mind and start allowing the higher mind access in your life. This vibrates above the senses and from a place of mental calmness. It works. In this book, centering is considered to be the most effective version of meditation, as this has been my experience. The book also outlines other methods. As with any practice, at first it may seem difficult, but with more and more practice, it becomes second nature and enjoyable. Don't give up. It will change your life.

Practice 13: Meditation

❖ Create a space where you can be quiet and uninterrupted. Perhaps you have created a small area with objects that are meaningful to you, such as flowers or a candle.

❖ Sit in a comfortable position, either cross-legged or on a chair, ensuring the spine is straight and not leaning against the back of the chair. Chin should be tucked slightly in; feet firmly on the ground if sitting on a chair.

❖ Close your eyes, bring your attention to your breath, and center.

❖ Just sit in allowing.

❖ Calm the mind with the breath and return always to your center and your breath.

❖ Regular practice is essential to establish connection to the higher aspects of your being. Practice for ten minutes per day initially, gradually extending this to anything between twenty and sixty minutes.

❖ This can be combined with your daily practice of centering. This is a great energy practice to bring you to a meditative state very quickly.

Have a journal nearby to record your experience afterward.

Commentary on Transference and Projection

This is where most people live most of the time. Behavioral patterns are developed based on what happened in a past experience, and the response to a present-day dilemma is an almost automatic one from the way the brain is now wired to perceive this new experience. There is no accountability because you are not aware you are creating all the experiences in life by your vibrational frequency. Every experience is perceived as happening to you rather than created by you and becomes projected out onto others in the form of praise or blame, depending on the experience.

Only when you own your creation do you have the power to change it. Until that time you give your power away and keep repeating the same creation and the same response. By recognizing this erroneous way of perceiving reality and becoming accountable for my own part in the creative process of my lived experiences, I have been able to transform every single relationship in my life to one of harmony, including relationships with those who have passed to other dimensions. When you change, the outer reality of the reflection automatically changes.

Practice 14: Transference and Projection

❖ Anytime you are responding to a situation in a disproportionate way, positive or negative, pause and take a deep breath.

❖ Allow your emotions to pass through your body. Do not throw them outward in blame to others. Just let them pass through.

❖ Breathe deeply. Ground and center (practices 2 and 3).

❖ Return to the spaciousness of your heart and breathe deeply.

❖ Use your compassionate observer to ask, "What is it that I am feeling, saying, or doing?"

❖ What does this circumstance remind me of? Who does this person remind me of? When did I feel like this before?

❖ Ask yourself, "Am I really responding to a present circumstance? What is really going on here?"

❖ Focus on your inner experience. Listen to the wisdom of the heart and your body. What is it telling you?

❖ Your goal is to come back into deep contact with yourself and your inner wisdom.

❖ Identify the transference.

Engage in this practice any time you are triggered into a highly emotional reaction.

I am here in this now moment. I am fully present.

I am the compassionate observer and the consciousness of the observed.

I am the experience and the creator of the experience.

Commentary on the Transforming Power of Love

I have been able to transform every relationship in my life to one of harmony—quite a statement.

As your consciousness expands and you are able to see how you give your power away, how you create repeating patterns of negative experience, and how from the reactions of the child within you have built images and protective measures to keep from accessing this information through fear, only then can you begin to see you are not only the victim but also the perpetrator. You have created it all. At some point in the journey, it all becomes clear that you are the creator of your own experience. This great intuitive mechanism of the soul's longing to express itself as love, wisdom, and compassion breaks through all the barriers to self–knowledge, and you begin to see experiences through and with the eyes of the transforming power of love. As you begin to truly love yourself and have compassion for yourself, so too are you able to have this for all others. You realize that while their circumstances may be different, all have the same erroneous ideas, and their behavior is about the same projective perceptions. The heart literally breaks open, and there is such a flood of compassion for self and others and the beginning of learning to truly love unconditionally, without judgment or condemnation of any act.

Practice 15: The Transforming Power of Love

❖ Ground and center (practices 2 and 3).

❖ Come to a seated position, keeping the spine straight, and breathe deeply with the whole of your lungs for several breaths.

❖ Come to your heart space.

❖ From the still point at the center of your heart, listen to the rhythmic beat of your heart.

❖ Visualize the energetic lotus flower at the heart center. This has nine vortices of energy that shape like petals radiating from the center, hiding within themselves another three central petals and concealing a central point of energy.

❖ Visualize a line of red iridescent energy streaming up from the earth to this central point and a line of golden white iridescent energy streaming down from the heavens to meet at the center point of your heart.

❖ The two streams of energy meet, and the twelve vortices, one by one, are filled with rose white light radiating out in a circular motion from the center point of the lotus, creating a tube toroidal shape.

❖ Bring any feelings of fear to this heart space of love's energy, breathing deeply. Feel the fear dissolve.

❖ Breathe deeply as this energy radiates out from your heart and fills your entire energy body with life and love. With your intention and your breath, extend this outward as far as you wish, connecting with all life.

Recommended daily

I am peace, I am light, I am love.

Commentary on Receiving Guidance

This is open to you at all times and through all media. Everything in your life can give you guidance, for it is you who have created or cocreated with another what shows up.

What is your life telling you about you? What is your experience of life showing you about you? If you need to make a decision about something, practice your connection to your higher self and check in. Is it for my highest good? If you are asking on behalf of another, check in. Is it for his or her highest good?

The more impediments to full connection with the higher frequencies you are able to clear, the more infallible the guidance becomes, and the clearer the way forward appears. You are always connected in; you just need to switch on the receiver.

Practice 16: Receiving Guidance

❖ It is possible to receive guidance anywhere. It is a case of opening your awareness to everything that manifests in your reality. All is information about the self. When you are not sure about something, *ask*.

❖ If there is a specific query, it is useful to create a quiet space. Use the location where you practice your meditation, as this is already a conditioned space of heightened awareness.

❖ Sit quietly and comfortably with straight spine. Ground and center and bring your attention to the breath.

❖ Set your intention to connect with your higher self and align with truth.

❖ Your purpose is to connect with the higher aspects of your being by surrendering the lower personality self to be guided and instructed by your soul aspect.

❖ Expand your consciousness to the higher levels of your bioenergy field and surrender to not knowing.

❖ Ask your question. Approach this with sincerity, and there is always an answer.

❖ Keep a journal nearby to record your impressions or downloads.

❖ It is good to practice this often as it builds and strengthens the energetic connection between the lower and higher aspects of your being.

I am aligned with truth and open to receive.

I am the joy of surrender.

Commentary on Addressing the Negative

What shows up in your reality of existence is just a mirror. What manifests in your life is you in all its aspects: the good, the bad, and the ugly. Your own negativity can be hard to admit and own. In my younger days my own negative belief systems developed and supported by religious dogma brought much trauma and abuse into my reality. How I thought and felt about myself attracted in many abusive personal relationships. Very often your negativity it is not in your conscious awareness. Use the mirror. Learn about yourself through this mirror. If something unpleasant is turning up what does this show you about how you think and feel and behave? What you detest in another is lurking unconsciously inside you. Similarly what you admire in another is also inside of you.

Practice 17: Addressing the Negative

❖ Ground, center, and invoking the higher self, set your intention to identify your negativity.

❖ *I am willing* to find, acknowledge, accept, and observe my negative attitudes.

❖ Bring your attention to your daily life interactions. Using the mirror of relationship, which behaviors do you most deplore in others? What does this show you about yourself? Whatever presses your buttons is sure to be what is masked or un-owned in yourself. Get used to looking in this mirror and seeing yourself. Your own negative attitudes are so familiar and can be hard to see, admit, and own. We criticize others for what we will not acknowledge in ourselves. Be very honest with yourself here. These are the ways we disown our power and sabotage our self.

> ➤ When do they manipulate, lie, control, compete, punish, gloat, grasp, blame, judge, resent, avenge, criticize, worry, merge, cling, scorn, sulk, withhold, withdraw, envy, condescend, flatter, collapse, whine, caretake? When do you?

> ➤ When you witness any thoughts or acts of brutality, inhumanity, exploitation, coldness, or meanness of others, can you see and acknowledge the part of you that behaves in this way to yourself or to others?

> ➤ Victimhood and self-pity are unattractive traits. When do you indulge or struggle with this in your life?

> ➤ When do you criticize others for feeling they deserve special attention, insist on being right, attention seek, feel superior, desire something

without making any effort? This very criticism points to the very same behavioral trait in you. Can you acknowledge how and when you adopt this kind of behavior?

> When and how do you maintain familiar feelings of negativity, guilt, fear, struggle, resignation, compliance, depression, anxiety?

❖ Now that you have identified your own negative behaviors, select one of these that you wish to change most. Invoke your higher self and write down what the destructive intentionality behind this behavior is. What is your attachment to it?

❖ Does it continue to feed your negative conclusions about yourself and life? Does it punish you? Does it punish those who you believe hurt you? Is this about revenge?

❖ Identify the pleasure you have in this situation. What is the part of you that enjoys the negative situation of unfulfillment, victimhood, or control? What feelings does it elicit? What is the negative pleasure payoff? Is it about familiarity and safety? Is it about reprising your original role in the family and upholding the original family pattern? Is it a compensatory and a familiar role for you?

❖ What is the impact this has on your life? What is the actual outcome? What is the harmful effect on self and others?

❖ Are you willing to transform this?

❖ Write down the positive attitude you wish to embrace, the positive will and positive pleasure you wish to substitute for the current negative behavior. How would you like to think and behave? What would you like to be able to do?

❖ Why is it important to make this change?

❖ Why is it important to do this now, and what are the negative consequences of not changing?

❖ What are the benefits of changing this behavior?

❖ Make the following three statements:

> ➢ I acknowledge … must change.
> ➢ I acknowledge *my positive intention* to change …
> ➢ I acknowledge *I am* changing this.

❖ If these statements make you feel uncomfortable, then go through the above steps once more, really deepening into the feelings of not making this change.

❖ Now you are deeply recognizing your negative behavior and the pleasure you gain from this.

❖ Allow this very deep connection to yourself and begin to feel the positive pleasure of surrendering yourself more deeply into this contact.

❖ Reclaim your power to transform your negative thoughts and actions on a daily basis.

I set my intention to …

Commentary on Anchoring the Positive

Remember who you are. You are a powerful, magnificent creator. What brings you the most joy, or what is the state you wish to substitute for your negative intentions? Align with this feeling now.

Practice 18: Anchoring the Positive

To imprint your new behavior into your physical body, you can create an anchor as follows:

- ❖ Ground, center, and invoke your higher self. Set your intention to anchor your new behavior, thought, words, action.
- ❖ Recall a time, a memory, when you experienced the desired state or attitude you wish to substitute for your negative behavior.
- ❖ Become fully immersed, absorbed, and associated with this memory, with full sensory involvement. See, feel, hear, smell, touch, taste.
- ❖ Create your own unique word or phrase concerning your new behavior and a physical sensation (maybe hand on heart or place palms over temples) while you are at the peak of this state.
- ❖ Break the state temporarily and repeat using a different memory.
- ❖ Repeat this reconditioning several times.
- ❖ Test the association you have created by using your word or phrase and the physical sensation.
- ❖ Find the positive ways you can think about life and your circumstances.

Review the *"I AM"* affirmations.
Select what is relevant for you.

Commentary on Visualization

As you continue clearing, you will find your manifestation capabilities are greatly enhanced and your thoughts begin to manifest very quickly. This is why it is so important to stabilize your thoughts and master the emotions. This takes practice and continuous self-inquiry. Be mindful that your thoughts always mirror your highest intention for yourself and others and your creations are in line with your higher purpose. If this is not the case, you will not create permanent solutions or outcomes.

Practice 19: Visualization

❖ After setting your intention with your conscious awareness at the heart center, infuse your intention with love, gratitude, and appreciation.

❖ Visualize what you wish to manifest. See it, hear it, taste it, smell it, feel it, and love it.

❖ Project it onto the mind screen.

❖ Invoke ("I call forth") the consciousness and active intelligence and the energy frequencies of *higher will, love/wisdom, and higher mind* to witness and inspire this creation for the highest good.

❖ Evoke ("I call forth and command in the name of my higher self") the consciousness and active intelligence of matter and the lower energy frequencies of substance to bring the creation forth into manifestation.

❖ Let go of the outcome or needing to know how.

❖ Stabilize the process by bringing your own conscious awareness to the earth, her energy matrix, and her crystalline core, making sure you are still grounded.

❖ Manifest—be aware and open to synchronicities that will appear.

❖ If what shows up feels right, take action.

Do this any time you wish to consciously manifest an outcome.

I am the science of manifestation.

I am the synchronized vibrations of coherence and wholeness and project this perfection in all my creations.

Commentary on Redirecting Resistance

This is another look at what fears and behaviors may be holding you back from living the fully abundant, harmonious, and joyful life you were born to live. As you move further along your path, you will find there are even deeper layers for you to explore. It may be time to reconfirm your commitment and investigate these resistances. Paradoxically, high resistance is a sign you are near to your goal. It has been my experience it shows up in a way that is directly proportionate to the treasure waiting to be uncovered. It is by overcoming this resistance that you soar and become rebalanced, energized, and harmonized. You transmute the lower frequencies into the highest vibration.

Practice 20: Redirecting Resistance

❖ Where do you separate yourself from another? Where do you insist you are better than, greater than? Where do you want to fix another? Where do you judge and say you are right and the other is wrong?

❖ Where do you insist it has to be your way? Where do you insist this is the only way?

❖ What do you fear? Where do you block your energy flow?

❖ What is your goal in life? Do you just wish to relieve symptoms of discomfort, or do you wish to be all that you can be? If the latter, can you persevere and recommit to this?

❖ Find the exact point your positive intentions became blocked and then question what part of your personality wants to hold onto this self-negating activity. Where have you held back? Where did you not want to expose your behavior?

If you are not manifesting your desired outcome this means there is resistance in the mind and therefore your energy system. Ask yourself these questions and answer them honestly any time you do not create your positive desired reality.

I am the freedom from polarized intention and the conscious agreement to harmonic patterns of creation.

Commentary on Repelling Negative Energy Field Forces

Your energy system is part of the morphogenetic holographic field of the species, humankind. Although you may have cleared your own system, you are still connected into the group energy template, which holds the records of all the energetic signatures of humanity in its entirety throughout time. Distortions in your own energetic anatomy and connection to the morphogenetic field cause your existing DNA to be inhibited and prevent the development of the additional DNA strands that are necessary for higher dimensional life. This is just one of the practices that can accelerate the clearing at the DNA level. This is for the advanced student and is only useful when used in the correct sequence. First, it is necessary to clear the personal bioenergy field of all energetic blocks and distortions and to approach this practice in a coherent state.

Practice 21: Repelling Negative Energy Field Forces

Invocation of the Violet Light Ray of Transformation, Transmutation, and Transfiguration

❖ Ground, center, and sit in meditation. Visualize your entire bioenergy field, including every particle at the cellular level, filling and extending outward to a complete 360-degree span with flaming violet iridescent light. Invoke your higher self (*I AM presence*).

❖ In the name of the violet light ray of transformation, transmutation, and transfiguration, it is *commanded* that all forces not for my highest good and containing low frequency intentions and lack of unconditional love, including all cause, effect, record, and memory and all binding soul contracts across all time lines and dimensions, are expelled without delay, thought, emotion, or hesitation from my soul record and holographic energy field and neutralized by the transforming power of the violet ray.

❖ I call forth the highest aspects of will, love/wisdom, and active intelligence, and together, as triune, we *requalify* this energy in harmony and love. We charge this command with golden rays of brilliance and ground it with the transformative power of the violet light energy so it is irrevocable and manifested instantly.

❖ *It is done. It is done. It is done.*

I am the harmonized, rebalanced, and rebirthed sacred blueprint of my DNA.

I am the spiraling strands of DNA vibrating in the highest frequencies of consciousness.

I am the DNA of source.

Commentary on At-One-Ment and Integration

This is a most beautiful practice, in which you connect to source energy and recognize your own divine essence and connection to all that is. You have worked so hard through many incarnations. You deserve this. This is your birthright: to live in this knowing and connection for infinity.

Go forth in peace and be a light unto the world.

Practice 22: At-One-Ment and Integration

- ❖ Come to your sacred space, clean and comfortably clothed.
- ❖ Inhale deeply and exhale deeply. Continue this deep, rhythmic breathing for several minutes.
- ❖ Ground and center, using your breath to align the line of light from deep in the earth's core up and into the power of the golden white sphere at the tan-tien. Use your breath to make this connection very strong and feel the heat in your tan-tien.
- ❖ On the next inhale, bring the line of energy upward to the heart, connecting with the soul light. Breathe deeply and feel the deepest longing of your soul. Feel your purpose.
- ❖ On the next inhale, bring the line of energy upward again to the point three feet above the head, connecting into the tiny vortex opening of the golden white sphere of energy there. Feel the line of energy being pulled in and connecting with the higher dimensions.
- ❖ The bridge of light between earth and the higher dimensions is strong, and you are aligning this through your physical body.
- ❖ Now bring your awareness to the brilliant white-gold crystalline sun shining one and a half inches above the belly button. This is your divine essence. You are one with source energy.
- ❖ Upwell this with your breath into the line of light connecting the lower aspects with the higher dimensions, through all three aspects on this line of energy.
- ❖ Then with your breath, expand this light out through all energy centers simultaneously and out into all the levels of your bioenergy field. This expands outward 360

degrees in all directions throughout the entire cosmic holographic field.

❖ Finally, breathe this light into every cell of your physical body, from the tips of your toes to the ends of your hair. Every single cell. See and feel this point of light in every particle of your hologram. Breathe in this conscious awareness. This is the *source of all life* within, the magnificence and blessing of who you are.

I AM THIS I AM

Appendix

The Electric Scalar Wave

There has been much controversy around the discovery of the electric scalar wave. It is of major significance to today's science even though it was first discovered in the 1880s by Tesla. Heinrich Hertz demonstrated experimentally the existence of transverse radio waves in 1887. After this, theoreticians (such as Heaviside, Gibbs, and others) revised James Clerk Maxwell's original equations in his *Theory of Electromagnetism* by writing out the scalar longitudinal wave component from the original theory. Up to that time, there was no empirical evidence of the existence of a scalar wave, and it was felt the mathematical framework should be made to agree with the experiment. The simplified equations gave us the successful AC/DC model. However, shortly after this, in 1889, Nikola Tesla (a prolific experimental physicist and inventor of AC) produced experimental evidence of the electric scalar longitudinal wave. This suggested that scalar waves could propagate as pure electric waves or as pure magnetic waves. Tesla also believed these waves carried a hitherto-unknown form of excess energy he referred to as "radiant." This result was said to have been verified by Lord Kelvin and others soon after.

These waves have unique properties. Their amplitude does not fluctuate up and down, but rather they are a vibration of electric potential that expands and contracts (like a concertina), giving a more field-like effect than wavelike, just like a normal longitudinal wave. However, unlike the normal longitudinal wave, *they can exceed the speed of light, tunnel through matter, pass through electromagnetic shielding, and propagate from space. They can act as a carrier, not only receiving and transmitting information but also amplifying it, rendering their effects cumulative in nature.* The critical components in creating scalar energy are the presence of an antenna and a potential vortex. Sadly, instead of combining their findings into a unified proof of Maxwell's original equations, Hertz and Tesla became antagonists.

Tesla was an electrical engineer and concerned with practical applications of his work and as such did not have a theory. Unfortunately for him, his work was not readily acknowledged during his lifetime. Since the days of Tesla, empirical work carried out by professional electrical engineers such as Eric Dollard, C. Monstein, Konstantin Meyl, Thomas Imlauer, and J.L. Naudin has clearly demonstrated their existence experimentally, even though the revised version of Maxwell's equations does not allow for this. It was believed that a vortex-like electric and/or magnetic wave existing in free space without the support of some kind of a viscous medium was impossible. However, later experiments carried out by Dayton Miller, Paul Sagnac, and E. W. Silvertooth support Tesla. More recently, Italian mathematician/physicist Daniele Funaro, American physicist-systems theorist Paul LaViolette, and British physicist Harold Aspden have all conceived of (and mathematically formulated) models for a free space that is dynamic, fluctuating, and self-organizing and supports the formation and propagation of scalar energy.[247,248,249]

In particular, Professor Konstantin Meyl has created a device that experimentally replicates Tesla's findings, and these experiments are now being replicated in many parts of Europe and around the world using Meyl's device.[250,251]

Magnetic Scalar Waves

Konstantin Meyl also describes the detection of the magnetic scalar wave. Meyl's discoveries started with his PhD work on vortex energy calculations in 1990. A vortex is a mass of energy rotating around an axis. Vortices of energy form to circulate and transmit energy from one location to another. Up to this point, science had been able to describe only the expanding, spiraling vortex, consisting of movement from inside outward. Nowhere in the science of electrical engineering was there a theory or equation that allowed for the contracting vortex, for example, a tornado, where pressure is applied from outside inward. It was not until nineteen years later, in 2009, with the discovery and acceptance of the magnetic monopole, predicted in 1931 by theoretical physicist Dirac, that finally Meyl's interpretation gained credence and acceptability.[252]

The implications of Tesla's now confirmed discoveries are extraordinary in what they could mean for mankind in all sorts of different applications, among them a new free energy source. The most important relevance for our purpose is to be aware of the existence of scalar energy and its intrinsic properties and be open to how this can account for phenomena of human experience that may be as yet unexplainable. These properties include their abilities to exceed the speed of light, tunnel through matter, propagate from space, and travel in a vacuum.

Vibration and Sound

The most common method to study the effects of sound is to take a flat surface, such as a large flat plate, and sprinkle a thin layer of particles, gel, or liquid. A frequency is then passed through the surface of the plate, and the particles begin to make geometrical patterns that correspond to the frequency applied. Each frequency creates a different pattern, but the pattern is always repeated for the same frequency. The patterns that emerge in the particles created from the sounds are analogous to the patterns of sacred geometry.

John Stuart Reid, a pioneer in acoustic and cymatic measurement, has become a world leader in the scientific exploration of cymatics or making sound visible. As coinventor of the CymaScope™, his research has shown that sound does not move through the air as a longitudinal wave as was previously believed. Reid recognized that the existing wave model of sound was not complete, because it did not take into account this spherical space-form of audible sound. The images created on the CymaScope™ and the geometries they revealed equated with the musical pitches of the sound or music that caused the pattern to form on the instrument's membrane. This incredible instrument actually allows us to see a circular section of the holographic, water sound bubble.

Sound in the air is defined as the transfer of vibrations between adjacent colliding atoms and molecules. Through the development of his CymaScope™, Reid has been able to show that sonic energy expands away from the site of these collisions as a spherical emanation or bubble with an oscillating surface. This bubble of energy expands and contracts with the same vibration as the original sound source. The collision between the atoms and molecules caused by the sound event initially causes the sonic energy to move in all directions simultaneously, but the distribution of energy in the sound bubble propagates on an axis away from the sound source. According to Reid, when sound passes through the air, every atom and molecule in its path becomes involved in transferring the energy. He uses the example of a human voice, a complex sound with a multitude of different vibrations that must be transmitted by all the atoms and molecules in the air; as each atom or molecule collides with its neighbor, it passes on the vibrations or sonic data of the voice with each collision. If the sonic bubble could be viewed, then all the atoms and molecules would be seen to be vibrating in unison with the particular vibration of the sound source. Reid is proposing that sound is holographic in nature in that every atom in the sonic bubble contains all the data of the sound source. However, we also know that when atoms and molecules collide, they produce a photon or electromagnetic energy. The frequency of the electromagnetism is determined not only by the collision but also by the velocity at which the particles are moving. Where the energy state is low and slow moving, then infrared or radio waves are created. If the particles are extremely high energy and moving very quickly, then X-ray or gamma rays at the other end of the scale are created. Reid proposes that when a sonic bubble is created, it is also accompanied by low-level light emissions, typically as either infrared light or radio waves. If the sound pressure is extremely high, in this case it would create visible light. He proposes sound and light are inextricably linked.[253]

Bibliography

Alexjander, Susan. "The Infrared Frequencies of DNA Bases as Science and Art." *IEEE Engineering In Medicine and Biology (1999)*: 74-79

Alfven, Hannes. "Model of the Plasma Universe." *IEEE Transactions on Plasma Science* (ISSN 0093-3813), vol. PS-14 (1986): 629–638.

Alfven, Hannes., and Arrenhius, Gustaf. *Evolution of the Solar System*. Washington, DC NASA, 1976.

Alfvén, Hannes., Carlqvist, Per "Currents in the Solar Atmosphere and a Theory of Solar Flares." *Solar Physics* 1 (1967): 220-228

Anderson, Carl A. "The Apparent Existence of Easily Deflectable Positives." *Science* Vol. 76 (1967) : 238–239.

Aposhyan, Susan. *Body-Mind Psychotherapy; Principles, Techniques and Practical Applications*. New York: W.W. Norton, 2004.

Aspden, Harold. "Standing Wave Interferometry." *Physics Essays* 3 (1990): 39–45.

Aspect, Alain., Philippe Grangier, and Gerard Roger. "Bell Test Experiments." *Physical Review Letters*. 49,(1982): 91-94.

Baconnier, S., S. B. Lang, M. Polomska, B. Hilczer, G. Berkovic, and G. Meshulam. "Calcite Microcrystals in the Pineal

Gland of the Human Brain: First Physical and Chemical Studies." *Bioelectromagnetics* 23, No.7 (2002): 488–495.

Bailey, Alice. *A Treatise on Cosmic Fire*. New York: Lucis Trust Publishing, 1979.

Bell, John S. "On the Einstein Podolsky Rosen Paradox." *Physics* 1(1964):195-200

Bennet, Charles. H., G. Brassard, C. Crepeau, R. Jozsa, A. Peres, and W. Woothers. "Teleporting an Unknown Quantum State via Dual Classical and EPR Channels." *Physics Review Letters* 70 (1993): 1895–99.

Biffi, Guilia., D. Tannahill, J. McCafferty, and S. Blasubramanian. "Quantitative Visualization of DNA G-Quadruplex Structures in Human Cells." *Nature Chemistry* 3 (2013): 182–186.

Bohm, David. *Wholeness and the Implicate Order*. London: Routledge, 1980.

Bohr, Niels. *The Philosophical Writings of Niels Bohr, Vol. I. Atomic Theory and the Description of Nature*. Woodbridge, Connecticut: Ox Bow Press, 1987

Bolwby, John. *A Secure Base:Parent Child Attachment and Healthy Human Development*. New York: Basic Books,1988.

Brennan, Barbara. A. *Hands of Light*. New York: Bantam Books, 1988.

Brewitt, Barbara. "Quantum Analysis of Electrical Skin Conductance in Diagnosis: Historical and Current Views of Bioelectric Medicine." *Journal of Naturopathic Medicine*. 6 No.1 (1996): 66-74

Budagovsky, A. V., N. I. Turovzeva, and I. A. Budagovsky. "Coherent Electromagnetic Irradiation in Distant Intercellular Interaction." *Biophysica* 46, No.5 (2001):894-900

Burr, Harold Saxton. *Blue Print for Immortality: The Electrical Patterns of Life*, London. C.W. Daniel, 1972.

Carlqvist, Per. "Current Limitation and Solar Flares." *Solar Physics* 7 (1969): 377-392

Casimir, Henrik B. G., and D. Polder. "The Influence of Retardation on the London Van Der Walls Forces." *Physical Review* 73. No.4 (1948):360-372.

Darwin, Charles. *On the Origin of Species by Means of Natural Selection, or the Preservation of Favoured Races in the Struggle for Life.* London:John Murray, 1859.

Del Guidice, Emilio., S. Doglia, M. Milani, J. M. Smith, and G. Vitiello. "Magnetic Flux Quantization & Josephson Behaviour in Living Systems." Physica Scripta 40 (1989):786-791.

Denton, Michael. *Evolution: A Theory in Crisis.* Parker, Colorado: Adler and Adler Pubishing 1985.

Deshpande, Pradeep B., K. P. Madappa, and K. Korotkov. "Can the Excellence of the Internal Be Measured, A Preliminary Study: Scientists Quantify & Graphically Chart Alignment of Human Chakras in Various Emotional States." *Journal of Consciousness Exploration & Research* 4, no.9 (2013): 977–987.

d'Espagnat, B. J. "The Quantum Theory and Reality." *Scientific American.*(November 1979): 158–181.

Dibble, W. E., and William A. Tiller. "Electronic Device Mediated pH Change in Water." *Journal of Scientific Exploration* 13, No. 2 (1999): 155-176

Dirac, Paul A. M. "Quantised Singularities in the Electromagnetic Field." *Journal of the Royal Proceedings of the Royal Society of London.*133 (1931): 610-624

Dobyns, York H. "Selection Versus Influence Revisited: New Methods and Conclusions." *Journal of Scientific Exploration* 10, No. 20 (1996): 253–268.

Dupont, Caroline Marie. *Enchanted Eating: Nourishment for Body and Soul.* Summertown, Tenesssee: Alive Books, 2006

Eckenhoff et al. "Direct Modulation of Microtubule Stability Contributes to Anthracene General Anasthaesia." *Journal of the American Chemical Society* 135, no. 14 (April 10, 2013): 5389–5398.

Einstein, Albert, Boris Podolsky, and Nathan Rosen. "Can Quantum-Mechanical Description of Physical Reality Be Considered Complete?" *Physical Review* 47, no. 10 (1935): 777–780.

Freedman, Stuart J., and John F. Clauser. "Experimental Test of Local Hidden-Variable Theories." *Physical Review Letters.* 28, vol.40 (1972): 938-941

Funaro, D. "Numerical Simulation of Electromagnetic Solitons and Their Interaction with Matter." *Journal of Scientific Computing.* 45, no. 1 (2010):259-271

Gariaev, Peter P., K.V. Grigoriev, A.A. Vasiliev, V.P. Poponin and V.A. Shcheglov. "Investigation of the Fluctuation Dynamics of DNA Solutions by Laser Correlation Spectroscopy." *Bulletin of the Lebedev Physics Institute,* Vol11 (1992): 23-30

Gariaev, P. P., M. J. Friedman, and E. A. Leonova-Gariaeva. "Principles of Linguistic-Wave Genetics." *DNA Decipher Journal* Vol1 issue1 (January 2011): 11–24.

Gariaev, P. P., P. J. Marcer, K. A. Leonova-Gariaeva, U. Kaempf, and V. D. Artjukh. "DNA as Basis for Quantum Biocomputer." *DNA Decipher Journal* 1, no. 1 (January 2011): 25–46.

Gariaev, P., and M. Pitkanen. "A Model for the Findings about Hologram Generating Properties of DNA." *DNA Decipher Journal* 1, no. 1 (January 2011): 47–72.

Gariaev, Peter P., V.I Chudin, G.G. Komissarov, A.A. Berezin, A.A. Vasiliev. "Holographic Associative Memory of Biological Systems." *Proceedings SPIE-The International Society of Optical Engineering, Optical Memory and Neural Networks Vol 1621 (1991):280-291*

Giertz, Hans W. "Extremely Low Frequency Electromagnetic Energy in the Air." *Journal of Atmospheric and Solar Terrestrial Physics* 72 (2010): 767–773.

Giorbran, Gevin. *Everything Forever: Learning to See Timelessness.* Seattle, WA: Enchanted Puzzle Publishing, 2007.

Gladwell, Malcolm. *The Tipping Point: How Little Things Can Make a Big Difference.* London:Little Brown, 2000.

Goldberger, Ary L., L. Amaral, J. M. Hausdorff, P. Ivanov, C. K. Peng, and H. E. Stanley. "Fractal Dynamics in Physiology: Alterations with Disease and Aging," *Proceedings of the National Academy of Sciences,* February 19, 2002, vol. 99, suppl. 1, 2466–2472.

Gurwitsch, A. G. *Das Problem der Zellteilung (The Problem of Cell Division).* Alexander Gavrilovich Gurwitsch, Moscow,1926.

Hameroff, Stuart, and Roger Penrose. "Consciousness in the Universe: A Review of the Orch OR Theory." *Physics of Life Reviews* 1, vol. 11 (2014): 39–78.

Hanada, M., Y. Hyakutake, G. Ishiki, and J. Nishimura. "Holographic Description of Quantum Black Hole on a Computer." *Science* Vol 344 (2014):882-885

Haramein, Nassim. "Quantum Gravity and the Holographic Mass." *Physical Review & Research International* Vol. 3 (2013):270-292

Hartley, Linda. *Wisdom of the Body Moving: An Introduction to Body-Mind Centering.* Berkeley, CA: North Atlantic Books, 1995.

Hartman, Hyman. "Speculations on the Evolution of the Genetic Code." *Origins of Life* Vol 6 (1991): 423–427.

Hatchard, Guy D., A. J. Deans, K. L. Cavanaugh, and D. Orme-Johnson. "The Maharishi Effect: A Model for Social Improvement. Time Series Analysis of a Phase Transition to Reduced Crime in Merseyside Metropolitan Area." *Journal Psychology, Crime and Law* 2, no. 3 (1996): 165–174.

Hathaway, David H. "The Solar Cycle." *Living Reviews in Solar Physics* 7 (2010):1-56

Hawkins, David. *Power vs. Force.* Carlsbad: Hay House, 2004.

Heisenberg, Werner. "Über den anschaulichen Inhalt der quantentheoretischen Kinematik und Mechanik,"

Zeitschrift für Physik (in German) 43, no. 3–4 (1927): 172–198. Accessed August 5, 2014.

Hirose, Kei, S. Tateno, Y. Ohishi, and Y. Tatsumi. "The Structure of Iron in Earth's Inner Core." *Science* 330, no. 6002 (2010): 359–361.

Ho, Mae-Wan. *The Rainbow and the Worm: The Physics of Organisms.* Singapore: World Scientific Publishing, 2008.

Ho, Mae-Wan. *Living Rainbow, H20.* Singapore: World Scientific Publishing, 2012.

Hu, Huping., Maoxin Wu, "Decipherment of the Secrets of DNA." *DNA Decipher Journal* 1, no. 1 (January 2011):1-10

Hyakutake, Yoshifumi. "Quantum Near Horizon Geometry of Black 0-Brane." *Progress of Theoretical and Experimental Physics.* 033BO4 (2014) 1-27

Hyman, Scott D., "A Powerful Bursting Radio Source Towards the Galactic Centre" *Nature* 434, (March 3, 2005) :50-52

Iyengar, B. K. S. *Light on Pranayama: The Definitive Guide to the Art of Breathing.* London: Harper Thorsons, 1981.

Jayanthan, R. "Electric Current in a Sunspot." *Solar Physics* 12 no. 1 (April 1970): 104–105.

Johnson, Stephen. M. *Character Styles.* New York: Norton, 1994.

Josephson, Brian. D. "Possible New Effects in Superconductive Tunnelling." *Physics Letters* 1 (1962): 253–255

Josephson, Brian. D. "Supercurrents Through Barriers." *Advances in Physics* 14 (1965): 419–451.

Kabat-Zinn, John. *Coming to Our Senses: Healing Ourselves and the World Through Mindfulness.* New York: Hyperion, 2005.

Karlicky, M. "Evolution of Force-Free Electric Currents in the Solar Atmosphere." *Astronomy and Astrophysics* 318 (1997): 289–292.

Kaznacheyev, V., et al. "Distant Intercellular Interactions in a System of Two Tissue Cultures." *Psychoenergetic Systems* 1, no. 3 (March 1976): 141–142.

Kirsch, Irving. The Emporer's New Drugs: An analysis of Antidepressant Medication submitted to the US Food and Drug Administration. *Prevention & Treatment*, Volume 5, Article 23 Copyright (2002)by the American Psychological Association: 1-10

Kirsch, Irving. *The Emporer's New Drugs:Exploding the Antidepressant Myth*. New York: Basic Books, 2011

Kohut, Heinz. "The Disorders of the Self and Their Treatment: An Outline." In H. Kohut, *The Search for the Self: Selected Writings of Heinz Kohut: 1978–1981*, 359–385. Madison: International Universities Press, Inc., 1978.

Korotkov, Konstantin G. and Ekaterina Jakovleva. *Electrophotonic Applications in Medicine:GDV Bioelectrography*. Colorado Springs, Colorado: Create Space Publishing,2013

Lamoreaux, Stephen K. "Demonstration of the Casimir Force in the 0.6 to 6μm Range." *Physical Review Letters*. 78, no. 1 (1997)1-8

Landaver, Rolf, IBM physicist. "Minimal Energy Requirements in Communication." *Science* 272 (1996): 1914–1918.

LaViolette, Paul. A. "Elevated Concentrations of Cosmic Dust in Wisconsin Stage Polar Ice." *Meteoritics* 18 (1983):337-338

LaViolette, Paul A. *Galactic Explosions, Cosmic Dust Invasions, and Climatic Change.* PhD dissertation, Portland State University, Portland, Oregon, August 1983.

LaViolette, Paul. A. "The Terminal Pleistocene Cosmic Event: Evidence for Recent Incursion of Nebular Material into the Solar System." *Eos, Transactions American Geophysical Union* Vol 74 Issue 44 (1993): 511

La Violette, Paul. A. "A Tesla Wave Physics for a Free Energy Universe." *Proceedings of the 1990 International Tesla Symposium*, 5: 1–20.

Ling, Gilbert N. *Life at the Cell and Below Cell Level*. New York: Pacific Press, 2001.

Lipton, Bruce. *The Biology of Belief: Unleashing the Power of Consciousness, Matter & Miracles*. Carlsbad:Hay House, 2011.

Mainster, Martin A. "The Fractal Properties of Retinal Vessels: Embryological and Clinical Implications." r^1 Eye 4 (1990), 235–241.

Maldacena, Juan M. "The Large N Limit of Superconformal Field Theories and Supergravity.". International Journal of Theoretical Physics 38 (1999) 1113–1133.

Maldacena, Juan, and Leonard Susskind. "Cool Horizons for Entangled Black Holes." Cornell University Library arXiv:1306.0533v2 11 July 2013 accessed 26 May 2015.

Mandelbrot, Benoit. B. The Fractal Geometry of Nature. New York: WH Freeman1983.

Mandelbrot, Benoit. B -Hunting the Hidden Dimension-Nova 2008   http://www.pbs.org/wgbh/nova/physics/... uploaded by teamfresh @ http://fractal.com / http://hd-fractals.com

Mc Comas, David., J.T. Gosling, E. Santiago-Munoz, R.M. Skoug, B.E. Goldstein, M. Neugebauer, P. Riley, A. Balogh. "Solar wind observations over Ulyssees' first full polar orbit.". Journal of Geophysical Research, Vol.105.(2000):10419–10433

McCarty, James. A., D. Elkins, and C. Rueckert. The Ra Material Books 1-4. Atglen, PA: Whitford Press, 1982–4.

McCraty, Rollin. "The Energetic Heart: Bioelectromagnetic Communication Within and Between People. Clinical Applications of Bioelectromagnetic Medicine. edited by P. J. Rosch and M. S. Markov. New York: Marcel Dekker, 2004: 541–562.

McCraty, Rollin, Mike Atkinson, and Raymond Trevor Bradley. "Electrophysiological Evidence of Intuition: Part 2. A System-Wide Process." Journal of Alternative and Complementary Medicine 10, no. 1 (2004): 133–143.

McCraty, Rollin, Mike Atkinson, William A. Tiller, Glen Rein, and Alan D. Watkins. "The Effects of Emotions on Short-Term Power Spectral Analysis of Heart Rate Variability." American Journal of Cardiology 76, no. 14 (1995): 1089–1093.

McCraty, Rollin, M. Atkinson, D. Tomasino, and R. T. Bradley. "The Coherent Heart: Heartbrain Interactions, Psychophysiological Coherence and the Emergence of System Wide Order." *Integral Review* Vol.5.2 (2009):11-114

McCraty, Rollin, M. Atkinson, D. Tomasino, and W. A. Tiller. "The Electricity of Touch: Detection and Measurement of Cardiac Energy Exchange Between People." In *Brain and Values: Is a Biological Science of Values Possible*. ed. Karl H. Pribram, 359–379. Mahwah, NJ: Lawrence Erlbaum Associates, Publishers, 1998.

McTaggart, Lynne. *The Field*. London: HarperCollins, 2001.

Meyl, Konstantin. "Scalar Waves Theory—Experiments." *Journal of Scientific Exploration* 15, no. 2 (2001): 199–205.

Meyl, Konstantin. "Cellular Communication by Magnetic Scalar Waves." *PIERS Proceedings, Progress in Electromagnetic Research, Technical University Moscow, Russia,* (2012):997-100:

Meyl, Konstantin. "About Vortex Physics and Vortex Losses." *Journal of Vortex Science and Technology* 1 (2012).1-10

Mills, Joy. "On Fohat." *Quest* 97, no. 1 (2009): 17–19.

Modena, I., G.B. Ricci, S. Barbanera, R. Leoni, G.L Romani, P. Carelli,"Biomagnetic Measurements of Spontaneous Brain Activity in Epileptic Patients." *Electroencephalography and Clinical Neurophysiology* 54 (1982): 622–628.

Montagnier, Luc, J. Aissa, E. D. Del Giudice, C. Lavallee, A. Tdeschi, and G. Vitiello. "DNA Waves and Water." (2011) *Journal of Physics: Conferences Series*. Vol 306. 1 article 012007:1-10

Mosley, B. "A Controlled Trial of Arthroscopic Surgery for Osteoarthritis of the Knee." *New England Journal of Medicine* 347 (2002): 81–88.

Muto, V., J. Halding, P. L. Christiansen, A. C. Scott. 1988 "Solitons in DNA." *Journal of Biomolecular Structural Dynamics* 4 (1988): 873–894.

Opher, M., F. Alouani Bibi, G. Toth, J.D. Richardson, V.V. Izmodenov, T.I. Gombosi. "A Strongly Tilted Magnetic Field near the Solar System." *Nature* 462 (2009) :1036-1038

Oschman, James. *Energy Medicine: The Scientific Basis.* Philadelphia, PA: Churchill Livingstone, Elsevier, 2000.

Oschman, James. *Energy Medicine in Therapeutics and Human Performance.* Philadelphia, PA: Butterworth Heinman, 2003:271-272

Oschman, James. *The Living Matrix* DVD. Hillsboro, OR: Beyond Words Publishing, 2009.

Pankskepp, Jaak. *Affective Neuroscience: The Foundations of Animal and Human Emotions.* New York: Oxford University Press, 1998.

Peratt, A. L. "Electric Space:Evolution of the Plasma Universe." *Astrophysics and Space Science.* (1996) 244: 89–103.

Pierrakos, Eva. *Complete Lectures of the Pathwork: Expanded Edition.* Charlottesville VA: Pathwork Press 2009

Pierrakos, Eva and D. Thesenga. *Fear No Evil: The Pathwork Method of Transforming the Lower Self.* Charlottesville, VA: Pathwork Press, 1993

Pierrakos, E., and D. Thesenga. *Surrender to God Within: Pathwork at the Soul Level.* Charlottesville, VA: Pathwork Press, 1997.

Pietsch, Paul. *Shufflebrain: The Quest for the Holographic Brain.* Boston: Houghton Mifflin, 1981.

Pollack, Gerald. *Cells, Gels and the Engines of Life.* Seattle, WA: Ebner and Sons, 2001.

Pollack, Gerald. *The Fourth Phase of Water: Beyond Solid, Liquid and Vapor.* Seattle, WA: Ebner and Sons, 2013.

Popp, Fritz Albert., W. Nagl, K. H. Li, W. Scholz, O. Weingärtner, and R. Wolf. "Biophoton Emission: New Evidence for Coherence and DNA as Source." *Cell Biophysics* 6, no. 1 (1984): 33–52

Popp, Fritz Albert., M. Rattemeyer, and W. Nagl. "Evidence of Photon Emission from DNA in Living Systems." *Nature Wissenshanften* 68, no. 11 (1981): 572–573.

Potemra, T.A. "Birkeland Currents in the Earth's Magnetosphere." *Astrophysics and Space Science* 144 (1988): 155–169.

Pribram, Karl. "The Neurophysiology of Remembering." *Scientific American*, vol. 220 (1969): 73-86.

Pribram, Karl. *Languages of the Brain.* Monterey, CA: Wadsworth Publishing, 1977.

Radin, Dean. *The Conscious Universe: The Scientific Truth of Psychic Phenomena.* New York: HarperCollins, 2009.

Radin, Dean. I., and Diane C. Ferrari. "Effects of Consciousness on the Fall of Dice: A Meta-Analysis." *Journal of Scientific Exploration* 5 (1991): 61–84.

Radin, Dean., G. Hayssen, M. Emoto, and T. Kizu. "Double Blind Test of the Effects of Distant Intention on Water Crystal Formation." *Explore* 2, no. 5 (2006):408-441

Radin, Dean., N. Lund, M. Emoto, and T. Kizu. "Effects of Distant Intention on Water Crystal Formation: A Triple-Blind Replication." *Journal of Scientific Exploration* 22, no. 4 (2008): 481–493.

Radin, Dean., L. Michel, K. Galdamez, P. Wendland, R. Rickenbach, and A. Delorme. "Consciousness and the Double-Slit Interference Pattern: Six Experiments." *Physics Essays* 25, no. 2 (2012):157-171

Radin, Dean. I., and Roger D. Nelson. "Evidence for Consciousness Related Anomalies in Random Physical Systems." *Foundations of Physics* 19 (1989): 1499–1514.

Rajneesh, Bhagwahn Shree. *A Cup of Tea; Letters.* New York: Osho International Foundation, 1983.

Randall, Lisa. *Higgs Discovery: The Power of Empty Space.* London:The Bodley Head 2012.

Reid, John. S. "The Special Relationship Between Sound and Light with Implications for Sound and Light Therapy."

Subtle Energies and Energy Medicine 117, no. 3 (2006): 215–231.

Rein, Glen. "Biological Effects of Scalar Acoustic Energy: Modulation of DNA." *Proceedings of the US Psychotronics Association, Columbus, Ohio,* July 1998.

Rein, Glen. and R. McCraty. "Modulation of DNA by Coherent Heart Frequencies." In *Proceedings of the Third Annual Conference of the International Society for the Study of Subtle Energy and Energy Medicine Monterey, California, 1993:* 58–62.

Rein, G., and R. McCraty. "Modulation of DNA by Coherent Heart Frequencies." *Journal of Scientific Exploration* 8, no. 3 (1994): 438–439.

Rein, G., and R. McCraty. "Structural Changes in Water and DNA Associated with New Physiologically Measurable States." *Journal of Scientific Exploration* 8, no. 3 (1994): 438–439.

Robbins, John, and J. Patton. *May All Be Fed: A Diet for a New World.* New York: Avon Books,1992

Sagan, Carl. *The Demon Haunted World: Science as a Candle in the Dark.* New York: Ballantine Books, 1996.

Schmidt, Helmut. 1993 "New PK Test with an Independent Observer." *Journal of Parapsychology* 57 (1993): 227–240.

Schmidt, Helmut. "Observation of a Psychokinetic Effect Under Highly Controlled Conditions." *Journal of Parapsychology* 57(1993): 351–72.

Schrödinger, Erwin. "An Undulatory Theory of the Mechanics of Atoms and Molecules." *Physical Review* 28, no. 6 (1926): 1049–1070.

Schumann, Winfried O. "Über die Dämpfung der elektromagnetischen Eigen schwingungen des Systems Erde-Luft-Ionosphäre." *Zeitschrift Fur Naturforschung- Journal for Natural Science Research Section A.* Vol. 7.(1952) 250-252

Schumann, Winfried O. "Über die strahlungslosen Eigenschwingungen einer leitenden Kugel, die von einer Luftschicht und einer Ionosphärenhülle umgeben ist." *Zeitschrift Fur Naturforschung –Journal for Natural Science Research Section A Sciences.* Vol.7 No 2 (1952):149-154

Scott, D. E. *The Electric Sky.* Happy Valley, Oregon Mikamar Publishing, 2006.

Seto, A., L. Kusaka, S. Nakazato, W. Huang, T. Sato, T. Hisamitsu, and C. Takeshige. "Detection of Extraordinary Large Bio-Magnetic Field Strength from Human Hands During External Qi Emission." *Acupuncture and Electro-Therapeutics Research International Journal* 17 (1992): 75–94.

Sheldrake, Rupert. *Morphic Resonance: The Nature of Formative Causation.* Rochester, Vermont: Park St. Press, 2009.

Shprits, Yuri., D. Subbotin, A. Drozdov, M.E. Usanova, A. Kellerman, K. Orlova, D.N. Baker, D.L. Turner, K-C. Kim. "Unusual Stable Trapping of the Ultrarelativistic Electrons in the Van Allen Radiation Belts." *Nature Physics* 9 (2013):699-703.

Strauss, H. R., and N. F. Otani. "Current Sheets in the Solar Corona." *Astrophysical Journal, Part 1* 326 (1988): 418–424.

Teresa E. Strzelecka, Michael W. Davidson, Randolph. L. Rill "Multiple Liquid Crystal Phases of DNA at High Concentrations." *Nature* 331 (1988): 457–460.

Talbot, Michael. *The Holographic Universe.* London: Harper Collins, 1996.

Taylor, Richard P. "Reduction of Physiological Stress Using Fractal Art and Architecture." *Leonardo* 39, (2006):245-251

Taylor, Richard P., Branka Spehar, Paul Von Donkelar, C.M. Hagerhall. "Perceptual and Physiological Responses to Jackson Pollock's Fractals." *Frontiers in Human Neuroscience* 5. Article 60(2011):1-13

Thesenga, S. J. *The Undefended Self: Living the Pathwork.* Charlottesville, VA: Pathwork Press, 2001, 246–247.

Thornhill, W., and D. Talbot. *The Electric Universe*. Happy Valley Oregon: Mikamar Publishing, 2007.

Tiller, William A., *Science and Human Transformation*. Walnut Creek, CA: Pavior Publishing,1997.

Tiller, W. A., W. E. Dibble, and M. J. Kohane. *Conscious Acts of Creation: The Emergence of a New Physics*. Walnut Creek, CA: Pavior Publishing, 2001.

Tolle, Eckhart. *The Power of Now: A Guide to Spiritual Development*. Novato, CA: New World Library 1999

Tsukamoto, I., and K. Ogli. Anaesthetic membrane interactions evaluated by Taft's Polarity Parameters." *Journal of Colloid and Interface Science* 154 (1992): 1-304.

West, G. B., J. H. Brown, and Brian J. Enquist. "The Fourth Dimension of Life: Fractal Geometry and Allometric Scaling of Organisms. *Science* 284 (1999):1677–1679.

Wever, Rutger. *The Circadian System of Man: Results of Experiments under Temporal Isolation*. New York: Springer-Verlag, 1979.

Wilcock, D. *The Source Field Investigations*. New York :Plume-Penguin, 2011.

World Health Organization. *"Obesity and Overweight-Key facts."* Fact sheet no. 311.

Young, Thomas. "The Bakerian Lecture: On the Theory of Light and Colours." *Philosophical Transactions of the Royal Society of London* 92 (1802): 12–48. Accessed August 5, 2014. JSTOR 107113. http://en.wikipedia.org/wiki/Double-slit_experiment. doi:10.1098/rstl.1802.0004.

Zaitsev, V. V., and A. V. Stepanov. "Towards the Circuit Theory of Solar Flares." *Solar Physics* 139, no. 2 (June 1992): 343–356.

Zimmerman, John. "Laying On of Hands Healing and Therapeutic Touch: A Testable Theory." *BEMI Currents, Journal of the Bio-electro Magnetics Institute* 2 (1990): 8–17.

Endnotes

1   Radin, *The Conscious Universe.*
2   Sagan, *The Demon Haunted World.*
3   Darwin, *On the Origin of Species*, 162.
4   Denton, *Evolution*, 250.
5   d'Espagnat, "The Quantum Theory and Reality,"
6   Vibration en.wikipedia.org/wiki/Vibration accessed 7August 2014
7   Frequency en.wikipedia.org/wiki/Frequency accessed 7August 2014
8   Resonance en.wikipedia.org/wiki/Resonance accessed 7 August 2014
9   Frenzel, Lou., Electronic Design. *What's the difference between EM near field and far field* ? 8 June 2012 http://electronicdesign.com/energy/what-s-difference-between-em-near-field-and-far-field accessed 7 Aug 2014
10 Force en.wikipedia.org/wiki/Force accessed 7 August 2014
11 Gravitation wikipedia.org/wiki/Gravitation accessed 7August 2014
12 Electromagnetism.wikipedia.org/wiki/Electromagnetism accessed 7 August 2014
13 Strong interaction en.wikipedia.org/wiki/Strong interaction accessed 7 August 2014
14 Weak Interaction.en.wikipedia.org/wiki/Weak interaction accessed 7 August 2014
15 See Appendix.
16 Kraus, Marian is a Gong Master and provides transformational sound meditations in the form of workshops, retreats and private sessions using sacred sound all over the world. His work is a testament to the transformative power of sound energy. http://gongsoundhealing.com/quotes/ accessed 19 Feb 2015

[17] Sonic Geometry consists of a team of researchers and moviemakers creating videos about the language of frequency and form; the connection between sound, geometric shapes and numerical sequences discovered when studying ancient places and peoples. www.sonicgeometry.com accessed 19 Feb 2015

[18] Reid, website dedicated to the Cymascope™ research into vibration and sound and a full description of his work is at www.cymascope.com accessed 4 Feb 2015

[19] See Appendix.

[20] Mandelbrot, *The Fractal Geometry of Nature*, 151–165.

[21] West, Brown, and Enquist, "The Fourth Dimension of Life,"

[22] Goldberger, Hausdorff, Ivanov, Peng, and Stanley, "Fractal Dynamics in Physiology."

[23] Mainster, "The Fractal Properties of Retinal Vessels," 235–241.

[24] Taylor, "Reduction of Physiological Stress."

[25] Taylor, "Perceptual and Physiological Responses to Jackson Pollock's Fractals." "Investigation of EEG Response to Fractal Patterns,"

[26] Hunting the Hidden Dimension Nova 2008 PBS.

[27] Sheldrake, *Morphic Resonance*. Official Website https://www.sheldrake.org Research: Morphic Resonance and Morphic Fields accessed 5 August 2014

[28] Lipton, Fractal Evolution. "Evolution by Bits and Pieces; An introduction to Fractal Evolution" *7 June https://www.brucelipton.com/resource/article/fractal-evolution* Resources : Bruce's Free Content accessed 6 August 2014

[29] Haramein, Nassim. The Resonance Project. www.resonance.is accessed 6 October 2014

[30] Einstein's key observation was that motion under gravity and motion in an accelerated frame are the same, and therefore, for example, since a beam of light will bend in a rocket that is accelerating, a light beam will also bend under gravity. His concept of curved space theorized that gravity is not a force at all but a distortion in space-time and planets move around the sun, not because of the gravitational pull but because planets are following the curvature of space created by the sun in the fabric of space-time. Humans remain fixed on earth, not because of the pull of gravity, but rather because space is pushing us down, creating the feeling of weight.

[31] Kaku and Holmes: Einstein In a Nutshell (2004) –Discover-Online Magazine September 2004 special issue under Cosmology -100 years of Genius without Limits http://discovermagazine.com/2004/sep/einstein-in-a-nutshell accessed 14 November 2014

32 CERN is the European Organization for Nuclear research. The Standard Model:The Standard Model explains how the basic building blocks of matter interact governed by four forces. home.web.cern.ch/about/physics/standard-model accessed 28 August 2014

33 http://physics.about.com/od/lightoptics/a/waveparticle.htm accessed 6 August 2014

34 Young, "The Bakerian Lecture."

35 Radin et al., "Consciousness and the Double-Slit Interference Pattern."

36 Schrödinger, "An Undulatory Theory of the Mechanics of Atoms and Molecules."

37 Heisenberg, "Über den anschaulichen Inhalt der quantentheoretischen Kinematik und Mechanik."

38 Niels Bohr, *The Copenahagen Interpretation*.

39 Dirac, "Quantised Singularities in the Electromagnetic Field."

40 Anderson, "The Apparent Existence of Easily Deflectable Positives."

41 Einstein, Podolsky, and Rosen, "Can Quantum-Mechanical Description of Physical Reality Be Considered Complete?"

42 Bell, "On the Einstein Podolsky Rosen Paradox."

43 Freedman, "Experimental Test of Local Hidden-Variable Theories."

44 Aspect, "Bell Test Experiments."

45 Landaver, "Minimal Energy Requirements in Communication."

46 Bennet, et al. "Teleporting an Unknown Quantum State via Dual Classical and EPR Channels."

47 Randall, *Higgs Discovery*, 39.

48 Wilson, How Stuff Works –How Holograms Work http://science.howstuffworks.com/hologram1.htm accesssed 27 August 2014

49 Talbot, *The Holographic Universe*.

50 Bohm, *Wholeness and the Implicate Order*, 182–186.

51 Ibid., 190–196.

52 Talbot, *The Holographic Universe*, 41–42.

53 http://physics.about.com/od/physicsatod/g/brane.htm accessed 27 Aug 2014

54 Maldacena, "The Large N Limit of Superconformal Field Theories and Supergravity.

55 Hyakutake, "Quantum Near Horizon Geometry of Black 0-Brane."

56 Hanada et al. "Holographic Description of Quantum Black Hole on a Computer."

57 Maldacena and Susskind, "Cool Horizons for Entangled Black Holes."

58 Haramein, "2013 Quantum Gravity and the Holographic Mass."

59 Pribram, *Languages of the Brain*.

60 Pietsch, *Shufflebrain*,81.

[61] Pribram, "The Neurophysiology of Remembering."

[62] "The Holographic Brain," "New Dimensions – Dec 2012 You Tube accessed 20 Aug 2014 www.youtube.com/watch?v=awFleswtH2Y.

[63] Hameroff and Penrose, "Consciousness in the Universe: A Review of the Orch OR Theory."

[64] Sahu et al., "Multi-Level Memory-Switching Properties of a Single Brain Microtubule."

[65] Eckenhoff et al., "Direct Modulation of Microtubule Stability Contributes to Anthracene General Anasthaesia."

[66] Chopra, "Reality and Consciousness: A view from the East": Comment on Consciousness in the Universe: A Review of the Orch OR Theory by Hammeroff and Penrose." http://www.sciencedirect.com/science/article/pii/S1571064513001590 accessed 8 Nov 2014

[67] Tiller, *Science and Human Transformation*, 46.

[68] Ibid., 55.

[69] Ibid., 63.

[70] Ibid., 58.

[71] Tehrani, The Omni Intelligencer – Video Interview with Dr William Tiller http://omniintelligencer.com/Science/Science/Interview-with-Dr.-William-Tiller-renowned-physicist.html#ixzz3Ixj04MSM accessed 9 Nov 2014

[72] Bohm, Wholeness and the Implicate Order, 242,243

[73] Bohm, *Wholeness and the Implicate Order*.

[74] Tiller *Science and Human Transformation*, 46.

[75] McTaggart, *The Field*, Element.

[76] Wilcock, *The Source Field Investigations*.

[77] Brennan, *Hands of Light*.

[78] Casimir and Polder, "The Influence of Retardation on the London Van Der Walls Forces."

[79] Lamoreaux, "Demonstration of the Casimir Force in the 0.6 to $6\mu m$ Range."

[80] Schumann, W.O., 1952 Über die strahlungslosen Eigenschwingungen einer leitenden Kugel, die von einer Luftschicht und einer Ionosphärenhülle umgeben ist, Naturforsch. 7a, 149)
Schumann, W.O., 1952 Über die Dämpfung der elektromagnetischen Eigen schwingungen des Systems Erde-Luft-Ionosphäre, Z. Naturforsch. 7a, 250

[81] Wever, *The Circadian System of Man*

[82] Montagnier et al., "DNA Waves and Water."

83 Ho, Mae-Wan., Institute Of Science in Society. Isis Report. DNA reconstituted from water memory 20 July 2011 http://www.i-sis.org.uk/DNA_sequence_reconstituted_from_Water_Memory.php accessed Nov 2014

84 Encyclopaedia Brittanica, Telluric Current, Geophysics –Definition www.britannica.com/EBchecked/topic/586372/telluric-current accessed 28 April 2015

85 Giertz, "Extremely Low Frequency Electromagnetic Energy in the Air."

86 Olcott, Earth Energy Blog-The Impact of Earth Energies on Life. http://www.jiroolcott.com/blog/earth-energy accessed September 2014

87 Hecht, New Scientist issue 2984, 30August 2014 "Earth's Tectonic Plates Have Doubled Their Speed." 27 August 2014 https://www.newscientist.com/article/mg22329843-000-earths-tectonic-plates-have-doubled-their-speed/ accessed 1 September 2014

88 Castro, News Discovery, Oceans of water locked 400 miles inside earth. 12 June 2014 Live Science 2014 http://news.discovery.com/earth/oceans/oceans-of-water-found-locked-deep-inside-earth140612.htm accessed 1/September 2014 http://www.livescience.com/46291-ocean-hidden-beneath-earth-photos.html

89 Hirose et al., "The Structure of Iron in Earth''s Inner Core."

90 Deborah Byrd and Bruce McClure –EarthSky.Org-Human World-Article When will the Age of Aquarius begin in FAQs | Human World on Jan 03, 2014 http://earthsky.org/human-world/when-will-the-age-of-aquarius-begin accessed 5 September 2014

91 Connelly, Timothy website www.shiftoftheage.com http://www.shiftoftheage.com/2009/11/02/precession-of-the-equinox-from-darkness-into-light-2/ accessed 5 September 2014

92 Opher et al "A Strong Highly Tilted Interstellar Magnetic Field near the Solar System."

93 Shprits et al., "Unusual Stable Trapping of the Ultrarelativistic Electrons in the Van Allen Radiation Belts."

94 Popp, Rattemeyer, and Nagl, "Evidence of Photon Emission from DNA in Living Systems."

95 Gariaev, Friedman, and Leonova-Gariaeva, "Principles of Linguistic-Wave Genetics."

96 Ferris, T., National Geographic, Solar Storms 2 June 2012 http://ngm.nationalgeographic.com/2012/06/solar-storms/ferris-text accessed 8 Sept 2014

97 Hathaway, "The Solar Cycle Living Rev."

98 Hannes Alfvén, "Currents in the Solar Atmosphere and a Theory of Solar Flares."

[99] Carlqvist, "Current Limitation and Solar Flares."

[100] Karlicky, "Evolution of Force-Free Electric Currents in the Solar Atmosphere."

[101] Zaitsev, "Towards the Circuit Theory of Solar Flares."

[102] Strauss and Otani, "Current Sheets in the Solar Corona."

[103] Jayanthan, "Electric Current in a Sunspot."

[104] NASA, Solar Physics. The Big Questions-http://solarscience.msfc.nasa.gov/quests.shtml accessed 10 Sept 2014

[105] http://sedonanomalies.weebly.com/earths-magnetic-field.html accessed 21 August 2014

[106] Hyman, "A Powerful Bursting Radio Source Towards the Galactic Centre"

[107] LaViolette, "Elevated Concentrations of Cosmic Dust in Wisconsin Stage Polar Ice."

[108] LaViolette, Galactic Explosions, Cosmic Dust Invasions, and Climatic Change.

[109] LaViolette, "The Terminal Pleistocene Cosmic Event."

[110] Scott, *The Electric Sky*, 92.

[111] Gallagher, "Plasma, Plasma Everywhere: A New Model of the Plasmasphere Surrounding Our World". 7 September 1999 *NASA Science News* http://science.nasa.gov/science-news/science-at-nasa/1999/ast07sep99 accessed 11 September 2014

[112] Potemra, "Birkeland Currents in the Earth's Magnetosphere."

[113] Alfven, "Model of the Plasma Universe"

[114] Peratt, "Electric Space:Evolution of the Plasma Universe."

[115] Alfven and Arrenhius, *Evolution of the Solar System*.

[116] Thornhill and Talbot, *The Electric Universe*. www.holoscience.com accessed 31 August 2015

[117] Sheldrake, *A New Science of Life*.

[118] Sheldrake, Articles and Papers, Morphic Resonance and Morphic Fields http://www.sheldrake.org/Articles&Papers/papers/morphic/morphic_intro.html accessed 22 September 2014

[119] Lipton, *The Biology of Belief.*

[120] Lipton, "Insight into Cellular Consciousness." Reprinted from Bridges, vol12 (2001):5 ISSEEM 7 July 2012 Resources : Bruce's Free Content https://www.brucelipton.com/resource/article/insight-cellular-consciousness accessed 6 August 2014

[121] Sheldrake, Morphic Resonance and Morphic Fields –An Introduction http://www.sheldrake.org/research/morphic-resonance/introduction accessed 22September 2014

[122] Gladwell, *The Tipping Point.*

[123] Oschman, *Energy Medicine*, 23, 27, 38.

[124] Ibid., 255.

[125] Burr, *Blue Print for Immortality.*

[126] Gurwitsch, *Das Problem der Zellteilung.*

[127] Popp, Rattemeyer, and Nagl, "Evidence of Photon Emission."

[128] Gurwitsch, *Das Problem der Zellteilung.*

[129] Modena et al., "Biomagnetic Measurements of Spontaneous Brain Activity."

[130] Brewitt, "Quantum Analysis of Electrical Skin Conductance in Diagnosis."

[131] Brewitt, "Journal of Bodywork and Movement Therapies."

[132] Josephson, "Possible New Effects in Superconductive Tunnelling."

[133] Josephson, "Supercurrents Through Barriers."

[134] Del Guidice et al., "Magnetic Flux Quantization & Josephson Behaviour in Living Systems."

[135] Zimmerman, "Laying On of Hands Healing and Therapeutic Touch."

[136] Seto et al., "Detection of Extraordinary Large Bio-Magnetic Field Strength from Human Hands During External Qi Emission."

[137] Oschman, "Energy Medicine in Therapeutics and Human Performance."

[138] Korotkov and Jakovleva. *Electrophotonic Applications in Medicine: GDV Bioelectrography.* See also www.korotkov.eu Dr Konstantin G. Korotkov's official website-The Human light System- Selected Papers – Scientific Basis of GDV Bioelectrography.12 July 2014 accessed 24 September 2014

[139] Deshpande, Madappa, and Korotkov."Can the Excellence of the Internal Be Measured."

[140] Hunt, Transcript of interview with Larry Triv http://healthontheedge.wordpress.com/2012/01/28/the-human-energy-field-an-interview-with-valerie-v-hunt-ph-d/ accessed 16 Sept 2014

[141] Ibid.

[142] Ibid.

[143] Meyl, "Cellular Communication by magnetic scalar waves."

[144] HeartMath Institute website http://www.heartmath.org/about-us/about-us-home/hearts-intuitive-intelligence accessed 14 September 2014

[145] McCraty et al., "The Effects of Emotions on Short-Term Power Spectral Analysis of Heart Rate Variability."

[146] McCraty et al., "The Coherent Heart."

[147] Ibid.

[148] www.heartmath.org/free-services/articles-of-the-heart/coherence.htm

[149] McCraty, Atkinson, and Bradley. "Electrophysiological Evidence of Intuition."

[150] McCraty et al., "The Electricity of Touch."

[151] McCraty, "The Energetic Heart."

[152] http://www.glcoherence.org/about-us/about.html accessed November 2014

[153] McCraty, *The Energetic Heart.*

[154] Hartman, "Speculations on the Evolution of the Genetic Code."

[155] Rein and McCraty, "Modulation of DNA by Coherent Heart Frequencies."

[156] Popp et al., "Biophoton Emission."

[157] Muto et al., "Solitons in DNA."

[158] Meyl, "Cellular Communication by Magnetic Scalar Waves"

[159] Strzelecka et al., "Multiple Liquid Crystal Phases of DNA at High Concentrations."

[160] Gariaev et al, Investigation of the Fluctuation Dynamics of DNA Solutions by Laser Correlation Spectroscopy

[161] Ibid.

[162] Montagnier et al., "DNA Waves and Water."

[163] Pollack, *The Fourth Phase of Water.*

[164] Gariaev et al., "DNA as Basis for Quantum Biocomputer."

[165] Gariaev and Pitk¨anen, "A Model for the Findings about Hologram Generating Properties of DNA."

[166] Kaznacheyev et al., "Distant Intercellular Interactions in a System of Two Tissue Cultures."

[167] Budagovsky et al., "Coherent Electromagnetic Irradiation in Distant Intercellular Interaction.

[168] Gariaev, Friedman, and Gariaeva. "Principles of Linguistic-Wave Genetics."

[169] Garyaev*, Wave Genetics. English website of Dr Peter Petrovich Gariaev founder of the Institute of Quantum Genetics in Moscow, Russia. Describes the complete history, theory, research, experiments, technology and applications of Wave Genetics. www.wavegenetics.org Accessed 28 August 2015 *(This website is also in Russsian. English spelling required to access English website.)

[170] Alexjander, "The Infrared Frequencies of DNA Bases, as Science and Art."

[171] Rein, "Biological Effects of Scalar Acoustic Energy."

[172] Rein and McCraty, "Modulation of DNA by Coherent Heart Frequencies."

[173] Rein and McCraty, "Structural Changes in Water and DNA Associated with New Physiologically Measurable States."

[174] Oschman, *Energy Medicine in Therapeutics and Human Performance*, 282.

[175] Oschman, *The Living Matrix*.

[176] Oshman, *Energy Medicine in Therapeutics and Human Performance*.

[177] Ibid., 158.

[178] Ho, *Living Rainbow H20*, 16.

[179] Ho, *The Rainbow and the Worm*, 237.

[180] Tsukamoto and Ogli, "Effects of Anaesthetics on the Interfacial Polarity of Membranes."

[181] Pollack, *Cells, Gels and the Engines of Life*.

[182] Pollack, *The Fourth Phase of Water*.

[183] Ling, *Life at the Cell and Below Cell Level*.

[184] Mercola, "Interview with Gerald Pollack." 16 August 2013 http://articles.mercola.com/sites/articles/archive/2013/08/18/exclusion-zone-water.aspx. Accessed May 3, 2015.

[185] Radin et al., "Consciousness and the Double-Slit Interference Pattern."

[186] Mosley, "A Controlled Trial of Arthroscopic Surgery for Osteoarthritis of the Knee."

[187] Kirsch, *The Emporer's New Drugs: Exploding the Antidepressant Myth*. Article by Kirsch in 2002 submitted to US Food and Drug Administration published by American Psychological Association eventually became a book published in 2009.

[188] Rankin,"Owning Pink: Redefining Women's Health:The Nocebo Effect: Negative Thoughts Can Harm Your Health." *Psychology Today* August 6, 2013. psychologytoday.com accessed October 7, 2014.

[189] Dibble, Tiller and Kohane, "Electronic Device Mediated pH Change in Water.".

[190] Radin, *The Conscious Universe: The Scientific Truth of Psychic Phenomena*.

[191] Ibid., 51.

[192] Radin and Ferrari, "Effects of Consciousness on the Fall of Dice."

[193] Ibid., 147.

[194] Radin and Nelson, "Evidence for Consciousness Related Anomalies in Random Physical Systems."

[195] Dobyns, "Selection Versus Influence Revisited."

[196] Ibid., 155.

[197] Schmidt, "New PK Test with an Independent Observer." Schmidt, "Observation of a Psychokinetic Effect Under Highly Controlled Conditions."

[198] Ibid., 156.

[199] Radin et al. "Double Blind Test of the Effects of Distant Intention on Water Crystal Formation."

[200] Radin et al. "Effects of Distant Intention on Water Crystal Formation."

[201] Puthoff, CIA initiated remote viewing at Stanford Research Institute. Detailed report by Puthoff in 1996 http://www.biomindsuperpowers. com/Pages/CIA-InitiatedRV.html accessed 8 October 2014

[202] Nelson, The Global Consciousness Project –global-mind.org 1998-2015 Formal results : Testing the Global Consciousness Project http://noosphere.princeton.edu/results.html#alldata accessed 8 October 2014 and 27 August 2015

[203] Ibid.

[204] Hatchard et al. "The Maharishi Effect."

[205] Ho, The Rainbow and the Worm.

[206] Mills, "On Fohat."

[207] McCarty, Elkins, and Rueckert, The Ra Material Books 1-4.

[208] Tolle, The Power of Now.

[209] Giorbran, Everything Forever.

[210] Bailey, A Treatise on Cosmic Fire.

[211] Ibid.

[212] Kabat-Zinn, Coming to Our Senses, 243.

[213] Hartley, Wisdom of the Body Moving,21.

[214] Cohen, Body Mind Centering : An Embodied Approach to Body Mind Consciousness. Cellular Intelligence Bonnie Bainbridge Cohen Blog http://www.bodymindcentering.com/bonnie-bainbridge-cohen accessed 25 November 2014

[215] Ibid.

[216] Iyengar, Light on Pranayama, 24–25.

[217] Brule, D http://www.breathmastery.com Breath Energy Training Dan Brule accessed 27 November 2014

[218] Robbins and Patton, May All Be Fed.

[219] World Health Organization; Fact sheet no. 311.

[220] Dupont, Enchanted Eating.

[221] Kim, The Truth About Alkalising Your Blood 4 July 2014 http:// drbenkim.com/ph-body-blood-foods-acid-alkaline.htm accessed 26 Nov 2014

[222] Dupont, Enchanted Eating,7 adapted from recommendations.

[223] The Importance of Water and Your Health. Website sponsored by APEC Water http://www.freedrinkingwater.com/water-education/water-health-page2.htm accessed 25 November 2014

[224] National Sleep Foundation website- adapted from Sleep Tools http:// sleepfoundation.org/sleep-tools-tips accessed 25 November 2014

225 Pierrakos. "Three Cosmic Principles: The Expanding, Restricting and Static Principles." (1959) Pathwork Guide Lecture 55. Pathwork Lectures 1996 ed.
226 Hawkins, *Power vs. Force*, 31.
227 Pierrakos and Thesenga. *Fear No Evil*, 73–75.
228 Pankskepp, *Affective Neuroscience*.
229 Bowlby., *A Secure Base: Parent-Child Attachment and Healthy Human Development*.
230 Hoyt, "An Overview of Heinz Kohut's Self Psychology and Object Relation Theory." Hoyt, Terence. J. 2011. http://www.practicalphilosophy.net/?page_id=426. Accessed December 4, 2014
231 Kohut, "The Disorders of the Self and Their Treatment."
232 Johnson, *Character Styles*.
233 Rajneesh, *A Cup of Tea; Letters*.
234 Pierrakos, "Resume of the Basic Principles of the Pathwork: Its Aim and Process."(1971). Pathwork Guide Lecture 193. Pathwork Lectures 1996 ed.
235 Staroversky, Staroversky Counseling and Psychotherapy. Three Minds: Conscious, Subconscious and Unconscious 23 May 2013 http://staroversky.com/blog/three-minds-conscious-subconscious-unconscious. Accessed 25 November 2014
236 Austin, Michelle., Adapted from Article for Sport Coach page vol 28 no4 by M. Austin, "Listening to the Voices in your Head: Identifying and Adapting Athletes Self-Talk" Website sponsored by Australian Government Sports Commission http://www.ausport.gov.au/sportscoachmag/psychology2/listening_to_the_voices_in_your_head_identifying_and_adapting_athletes_self-talk. Accessed 26 November 2014
237 Mayo clinic website outlines the various elements of meditation. Tests and Procedures; Meditation. Mayo Clinic Staff. http://www.mayoclinic.org/tests-procedures/meditation/in-depth/meditation/art-20045858?pg=2 accessed 31 August 2015
238 Bailey, *A Treatise on Cosmic Fire*, 816–869.
239 Thesenga, *The Undefended Self*, 246–247.
240 Cromie, W. J. "New Findings May lead to Better Painkillers: Pleasure and Pain activate the same part of the brain." *Harvard University Gazette* 2002. Online news magazine owned by President and Fellowes of Harvard College http://news.harvard.edu/gazette/2002/01.31/01-pain.html. Accessed 4 January 2015
241 Pierrakos and Thesenga, *Fear No Evil*.

242   Adapted from Barbara Moreau <u>www.ancientwisdomtrails.com</u> First Nation Healers website owned by Frank J Austin, Barbara Moreau, Manyhorses and Angel Who Dances On The Clouds. 2012-2016 accessed 4 October 2014

243   Baconnier et al., "Calcite Microcrystals in the Pineal Gland of the Human Brain: First Physical and Chemical Studies".

244   Pierrakos and Thesenga, *Surrender to God Within*, 63.

245   Ibid., 145–147.

246   Biffi et al. "Quantitative Visualization of DNA G-Quadruplex Structures in Human Cells.

247   Funaro, "Numerical Simulation of Electromagnetic Solitons and Their Interaction with Matter."

248   La Violette, "A Tesla Wave Physics for a Free Energy Universe."

249   Aspden, "'Standing Wave Interferometry.'"

250   Meyl, "Scalar Waves Theory—Experiments."

251   Tesla's scalar fields: The superluminal (faster than light) scalar or longitudinal waves Nikola Tesla used to magnify and wirelessly transmit power are not just a thing of the past. March 24, 2011, Steve Jackson held a presentation and demonstration of a scalar wave transmitter and receiver at a local IEEE meeting at McMaster University in Ontario, Canada. <u>Accessed August 10, 2014. http://pesn. com/2011/03/26/9501797 Teslas Scalar Waves Replicated by Steve Jackson/.</u>

252   Meyl, "About Vortex Physics and Vortex Losses."

253   Reid, "The Special Relationship Between Sound and Light with Implications for Sound and Light Therapy."

Index

Biophoton 99, 117, 122, 124, 132, 352, 364
biophysics 4, 92, 352
Bioscalar Energy 104
blueprint 90, 92-4, 98-9, 116-17, 122, 150, 211, 262, 271-2, 332
body xxxvi-xxxvii, 30-1, 95-102, 104-11, 121-3, 130-7, 167-8, 176-85, 187-9, 193, 208, 233-7, 284-9, 293-9, 366
brain 9, 52-6, 65-6, 107-8, 110-13, 115, 131-2, 134-5, 208, 236-7, 253-4, 264-5, 351-3, 359-60, 367-8
breath xxxvii, 154, 163, 181, 183-6, 189, 203, 223, 232, 234-5, 285, 293-5, 303, 313, 334
breathwork 294-5
Business xviii, xx, 243, 252

C

carrier 80, 106, 111, 113, 123-4, 130, 132, 338
Causal xxxvii, 96, 162, 167, 169, 171, 202, 231
cause and effect xxxvi, 9, 163, 274-5
cell xxviii, 11, 29-30, 93-4, 99, 121-3, 125, 130, 133, 135, 179, 271-2, 335, 349, 365
Centre 83, 348, 362
child consciousness xxxvii, 219-21, 250, 306-7
Chromosome 124-5
Cocreator xxix, 155, 230, 241
codes xxxix, 9, 25, 117, 124-5, 272
codons 117, 123, 126
coherence xxxiv, xxxvi, 67, 108-10, 112-13, 130, 132, 139, 142, 172-3, 176-7, 182, 191, 237-8, 351-2

Coherence xxxiv, xxxvi, 67, 108-10, 112-13, 130, 132, 139, 142, 172-3, 176-7, 182, 191, 237-8, 351-2
community xix, xxix-xxx, 5-6, 19, 42, 52, 56, 84, 116, 143, 212
competition 29, 216-17
conditioning xxxi, xxxvii, 174, 179, 208-9, 242-3, 247, 253, 272, 284, 300, 306
conductor 68, 86
connection xxv-xxvi, xxx, xxxii, xxxviii, 21, 112-13, 179-80, 235, 246-8, 264, 274-5, 288-91, 312-13, 318-19, 333-4
connective tissue 132-3, 137
consciousness xxxii-xxxix, 54-60, 137-9, 145-8, 153-6, 159-62, 164-8, 171-2, 203-6, 219-22, 231-3, 248-51, 253-8, 267-70, 274-5
constructive 74, 199, 260, 270, 275
control 93-4, 116, 142-4, 156, 184-5, 195, 215, 218, 228, 239, 252, 266, 321-2
correspondence 162
cosmic xxi, xxxvi, 24, 38, 62, 64, 75-7, 84, 91, 95-6, 164-5, 204-6, 349, 362, 366-7
cosmology 4, 11, 33, 48, 72, 86, 89-90, 104, 358
cosmos xxiv, xxxii, xxxvi, 5, 11, 30, 48, 51, 57, 72, 86, 89, 115, 153-4, 156
crisis 8, 89, 229, 269-70, 345
Crystal 70-1, 93, 117, 121, 125, 133, 145, 200, 353, 355, 364, 366
crystalline matrix 131, 134-5, 137
Cymaglyph 22-4, 129
Cymascope™ 22, 340, 358
cymatics 4, 21, 340

S

safety xxx, 211, 227-8, 307, 322

scalar energy xix, 20, 78, 90, 97, 105-6, 117, 338-9

scalar waves 19, 87, 106, 128, 150, 337, 339, 351, 363-4, 368

science xix-xx, xxix-xxx, xxxii-xxxiv, 3-6, 8-12, 18-21, 41-2, 52, 56-7, 59-60, 76, 89-90, 92-7, 351-6, 359-62

Self-Concept 214

self-esteem 210, 214-15, 224-5, 228

self-talk 224-5, 258, 294, 367

Senses 7, 16, 54, 57, 110, 138, 168, 177, 179, 208, 222, 233, 253-5, 266, 274

sex 144, 206, 217

Sexuality xxxvii, 205-6, 216

Signature xx, xxxvi, 202-3, 210-13, 215-18, 220, 230, 241, 259, 262-3, 310

solar system xxxviii, 11, 30, 51, 57, 73, 75-7, 80, 82, 86, 89, 91, 156, 165, 361-2

Soliton 133

soul xxiii-xxvi, xxxvii, 96, 154-6, 162, 167, 171, 175, 231-2, 236-41, 248-9, 251, 277, 331, 334

sound xxxviii-xxxix, 13-14, 21-4, 30, 117-18, 124-6, 128, 130-3, 149-50, 154-5, 261-3, 285-6, 295, 340-1, 357-8

source xxvi, xxviii-xxix, xxxi-xxxii, xxxv-xxxvi, 5-6, 24, 36, 51, 75, 83, 155-6, 172-4, 241, 332-5, 339-41

space 9, 15, 17, 33, 38-41, 47, 49-51, 55-64, 78-9, 81-9, 154-8, 167-8, 338-40, 352-3, 358

speech xxxviii, 124, 130, 150, 262-3

spirituality xxix, 1, 5-6, 252

SQUID 100

stability xxxvii, 4, 184, 207, 209, 307, 345, 360

structured water 121, 130, 135

subconscious xxxviii, 224, 367

sun xxv, 22-3, 65, 68, 74, 76, 78-82, 86-9, 91, 104, 136, 149, 172, 186, 358

superposition 37-9, 203

surrender xxiv, xxxviii-xxxix, 175, 184-5, 202, 215, 251-3, 256-7, 265, 300, 319, 352, 368

synchronicity 201, 268, 277

synergy xxix, xxxiv, 1, 4

synthesis xxix-xxx, xxxiv, 1, 4, 165, 238-9

T

Tai Chi 234

template xix-xxi, xxxvi, 67, 70, 95, 98, 115, 122, 150, 167, 179, 182, 271, 330

Tesla 1, 19, 64, 105-6, 127, 337-9, 349, 368

Thermal 13

Thought xxxv-xxxvi, 11, 20, 24, 33, 38, 105, 198, 220, 234, 237-40, 262-3, 275, 290-1, 308

Time xviii-xxi, 9-10, 32-3, 37-41, 49-52, 55-62, 74-6, 156-8, 167-8, 171-4, 177-81, 221, 237-8, 252-5, 327-31

transference 56, 242, 246, 258, 314-15

transfiguration 265, 331

transfigure 272

transformation xxi, xxiv, xxvii-xxviii, xxxi, 178, 180, 264-5, 284, 293, 310, 331, 356, 360

Printed in the United States
By Bookmasters